CAMARO & FIREBIRD
1970-1981 PERFORMANCE PROJECTS

Jeff Tann

CarTech®

CarTech®

CarTech®, Inc.
838 Lake Street South
Forest Lake, MN 55025
Phone: 651-277-1200 or 800-551-4754
Fax: 651-277-1203
www.cartechbooks.com

© 2013 by Jeff Tann

All rights reserved. No part of this publication may be reproduced or utilized in any form or by any means, electronic or mechanical, including photocopying, recording, or by any information storage and retrieval system, without prior permission from the Publisher. All text, photographs, and artwork are the property of the Author unless otherwise noted or credited.

The information in this work is true and complete to the best of our knowledge. However, all information is presented without any guarantee on the part of the Author or Publisher, who also disclaim any liability incurred in connection with the use of the information and any implied warranties of merchantability or fitness for a particular purpose. Readers are responsible for taking suitable and appropriate safety measures when performing any of the operations or activities described in this work.

All trademarks, trade names, model names and numbers, and other product designations referred to herein are the property of their respective owners and are used solely for identification purposes. This work is a publication of CarTech, Inc., and has not been licensed, approved, sponsored, or endorsed by any other person or entity. The publisher is not associated with any product, service, or vendor mentioned in this book, and does not endorse the products or services of any vendor mentioned in this book.

Edit by Paul Johnson
Layout by Monica Seiberlich

ISBN 978-1-61325-370-0
Item No. SA237P

Library of Congress Cataloging-in-Publication Data

Tann, Jeff.
Camaro & Firebird performance projects, 1970-1981 / by Jeff Tann.
    pages cm
  ISBN 978-1-61325-014-3
1. Camaro automobile–Performance. 2. Camaro automobile–Motors–Modification. 3. Firebird automobile–Performance. 4. Firebird automobile–Motors–Modification. I. Title. II. Title: Camaro and Firebird performance projects, 1970-1981.
  TL215.C33T36 2013
  629.28'722--dc23
                    2012036008

Printed in USA

Front Cover: An LS7 is lowered into the engine bay of this immaculate 1970-1/2 Z28 Camaro. The LS7 uses a forged crank and CNC ported heads, which promote excellent flow. The Chevy Performance LS7 crate engine produces 505 hp and 475 ft-lbs of torque. (Photo courtesy Jeff Tann)

Title Page: This 1970 Z/28 features a super-low stance due to a custom front and rear subframe installation. Check out the large-diameter wheels and extra-wide, low-profile tires. This is definitely a very nice Pro Touring car with fantastic handling ability.

Back Cover Photos

Top Left: Installing a set of roller rockers is a popular upgrade to the valvetrain. Roller rockers reduce friction and provide excellent valve actuation. These rocker arms need to be set at zero lash.

Top Right: The Detroit Speed subframe was raised high enough to get it on the car lift. This was done by holding the front of the new subframe with a "cherry picker" while the rear was lifted using manpower. Wood strips were placed on the car lift to keep the rotors looking nice as the subframe was rolled under the Camaro.

Middle Left: Stepping back, you can see the complete differential installation that includes the four-link design, the large strong panhard bar, and the top-quality coil-over shocks that display plenty of adjustability. The differential is a Ford 9-inch with a limited-slip unit. Gear selections can be made for street driving, road racing, or even low gears for drag racing.

Middle Right: Modern aftermarket wheels allow you to use much larger disc brakes. If you look through the windows in the wheels, you can see the aluminum Baer Racing Brakes. They dramatically increase the stopping power of the car, plus the brakes are much lighter than the stock units.

Bottom Left: The dual-piston SSBC caliper and slotted/drilled rotor deliver a huge improvement in braking performance and safety. This brake uses hydraulic pressure for braking and mechanical activation for the parking brake. Aftermarket brake cables need to be installed to activate the parking brake.

Bottom Right: Original ignition parts do not provide cutting-edge spark performance. Here, a modern distributor is installed. Insert the distributor shaft into the block with the vacuum module facing the passenger side of the engine. Look closely at the bottom of the gear on the shaft where you find a slot that must align with a depression in the oil pump gear driveshaft.

CONTENTS

Introduction 4

Chapter 1: Planning and Organizing 8
   Choose Your Application 9
   Choose Your Process 10
   Project Your Time and Expenses 10
   Organize Your Parts 11
   Think about Safety 12
   Buildup Overview 13

Chapter 2: Engine Performance 15
   Small-Block versus Big-Block 15
   Cylinder Heads 16
   Project 1: Aluminum Head Installation 17

Chapter 3: Selecting and Installing a Camshaft ... 22
   Emission and Mileage Standards 22
   Hydraulic Lifters 23
   Solid Lifters 23
   Roller Cams 23
   Project 1: Hydraulic Roller Camshaft Installation ... 24

Chapter 4: Intake Manifolds and Carburetion 31
   Intake Manifolds 31
   Selecting a Carburetor 34
   Project 1: Intake Manifold and Carburetor Installation .. 36

Chapter 5: Ignition System 40
   Project 1: Distributor, Spark Plug Wires
      and Coil Installation 42

Chapter 6: Exhaust System 48
   Header Selection Tips 49
   Emissions Standards 50

Chapter 7: Installing a Crate Engine 52
   To Crate or Not to Crate 53
   Chevrolet Performance Small-Block and Big-Block ... 54
   LS Crate Engine Sources 55

Chapter 8: Performance Transmission 58
   Second-Generation OEM Options 59
   Transmission Sources 60

Chapter 9: Chassis Upgrades 63
   Suspension Component Sources 64
   Project 1: Subframe Connectors Installation 67
   Project 2: Rear Wheel Tubs Installation 73

Chapter 10: Front Suspension 86
   Front Suspension Sources 87
   Project 1: Front Subframe Installation 89

Chapter 11: Rear Suspension 100
   Eaton Detroit Springs 100
   Project 1: Rear Spring Installation 101
   Detroit Speed 106
   Project 2: Rear Suspension System Installation .. 106

Chapter 12: Performance Brakes 120
   Brake Sources 120
   Project 1: Front Brake and Shock Installation .. 121
   Project 2: Drum to Disc Brake Conversion 126

Chapter 13: Cooling System 132
   Radiator 133
   Water Pump 136
   Fans 137
   Thermostat 138

Chapter 14: Weight-Saving Measures 139

Chapter 15: Wheels and Tires 143
   Sidewall Flex 144
   Wheel Design 145

Chapter 16: Interior 148
   Seats 148
   Project 1: Seat Reupholstery 151
   Dash and Gauges 161
   Steering Wheel 164
   Sound System 165

Chapter 17: Electrical System and Wiring 166
   DIY or Outsource? 166
   Project 1: Power Window Installation 168

Afterword 172
Source Guide 174

INTRODUCTION

When Chevy enthusiasts are asked about their favorite muscle car, the Camaro tops the list by a large margin. The Camaro was Chevrolet's answer to the Ford Mustang, and since the introduction of the Camaro in 1967, the competition between the two in sales and performance has been fierce, and that competition continues today. Chevy enthusiasts revere the first-generation Camaro because it is small, light, nimble, and attractive, and the sporty coupes and convertibles were available with a wide variety of high-horsepower engine options.

Designing and Building the Camaro

When Chevrolet management decided to build a car to compete head-on with the extremely popular Mustang, the designers, stylists, and engineers were given the difficult challenge to build a Mustang-size car that was more attractive and better engineered than the Mustang. The stylists and engineers had to come up with a new car very quickly, so they looked at the platforms that were under construction.

Using the reengineered and vastly improved Nova platform that was going to be used in 1968, the Chevy engineers and stylists fast tracked the platform and created a new fastback unibody that could compete successfully with the Mustang. The new platform eliminated the shock towers used in the previous Nova design and similar to what the Mustang was using. The engineers came up with a unitized body that utilized a front subframe that was bolted to the body structure. The Chevy stylists and engineers were smart economically by coming out with only one body style that could compete with Mustang's fastback and notchback body styles. They also had to release a convertible model to compete with the convertible Mustang.

When Chevrolet was designing the Camaro, the Pontiac division, which was already very successful with the GTO muscle car, wanted to get in on the action with an upscale version of the Camaro called the Firebird. Ford also had an upscale model called the Mercury Cougar so the Firebird competed with the Mustang and the Cougar as well as the Camaro. Even with a very limited production run between February and July 1967, Pontiac sold 82,560 Firebirds, affecting Camaro, Mustang, and Cougar sales.

When the Camaro was released, many people thought the new car was substantially superior to the Mustang, both visually and mechanically. The new Camaro featured a crisp, clean, fastback unibody that connected to a separate front subframe featuring a dual A-arm front

The owner of this Trans Am restored the car because it is a rare 1978 Gold Special Edition. Only a small number of these cars were built between February 1978 and July 1978. The cars were equipped with a Pontiac 400 engine, except for California, where they were outfitted with a 403 Olds engine. All engines were backed by a Turbo 350 automatic transmission or a Super T-10 4-speed; however, in California no 4-speed could be sold.

INTRODUCTION

suspension and parallel leaf rear suspension. The coil-spring dual A-arm suspension was similar to the suspension used in the more expensive larger cars, such as the Chevelle, and because there were no spring towers, the design enabled Chevrolet to install a large selection of engines in the Camaro, including the big-block 396-ci engine.

When the Camaro was introduced, it could be ordered with a base 140-hp, 230-ci, six-cylinder engine; a 210-hp, 327-ci, V-8 engine; a completely new 295-hp, 350-ci Super Sport base V-8 engine; a 396, Super Sport V-8 engine with the buyers choice of 325 or 350 hp; or a high-performance 290-hp, 302-ci, solid-lifter V-8 engine used in the Z28 Camaro. In addition, drag racers could order a 375-hp, solid-lifter 396-ci V-8 engine for the Camaro, but because of liability issues, production was limited.

After the introduction of the Camaro in 1967, the Sports Car Club of America (SCCA) sanctioned a new road race for American sedans called Trans-Am racing (short for Trans-American). The Ford Mustang dominated sedan road racing in 1965 and 1966, and like so many times before, Chevrolet wanted to beat Ford and all other competitors.

The Race-Proven Camaro

General Motors took the opportunity to showcase its new entry into what the automotive press called the pony car market. In 1969, Mark Donahue, racing the Penske Sunoco Z28, won the Trans-Am championship and captured several race victories en route to the title. The Z28 302-ci Camaro engines were built with a variety of off-the-shelf Corvette parts, including big port and valve fuel-injection heads, a hot solid-lifter cam, an aluminum high-rise intake manifold, and a 780-cfm Holley carburetor. Powered by this high-performance, 290-hp (actually closer to 350 hp), 302-ci engine, combined with excellent suspension tuning, the Camaro quickly dominated Trans-Am racing. The Ford 302 engine wasn't competitive in 1967 because the factory head ports were too small to match the Chevy engine's horsepower.

After Chevrolet introduced the Camaro, Pontiac released a nice-looking pony car, the upscale Firebird. The Firebird shared the same basic Camaro body with a Pontiac-designed front-and rear-end body treatment. The new Firebirds were powered by a variety of Pontiac engines including the powerful GTO 400. Pontiac also entered into Trans-Am racing, but they weren't as successful as the Chevy entry because Pontiac didn't have an engine that could be successfully downsized to meet the Trans-Am series 305-ci engine limitation.

Pontiac's engineers did work on a 303-ci engine but it was never competitive and wasn't offered to the public. Pontiac was smart, however, because it did purchase the Trans Am name from the SCCA, and even though it didn't have a winner, the name was retained long after the races were discontinued. As it turned out, the name Trans Am was a winner for Pontiac throughout the car's long distinguished lifespan.

Designing the 1970 Camaro

General Motors' management was so pleased and excited about the 1967 Camaro's sales of 220,917 units and the Firebird's sales of 82,560, they decided to continue to develop new models that were going to be released in 1970. The styling and management teams were given a blank sheet of paper to design an all-new Camaro and Firebird for release in 1970. The actual design work had started in late 1966 when the management saw that the Camaros and Firebirds were going to be a huge success. The Chevrolet division took the lead on the new car but the Pontiac division had more input on the 1970 model, especially with regard to the suspension design. The Camaro was totally redesigned and this time the Nova borrowed the platform from the Camaro. The Firebird received small body changes from the Camaro, but the suspension parts, floorpan, and basic sheet metal remained very similar.

The new Camaro and Firebird were supposed to be a 1970-model car, but instead of the normal release in September 1969, they were pushed back due to small problems until February 1970. The 1969 Camaro had an extended run through January, although sales were low.

The engineers worked diligently to get the new Camaro finished to meet the September deadline but a few small problems surfaced. Any weakness associated with the first-generation cars was revised and improved upon. For example, the first-generation Camaros and Firebirds were in need of suspension and steering changes to improve ride and handling so those improvements were incorporated into the second-generation cars. Also, the basic unibody and subframe design remained similar but improvements were made in the basic engineering of the car, which included changing the steering location to improve handling.

INTRODUCTION

In 1970 the Camaros and Firebirds were offered with the same high-performance engine options as in the previous cars but changes were coming in engine performance as the EPA rules were phased in. The management at Chevrolet and Pontiac had different approaches to dealing with the EPA rules. Chevrolet went the more conservative route and started building cars with reduced horsepower and even discontinued the Z28 option for a few years. Pontiac didn't want to give up the big-cube engines and continued offering a 400 engine right up to the 1979 model year.

The second-generation Camaros and Firebirds were built to last a few years longer than the previous cars that were dramatically changed every two years. The new cars had such a low, sleek, and sexy body design that the stylists could use their imagination and improve the cars by only changing the nose and tail design of the cars. The rear window design was also changed in 1974 but other than that, the basic body design remained essentially the same. What couldn't be seen were improvements in the body structure to make the cars stiffer and more durable year by year.

General Motors also wanted to make the cars more appealing to a wide variety of buyers—from teenagers to middle-age people—so the company decided to make the cars more luxurious with a wide variety of power options. This also meant that the cars had to be quiet and comfortable and they succeeded in accomplishing that goal. All you have to do is ride in an early Camaro and then a mid-1970s Camaro; the difference is astonishing. Even though the second-generation Camaros were more attractive and vastly improved over the first-generation cars they didn't become as collectable, probably because engine performance was declining.

High-Performance Upgrades

Throughout this book I show you a wide variety of performance improvements for second-generation Camaros and Firebirds. The two cars were almost identical in body structure but they were different in engine selections; although, in the mid 1970s, Firebirds were offered with Chevy engines (now called corporate engines) as an economical option. Pontiac enthusiasts ordering a Trans Am were still able to order a Pontiac 400 engine except in California where the factory installed a 403 Olds engine because the cost of certifying the 400 for California emissions was prohibitive.

I also show you performance tips for the Camaro's small- and big-block Chevy engines. But remember that most of the performance tips also apply to Pontiac and Oldsmobile engines.

General Motors was changing body styles on even years and improving the cars mechanically on odd years. Chevrolet was using that plan also, but there were a few years when that policy couldn't be used. When the second-generation Camaro and Firebird were being styled and designed, the new cars had to have a body that would last longer than two years. The idea was to build a car that could be changed every two years with small front and rear styling improvements. The basic body remained the same for several years, but few realized the car would endure for 11 years.

The reason for the longer body run was to save money because changing the body tooling was very expensive. When you have a good thing that is selling, well, why change it? Also, General Motors was comprised of several divisions that were competing with each other. Instead of building a separate engine at each division, the divisions eventually shared engines, similar to the way Ford and Chrysler were. The small-block Chevy engine, which could be produced economically and could produce a variety of horsepower variations by simple cam-and-intake combinations and cubic-inch sizes, became the corporate engine shared by all divisions. It was in the mid 1970s that the divisions started losing their individual identity.

Selecting a Camaro or Firebird

It's hard to believe that the 1970 Camaros and Firebirds were released more than 40 years ago. The 1970 through 1981 cars don't necessarily seem old because their body styles are sleek and timeless. In my estimation, they are better looking that any of the Camaros or Firebirds that followed. Think about it. When is the last time you saw a 1970s Camaro or Firebird being used as daily transportation? General Motors cranked out several million Camaros and Firebirds from 1970 to 1981, so these second-generation cars are still available and somewhat affordable, particularly compared to other performance cars of an earlier era.

During the 1970s, General Motors sold more than one million economy, six-cylinder Camaros and Firebirds. In addition, there are many 305, 350-equipped Camaros. While many

INTRODUCTION

Here is an artist's rendering of a car that is currently being built at Pure Vision in Simi Valley, California. This Camaro is going to be a Pro Touring car with a very impressive twin-turbocharged Chevy small-block. The pro touring style of building is very popular these days. This car is slated to compete in the Goodguys Street Machine of the Year competition in Columbus, Ohio. (Photo Courtesy Pure Vision)

of the remaining cars are six-cylinder Berlinettas or smog-equipped V-8s, the second-generation cars are much more plentiful than 1967–1969 Camaros and Firebirds.

Therefore, the first-generation (1967–1969) Camaros and Firebirds have higher collector values than the second-generation cars (1970–1981), so many of the second-generation F-Bodies ended up in wrecking yards, rather than being preserved as the earlier ones were. The second-generation Camaros and Firebirds made during the peak and trailing end of the muscle car era are the most valuable collector cars and command the highest prices.

1970–1974

In particular, the 1970–1973 Camaro Z28s equipped with LT1 engines are very popular and command top dollar in good condition. These were gracefully styled, tasteful, high-performance cars. Many featured split or low-impact bumpers, Coke-bottle-style taillights, and body cues reminiscent of Ferrari. In addition Camaro Super Sports from the same era carrying a big-block engine are very valuable collector cars and often sell for $25,000 if perfectly restored.

On the Pontiac side, the 1970–1974 Trans Am Firebirds with 455 Super Duty engines are enduring classics and have exceptionally high collector interest. The Trans Am Firebirds were in particular low production from 1971 to 1974. For 1972, only 1,300 Trans Am Firebirds were manufactured, so these are particularly desirable. In addition, the Formula 400 Firebirds are another highly sought after model with high purchase prices.

You need to keep in mind that if you do find an early 1970 through 1974 Z28 Camaro or Trans Am, the car will probably be worth more if it is restored and, therefore, it's not the ideal candidate for a hot street or Pro Touring buildup. However, some invisible performance improvements can be made without changing their value. If the higher purchase price of a real Z28 or Trans Am isn't a problem, you are not a purist, and you want a highly modified example, go for it. There are no laws stating that you can't modify a collector car; however, many enthusiasts don't think it is a good idea.

1974–1981

The early 1974–1981 Camaros and Firebirds are the most desirable for building into high-performance street and competition machines because of their lower prices. But before you buy a Camaro or Firebird, you need to consider the cost of car and emissions laws of your particular state. In some states you can modify a later-model Camaro or Firebird and in some, such as California, you have to make the car emissions compliable. The 1975-and-up models are very affordable if you can find one in original condition.

You can purchase a six-cylinder or a base-model second-generation F-Body with a solid body for $4,000 or less. Restored cars sell for a much higher price, so you have to decide if you want a nice driver to fix up or a deteriorated car that needs everything. I have found that a daily driver in good condition eventually needs the same things as a restorable car. These include new paint, an interior upgrade, an engine upgrade, a suspension upgrade, and a variety of other improvements. If the car in good condition sold for $12,000 and the bad one sold for $2,000, the final investment after improvements were made you will probably spend more than $10,000 to restore it to good condition. If you buy and restore the car in poor condition you will have $12,000 invested in it. If you purchase the better car for $12,000 and then upgrade to perfect condition you will have $22,000 invested. It would be cost effective to purchase the car that was in poor condition.

It only makes sense that if you are planning to build a modified street machine or Pro Touring Camaro or Firebird you should start with a base model that can be purchased for a considerably lower price. In order to keep the cost even lower you may want to find a body or rolling chassis that doesn't have an engine or transmission because if you are modifying the car, the engine and transmission will most likely be upgraded with a high-horsepower engine and a performance transmission anyway.

CHAPTER 1

PLANNING AND ORGANIZING

Selecting the right project car is critical. If you already own one and it has a solid body, frame, and suspension system, you won't have to look at online listings, the local newspaper, or automotive sales magazines, and such. On the other hand, if you need to buy the car you're going to build up you have to decide which one you really want and then start looking for it.

When I am looking for a particular car I contact all of my automotive enthusiast friends and start spreading the word. I also spend time online on eBay and Craigslist to see if what I am looking for is available. I generally have more luck with my friends telling me about cars that I might be interested in. Recently one of the cars I purchased was advertised briefly on Craigslist and the other was purchased from a friend. The old 1970–1981 Camaros and Firebirds are becoming more difficult to find, but they are out there and with a little searching they can still be found.

Few enthusiasts have the knowledge, tools, ability, and training to build a car without help from professionals. I have seen too many cars sitting in a person's driveway for decades. The car is going downhill every year, but when you talk to the owner, he tells you that he is going to "fix up that car someday." The problem is someday never comes. The point is that a car is not going to fix itself, so you need to have mechanical and body-working talent or a fist full of money.

Before you start installing parts on your Camaro or Firebird, you should plan how you want the car to turn out. Professional shops generally commission an artist's rendering for the builder to follow as the car is being assembled. If you are computer savvy you can take a picture of your car and start working up a computer picture of how you would like the car to look after it is finished. This can be done using photo manipulation programs such as Adobe Photoshop where you can install different wheels, alter the color, and make other changes.

I still prefer the old-fashioned way of hiring an artist such as Chip Foose, Thom Taylor, or Steve Stanford to design the cars because they work with your ideas and add some of their own. These artists are very well known and have worked with many of the best shops in the country, but you pay a good price for their expertise.

An artist's rendering is generally used when the car is going to be changed radically from the factory design. It is not necessary when you are building a mildly modified car, such as a street machine or resto-mod without a lot of body changes. Remember that a mild upgrade, such as a restoration or resto-mod, costs less than a wild, no-expenses-spared, Pro Touring car because you do not have exotic body changes, high-end aftermarket engines, or related parts. Some of the cars I've seen currently competing for event honors, such as the Goodguys Street Machine of The Year, are getting away from what a clean muscle car should look like because they are too busy. Others look nice, so it is just a matter of how far you want to go. What makes a second-generation Camaro or Firebird look nice is the cleanliness of the design. They don't require body changes for improvement.

PLANNING AND ORGANIZING

Choose Your Application

You need to define what Camaro or Firebird you want to build, and certainly there is more than one way to modify a second-generation F-Body. The application (such as high-performance street, rectified, street/strip, Pro Touring) dictates the car you build. Your budget is also a factor in what car you build.

The following are general definitions, and a certain F-Body may carry elements from more than one category. In the various chapters you will find projects that fit several categories, and it's up to you to select the projects that help build the car of your goals.

High-Performance Street

A car that fits into this category has many chassis, suspension, and powertrain upgrades, and many of these elements are also found in a restified car. This covers a broad range of vehicles, but it is generally accepted that a high-performance street car has substantially modified suspension that includes shocks, A-arms, and sway bars. In addition, the Camaro carries high-performance heads, cam, intake, carb, and exhaust. Often, a car of this type carries the original block and horsepower is 500 and above. But it doesn't preclude from a complete high-performance engine build with forged rotating assembly and aluminum aftermarket block.

Rectified

Often with this type of car, the original or original-type engine is retained, but the stock engine is just a starting point. A forged crank, rods, and pistons are part of the engine build. On the top end, a set of high-flow aluminum heads, an aluminum dual-plane intake, and a larger carb to supply enough fuel to the engine are selected. And a high-lift, long-duration hydraulic roller camshaft is often added. When it comes to the transmission, an aftermarket automatic overdrive or a close-ratio 5- or 6-speed may be added.

On the suspension side, the front subframe and rear leaf springs are commonly retained, but extensive work is done from there. Tubular A-arms, high-durometer bushings, larger sway bars, and coil-over shocks are often added to vastly improve handling. In many cases, however, owners don't completely replace the front and rear suspensions.

In addition, high-performance aftermarket brakes are added to this seriously upgraded package because old drum and disc brake systems are often not up to the task of handling the increased performance. A high-performance Baer or Wilwood disc brake system to fit the wheels is a popular choice.

Street/Strip

When you build a street/strip car, you're building a car that can cruise Main Street and also turn consistent times at the drag strip as a bracket car. Therefore, your F-Body should be able to idle in traffic and cleanly pull away from a stoplight without excessive revving or difficulty. When at the drag strip, it should provide impressive top-end speed to make the run fun and exciting.

Many owners want to dabble in drag racing at True Street competitions, nostalgia shows, and even national sanctioned events, but they don't want an unruly street beast that needs to be trailered to the event. A second-generation F-Body can be built into an impressive weekend warrior for the drag strip. The key element here is to have a high-performance package that isn't too aggressive for the street and can be easily designed for consistency.

While some may add superchargers and turbos, I recommend keeping the engine package easy to understand and set up. After all, you don't want the engine to be overheating, destroying the cam, folding up the rear suspension, or bilging the transmission. So, as always, all the parts of the car need to be compatible and complementary so you have a strong, reliable, and consistent car at the strip. If you can't hit your quarter-mile times within a few tenths, you're not going to win races.

Pro Touring

A Pro Touring car can be built to several levels, and therefore, this type of car can cross the line into high-performance street and restification. However, a Pro Touring is typically regarded as a vintage muscle car that carries extensive, high-grade suspension and drivetrain improvements. A Camaro or Firebird could also be built into a mild to wild Pro Touring car, depending on how much money you want to invest.

In essence, a second-generation F-Body Pro Touring car has been transformed from a classic muscle car with antiquated stock equipment to a high-performance handling machine with a selection of modern suspension, brake, steering, and powertrain equipment. A Pro Touring car can often outperform a late-model muscle car.

In the 1980s, Jeff Smith, an editor at *Car Craft* magazine, thought a respectable street machine should be able to handle like a sports car, have a strong yet dependable engine that was fast in the quarter-mile, and be able to drive to events. He owned and promoted that type of car, and today the style he envisioned is now called a Pro Touring car. Professional builders today have taken that simple idea and gone wild, even when it doesn't improve the looks or performance of the car.

Many Pro Touring cars carry cutting-edge suspension, chassis, engine, and drivetrain hardware so that the performance is more than a match for a late-model muscle car. For a second-generation F-Body, upgrades include (but are not restricted to) an LS crate engine, complete aftermarket front subframe, chassis subframe connectors, big-rotor slotted and drilled aftermarket brakes, rack-and-pinion steering, other enhancement products, complete multi-link rear suspensions, 5- or 6-speed manual transmissions, wide 18- to 20-inch wheels, and many more modifications.

In many instances, Pro Touring muscle cars have performance that rivals or exceeds a Z06 Corvette. And part of the fun and challenge of Pro Touring is building a second-generation Camaro or Firebird into a car that's far better handling, performing, and faster than anyone ever thought it could be.

Choose Your Process

There are a variety of options for modifying and improving the performance of your 1970 to 1981 Camaro or Firebird. In order to build a high-performance second-generation Camaro or Firebird, you need to start with a solid, rust-free body and strong chassis.

Restoration

A straight restoration is the least expensive path but it only makes sense on a special model such as a Z28 or Trans Am.

Restoring a car can range from reasonably to moderately expensive, depending on how rough the car is and how much of the work has to be farmed out to professionals. Restoration is not covered in this book.

Modification

The second-generation F-Body car stands virtually alone as an affordable performance car because most of its body pieces are offered as reproductions. Also, if you need to restore or repair the body before you build it into a high-performance machine, most of the parts are readily available and also quite affordable. While certain trim pieces may have to be sourced from an auto recycling establishment, all of the other parts are available from the aftermarket. For example, bumper covers and other body pieces that were not being offered for years are now available.

The difference between a restoration and a modification is the restored car does not have to be built with expensive aftermarket engine and suspension performance parts. The most expensive part of the restoration is generally the bodywork and paint, and today both are very expensive unless you can do it yourself. Bodywork can take months to complete, and that doesn't include painting the car. Also, when you are paying a professional more than $75 per hour the bill can get very high very fast. I know painters who prep and paint a car for as little as $10,000 to as much as $35,000, so be prepared for some sticker shock. That is probably why there are so many rat rods running around in primer. Paint is very expensive, so even if you can do the paint prep and paint work you will be spending around $2,000 just for the materials.

Here's a good example: I went to my local paint shop and priced out a gallon of Viper Red paint. It was $790, and that didn't include reducer. I also priced out a top-quality clearcoat, which listed for $633, including the hardener. When you add in a gallon or two of primer and sanding supplies it is easy to get to that $2,000 price I mentioned. I recommend that if you want to save money, find a friend who knows how to do bodywork and paint and have him show you how to do it. The paint is expensive but it is the labor cost that breaks the bank.

Restification

This is a blend of restoration and modification. Restification typically fits between a strictly stock restoration of a muscle car and the ultimate modification of a muscle car in the form of a Pro Touring car. As such, the car typically retains much of the original bodywork and interior, so it keeps the classic muscle car style, but substantial drivetrain and suspension mods are performed. It's not until you closely scrutinize the car that you recognize the modifications.

Project Your Time and Expenses

Before you embark on any project, you need to properly plan and budget for the work to be completed. If you don't plan and budget according to your goals, you may run out of money and not complete the car.

A good way to establish your priorities is to create a Gantt chart in Excel or a similar spread-sheet program:

- In column one, list each performance goal in descending order of priority.
- In column two, specify the start time.
- In column three, specify the finish time.
- In column four, specify the duration.

This way you can track the highest priority projects and you can forecast the amount of time required to complete them. This allows you to identify the projects that are going to make the biggest performance improvements, and it allows you to focus on those while assigning a secondary priority to the upgrades that will not make the biggest impact.

Now that you've established a priority list, you need to create a budget and a time schedule as well. They help you determine how much time and money you need to dedicate to each particular task or project. For instance, an owner may want to complete the suspension, chassis, and drivetrain upgrades and put bodywork and paint on the back burner.

Another spreadsheet works great for this. You will want to use a priority rating system, such as 1 being the highest and 4 being the lowest.

- In column one, place the highest priority projects at the top and the lowest ones at the bottom.
- In column two, list all the tasks for that project.
- In column three, list your budgeted cost.
- In column four, list your actual cost.
- In column five, list your budgeted hours.
- In column six, list your actual hours.

For column three, you can research prices from online parts vendors and magazines.

For column four, you can refer to magazine articles, club members who have done the work, and shop owners to project the average time it takes to complete the work. But keep in mind that your level of proficiency is not going to be close to that of a working professional, especially if this is the first time you're doing a task. So be sure to make realistic and accurate time projections.

When you also consider your investment in tools and material to complete the task, you may come to the conclusion that you're better off subcontracting the work to a shop. It's all up to you, but the moral of the story is: Don't kid yourself; sweat equity in a project only goes so far.

Organize Your Parts

You need to organize your parts to save time and hassle. For a particular project you should have all the necessary parts organized in one area on a shelf. My recommendation is to mark the boxes with color-coded tags or markers. If a part is standing alone, put a color-coded tag on it. Large parts should remain stored in their box. To keep small parts organized and safe they can be placed in a zip-bag and tagged.

Many parts are exposed to the environment, particularly suspension, chassis, exhaust, and related parts. Before you start your project, all parts should be properly stored and protected. If a body panel needs to be hung, hang it in the proper fashion. If a bare-metal part needs protection, cover it with WD40 or, ideally, rust inhibitor. Remember, you are making a sizable invest in upgrading your second-generation F-Body, so you don't want that investment to go to waste because the parts were damaged due to improper storage.

Home improvement stores offer a variety of storage options, including shelving necessary. Do not haphazardly stack heavy parts on top of one another; I know it seems like common sense but you'd be surprised

This 1972 Formula Firebird looks original, but it actually has several improvements in handling and performance. This Firebird is running Trans Am snowflake wheels and is powered by a strong-running 455-ci engine.

how many times owners just don't stop and think. Months later, after all the damage has been done to the parts, the thought crosses the owner's mind that more time and care should have been exercised.

Do not expose parts to excess humidity, heat, or cold. Also make sure no mice, rats, or other animals can get into the parts and ruin them.

Keep the area free of clutter and don't store hazardous chemicals on top of boxes holding parts. Once again, it may seem like common sense, but people sometimes get in a hurry and put chemicals on top of parts boxes. Of course, it gets knocked over or leaks, which damages or ruins the parts.

If you're doing your build-up in stages, it's often better to order the parts as you need them because they often take up much more garage space than anticipated. Storage space takes away from work space and you don't want to fill up the garage with parts and have no place to work.

Buying a bunch of parts for multiple installation projects at the same time is a risky endeavor. Here's why. Often, owners run into unforeseen demands on their time...family, friends, work, and many other factors. They have to stop a project, and sometimes months or years pass before they return to the project. If you have the wrong part, it's defective, or has been discontinued, you're out of luck and you eat the cost and have to buy the same part over again. If you buy parts as you go, you should save time, frustration, and money in the end.

Your workbench should be used for its intended purpose, and that's working on your product install. It shouldn't be a storage area for your parts because they take up valuable space. I don't know about you but one of my pet peeves is having a cluttered bench when I'm trying to get something done and then having to stop and clean up the clutter. It doesn't have to be operating-room clean or look like Felix Unger was there but keep it free of clutter and reduce the annoyance.

Think about Safety

Never, ever, under any circumstances compromise your safety. Let me say that again, in the strongest and most emphatic way possible: Don't take any chances with safety. It simply isn't worth risking life or limb to build up a car. If you don't feel comfortable performing a procedure or you can't do it safely, don't do it. Having a professional complete work you can't do safely is smart; it's not showing a lack of skill.

Products come with safety precautions. Follow them and don't get sloppy or lazy. When you're working under the car, have all the jack stands located in the proper locations. Don't work under a car that's just supported by a floor jack. If it fails, it can crush you. When you're welding, you need to wear welding gloves, mask, and cover up any exposed skin. In addition, you should wear a respirator to protect your lungs from the toxic gas that's released during welding. Sad to say, many welders don't wear respirators. Don't be one of them.

When working with a power tool always have firm and confident control of the tools and don't get yourself into awkward situations. When performing any kind of bodywork, you need to wear the proper safety equipment. This includes a clear face mask for proper eye and face protection. It's always easy to get complacent and leave the shop glasses on the bench. Wear a

The early Camaros have always been popular—this one features a hot small-block Chevy engine and a variety of handling modifications. The engine in this car started out as a low-horsepower, small-block 350-ci engine, but with improvements it now makes more horsepower than the famous LT-1 engine used in Z28 models.

long-sleeved shirt and short gloves or a short-sleeved shirt and long gloves. When cutting sheet metal, hot shards of metal can be thrown off the work area, and you don't want them to penetrate your skin.

Just use common sense and keep yourself safe.

Buildup Overview

The last car I built took five months to build from start to finish; some people require years to finish a car. In a nutshell, here are the general steps I follow after I've found the right car.

Disassembly

To start the disassembly work, I remove the engine, transmission, front bumper, and sheet metal. Then I gut the interior. If I am going to use the original engine, in the case of a 350 or 396 Chevy or 400 Pontiac, I disassemble it and take it to a machine shop for any necessary upgrading. I select the new engine parts (such as the rings, bearings, pistons, and camshaft) and then assemble the engine after the machine work is finished. If the car is equipped with a 4-speed I rebuild it. If it is an automatic I send it out for rebuilding.

Bodywork

While the engine and transmission are being machined or rebuilt I start the bodywork. I generally strip the body to bare metal because with the paints that are available now it is better to start out with a blank canvas. I send some of the parts (such as the doors, trunk, hood, front fenders, inner fender panels, and chassis parts) to a professional sandblasting shop that specializes in automotive parts.

I pull out any dents, remove and rework old bodywork, cut out rusty areas, install new metal, and remove and restore the trim. I buff stainless-steel trim such as window moldings. In the case of the later Camaros and Trans Ams I send the window trim to a powder coater where semi-gloss black is applied.

After all of the dents and imperfections are taken care of, I paint the body with an etching primer, followed by a filler primer. At this point the body has to be block sanded until all of the panels are perfect. I use a long rubber sander on flat panels and a variety of other blocks on curved panels. I have found that a paint stick covered with sandpaper works well on small, flat, and slightly curved areas.

After the car is block sanded more primer can be applied, and this process continues until the car is dent and wave free. Certain primers from some companies, such as PPG, dry to a semi-gloss finish so it is easy to spot problem areas. After the final primer is completed and the body is dent free, I do the final sanding with 400-grit sandpaper; then the car is ready for the topcoat.

In certain parts of the country, you can paint the car with solvent-based paint. If you live in most parts of California you have to use a water-based paint. Fortunately the clear coat used in California and other states is still solvent based so after applying the color coat, the clear can be sprayed on. Every painter has his or her own way of doing things; I generally apply four coats of clear over the paint. This allows a thick coating that can be sanded flat before the buffing. Other painters say two coats are enough.

Using progressively finer sandpaper I sand the surface until it is flat. You can use small air-driven palm sanders and super-fine sandpaper to sand large, flat areas of the body to speed things up. When the body is sanded flat I buff the paint to a shine using 3M 6085 Rubbing Compound with a wool pad followed by 3M 6068 Ultra Fine Machine Polish with a foam pad.

The inner fender panels and subframe components have to be restored after they are sandblasted to bare metal. I paint the inner fender wells and chassis components with PPG DP 90 black etching primer first. Then I spray the engine components with special semi-gloss black from The Eastwood Company. Of course, this is done when the project is going to be a restored car or a resto-mod. If the project is a wildly modified car I paint the engine compartment the body color and I often smooth the firewall and make other nice changes.

Engine Building

I prefer to build the engine because that to me is the fun part. It is very satisfying to build a strong-running engine using the parts I know work for building power. This also allows me to detail the engine in a restored form or as a wild polished-and-chrome-plated jewel for a street machine. If the car was built between 1970 and 1975 I can build the engine to produce plenty of power. If it is a 1976-or-newer car I build the engine with parts that are legal in California so the car will pass the smog laws.

I don't use crate engines but they are available; many are strong-running engines and that is certainly another way to go if you want instant gratification. Many enthusiasts opt for one of the new LS Corvette engines, which certainly build substantial horsepower. The only problem you run into is hooking up all of the wiring the new engine needs.

Reassembly

After all of the parts are painted and the engine is rebuilt and detailed, the car is ready for reassembly, and that is the real fun part of building the car. As I disassemble a car I take pictures of how it comes apart so I can use them when I reassemble the car. Assembling most of a car is pretty straightforward but some of the grille and tail-end assemblies used in the 1970s can be confusing if you don't have something to look at. Some of the assembly manuals aren't particularly helpful.

It is important to do the assembly work (such as installing the inner fender panels in the fenders) on a surface that is soft and non-abrasive so the parts don't get scratched in the process. It is also important to put masking tape along the edges of the body when the doors and fenders are installed. It is a good idea to have a few friends help you install the trunk and, especially, the hood to keep it balanced and safe while the bolts are being installed.

Interior

The final part of building the car is finishing the interior, and that can be done with reproduction interior components from your favorite restoration supplier if you are building a restored car or a resto-mod. If you prefer a wild interior you have to turn the car over to a professional auto upholstery shop.

When you buy an interior from a reproduction supplier you can have a complete interior in your car for around $2,000. If you have an upholstery shop do the interior, it may be $10,000 or more. It's not unusual to see interiors that approach $20,000!

Engine Test

After the interior is finished the last thing that has to be done is to fire up the engine for the first time. First I find top dead center (TDC) of the engine and then make sure the rotor is facing the number-1 position and the spark plug wires are hooked up correctly following the firing order of the engine. Chevy engines turn in a clockwise direction and the Pontiac engines turn in a counter clockwise direction. The firing order is the same.

After I find the firing order and the rotor position, I find the starting point of the engine. The engine should be filled with oil, the automatic transmission should have a few quarts of transmission fluid for fire-up, and if the car has a manual transmission it should be filled with oil. The brakes should also be bled and working before the car is fired up. Providing that all the wires are hooked up properly and there is gas in the tank, the engine is ready to be fired up.

I generally pour a little gas down the carburetor and then turn the key. If the engine starts to fire up I know I am close. The radiator should be filled with water for the break-in period because if there are any leaks it will only be water. After the car is running I drain the water and install the proper coolant mix. If the car is running a flat-tappet or hydraulic cam the engine has to be run at 2,000 rpm for about 20 minutes to break in the cam. It is also very important to use an oil such as Comp Cams Break-In Oil that is zinc enhanced. After the cam break-in is finished, the engine requires timing and tuning to get it running perfect.

Tools

Whether you plan to build or modify a car you need a good variety of tools. A small tool set from Harbor Freight or Sears is a good start but it is necessary to have at least two wrenches of every size. You also need a good assortment of sockets in 1/2-, 3/8-, and 1/4-inch drive sizes, along with normal sockets and deep-drive sockets.

I also recommend having air tools, such as air-driven ratchet wrenches, of the same three sizes and large and small impact guns. The air tools are great when a car is being disassembled.

A good assortment of screwdrivers (straight and Phillip's head) are also important to have, plus a variety of other screwdriver bits. I also recommend a full set of Allen-head wrenches in T-handle drives and for use on socket wrenches.

You will need a good assortment of bodyworking tools, such as hammers and dollys, an electric dent puller, air sanders and grinders, spray guns, and a MIG welder for rust repair. It is also important to have bench sanders, a drill press, and a hydraulic press.

Other tools that come in handy are a pressure washer and a small portable sandblaster. A sandblast cabinet is another tool that comes in handy for small-part sandblasting. A car lift comes in handy when you are working on the bottom the car.

If you have most of the aforementioned tools you are in good shape to build a car but if you don't, you may run into some problems along the way.

CHAPTER 2

ENGINE PERFORMANCE

Most second-generation F-Body cars were equipped with a mild six-cylinder or a V-8 engine. While the early 1970s Trans Ams and Formula 400s, and Camaro Z28s and Super Sports provided soul-stirring performance, many of the second-generation cars housed mild 305s, 350s, and six-cylinder engines. These mild V-8 engines need a lot of work and performance parts to transform them into high-performance engines.

Since these cars rolled out of the factory, aftermarket engine technology has marched forward, and you can build a high-performance V-8 engine on a very reasonable budget. You can use these cars as a platform for building a quick and fun street or competition car. Head development has raged forward for the Chevy small- and big-block, as well as for the Pontiac V-8. Aftermarket high-flow heads can improve horsepower output by 50 or more. But beyond improving performance, aluminum heads weigh much less than OEM cast-iron heads, and replacing them saves a lot of weight on the front end of the car.

Before you tear into the engine, consider the following. The EPA was established in 1970, which became a transitional year for car manufacturers. The bureaucrats were cracking down on the car manufacturers for what they though was too much horsepower and excessive fuel usage. In 1971 they started mandating fuel economy and air pollution standards to clean up the environment. Part of this push was the elimination of lead in gasoline, even though many of the cars produced a year earlier required high-octane gasoline.

As the standards got tougher, engine compression ratios and power decreased, but these cars featured improved suspension geometry, more efficient aerodynamics, and alluring body style, and that's why the second-generation F-Body cars are an exceptional platform for building a serious street machine. Today, many of the early Camaros and Firebirds are no longer restricted, so enthusiasts can install a performance-oriented engine.

Small-Block versus Big-Block

The small-block Chevy was commonly found in the second-generation Camaro, and available throughout its production run. The Pontiac V-8 was produced in massive numbers in second-generation Trans Ams and Firebirds. And it's widely accepted that the Trans Am was the only muscle car in the mid and late 1970s.

A massive range of aftermarket engine performance parts can be used to upgrade and even transform both the Pontiac V-8 and small-block Chevy. In particular, the number of high-performance engine products for the 350 Chevy and 350 Pontiac engines is almost overwhelming. If you have one of these engines, you have a good foundation for a high-performance buildup. However, the second-generation car can easily accept a myriad of engines, so these small-blocks are not your only option. But, with an entire universe of top-quality products, the majority of Camaro owners opt to build up a small-block because they can find the right parts at the right price. These include performance camshafts, heads, carburetors, ignition systems, headers, and appearance improvements.

While the Mark IV 396-ci big-block made its way into a small number of 1971 and 1972 Camaros, an original big-block car is so rare that most wouldn't degrade the collector value by building it into a

CHAPTER 2

If you are looking for the ultimate high-performance LS1/LS2/LS6 engine, install a set of AFR aluminum cylinder heads. These emissions-legal heads are specifically designed for 1997-to-present Gen-III Chevy Corvettes, Camaros, and trucks using a 3.900-inch bore. AFR's LSX Mongoose Street aluminum cylinder heads offer unmatched flow performance and feature 2.02-inch intake valves and 1.60-inch exhaust valves with AFR's iron ductile interlocking valve seats. The heads add horsepower to the engines due to the larger ports and improved port designs. The LS engines are difficult to improve upon, but these heads make a difference.

high-performance street or track machine. But there's nothing to stop you from buying a vintage big-block from a private seller or sourcing a classic big-block crate engine, slotting it into an original small-block or six-cylinder Camaro, and then making the necessary chassis and suspension upgrades.

Of course, building and installing a big-block does come with some trade-offs. The larger engine places an additional 150 pounds over the front wheels compared to a small-block. Another consideration is that the components are much more expensive than those for a small-block. And small-block stroker kits allow owners to take a big leap in performance yet reliably retain the small-block. 383 stroker kits for the Chevy 350 are so abundant, and a huge number of 383 kits are available from every manufacturer. Most enthusiasts won't do a stock rebuild and opt for a 383 stroker kit. But 396 and 408 stroker kits are available for the small-block that push performance into the big-block territory without the weight penalty of the big-block, making small-block strokers very popular. While the small-block has many more high-performance and stroker parts options, many also agree that there's no substitute for the thundering power of the big-block.

If a small-block Chevy powers your 1970–1981 Camaro, you have the strong foundation for a high-performance engine. The aftermarket offers more high-performance parts for the small-block than any other American V-8 engine. You can find nearly an endless variety of parts for the Chevy small-block.

Cylinder Heads

The installation of performance cylinder heads can make a huge horsepower increase on any engine. Starting in 1955, small-block Chevy engines were available with standard heads and 2-barrel carburetors. If you wanted an upgrade you could order a power-pack engine that featured improved power-pack heads and a 4-barrel carburetor. Corvette engines featured heads with larger ports and valves, and they were equipped with dual-quad carburetors or fuel injection. For years, Chevy enthusiasts searched for original high-performance "double-hump" or "camel-hump" fuel-injection heads because there were no aftermarket versions.

Learning from what car manufacturers were doing, it was easy to see that improved heads and better

Installing a set of AFR oval-port Magnum aluminum cylinder heads provides excellent bottom-end torque, tremendous throttle response, and great all-around power for 396- to 468-ci big-block Chevy engines. The heads feature lightweight stainless-steel 2.19-inch intake valves and 1.88-inch exhaust valves. The heads also have double springs, 10-degree locks and retainers, and high-quality studs and guide plates. The oval-port Magnum heads are designed for improved street performance where low-end smooth performance is desired, but they also work great in high-RPM drag racing applications.

ENGINE PERFORMANCE

carburetion increased horsepower when used with the right camshaft. The aftermarket companies knew that cylinder heads with large ports and valves could direct a larger fuel/air mixture into the cylinders. When they are used along with a high-performance intake manifold and carburetor and a performance camshaft you can turn a mild-mannered 350-ci engine into one with performance to spare.

Heads are such an important engine component that a wide variety of companies started manufacturing high-performance cast-iron and aluminum heads. Aluminum heads are better than steel ones because they weigh half as much, and that is good for both drag racing and road racing.

Project 1: Aluminum Head Installation

Getting fuel into the engine efficiently and evacuating the exhaust quickly increases horsepower. Carburetor, intake manifold, heads, and camshaft are the crucial parts of any engine system. To maximize output and efficiency, these parts need to complement each other. In my estimation, heads are probably the most important part of this equation. After all, you can have the best intake manifold and carburetor and even a good camshaft, but without free-flowing heads, engine performance is limited.

The heads you choose need to work with the intake manifold, and a cam should be selected that works with the other two components to create a cohesive package. If you have built a few engines that have achieved their power potential, you know how to select the parts for your next engine, and you shouldn't have to go through the first-timer's trial-and-error process. If this is your first engine buildup, Edelbrock can help you out because it offers several package combinations, which are designed to work together to optimize output. The engine shown here uses the best of everything for high-performance street use. Edelbrock has designed a selection of aluminum head designs for a variety of engine uses, from hot street performance to all-out racing. The Performer RPM heads are for high-performance street and track use. The company also offers larger heads for racing endeavors and high-RPM use such as drag racing and circle-track racing.

Follow along as I install Edelbrock aluminum heads on a Chevy 350-ci engine block; you can do the same thing on your Camaro engine. If you have a second-generation Firebird, similar aluminum Pontiac Edelbrock heads can be used, and the installation instructions translate to the Pontiac engine.

Edelbrock offers several aluminum heads for Chevy engines. I installed Edelbrock Performer RPM heads (PN 60899) with straight plugs on my Chevy 350-ci engine. These heads feature 64-cc chambers and the engine has flat-top pistons, so the engine runs 10:1 compression. I selected the as-cast finish because it looks nice and gives the engine a business-only appearance. I selected straight-plug heads because there is a larger number of headers and exhaust products designed to work with them. I also used Edelbrock head gaskets and ARP head bolts that are designed to work with aluminum heads.

CHAPTER 2

Clean Cylinder Deck

1 After the pistons have been installed, oil is often left on the deck surface, so wipe the decks with acetone or lacquer thinner before the gaskets are installed. The heads are assembled at the factory with new valve seats, stainless-steel valves, and the correct valveguide clearance. Prior to installation, inspect those items for inconsistencies, flaws, and factory assembly problems.

For this project, I am using an Edelbrock camshaft, so the valve seat pressure of the heads is correct for the camshaft. Edelbrock heads have a seat pressure of 135 pounds and work fine for both flat-tappet and hydraulic-lifter camshafts. If you are using a very high lift cam (which I am not), check the valve-to-piston clearance. For the cam lift I am using, .516 inch is not going to be a problem.

Lubricate and Chase Head Bolt Holes

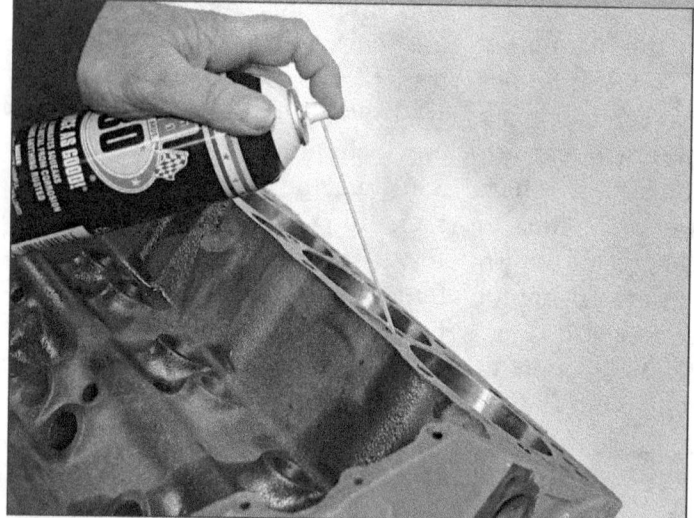

2 Spray JB80 or similar penetrating oil on all of the head bolt holes in the block and then run a tap through the threads. Even though the block has been cleaned, there might be some dirt trapped in the holes.

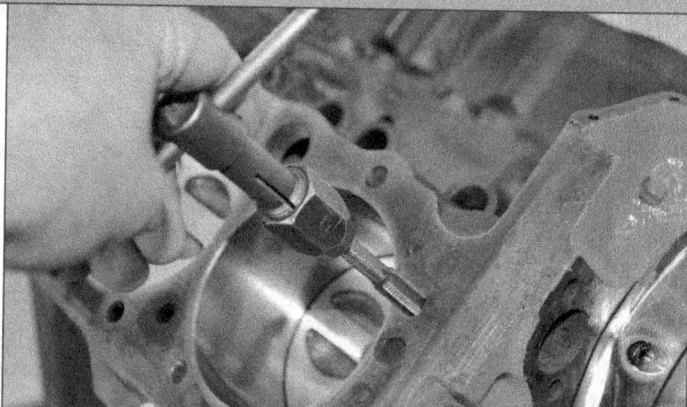

3 Chasing the threads in the block can be done before or after the pistons have been installed. I recommend doing it after and loading the threads with JB80 penetrating oil because the dirt sticks to the tap. Wipe down the tap to remove the dirt after each hole has been tapped. This makes it easier to start the new bolts and also provides more accurate torquing of the fasteners.

Apply Silicone to Head Bolts through Water Jacket

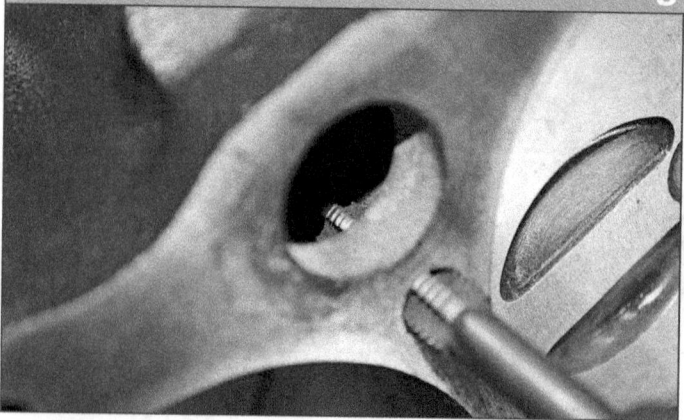

4 If you look closely, you can see that a few of the bolt holes go right into the water passage. Coat the threads on these bolts with silicone to prevent water leaks. The silicone seals the bolt holes and prevents coolant from seeping out.

Fit Head Gasket and Drill Steam Holes

5 Lay the head gasket on the deck before installing the aluminum head. (Edelbrock recommends Fel-Pro head gaskets.) Line up the gasket with the two dowel holes on each side of the block.

If you have a 400-ci engine, drill three steam holes into the head at the locations outlined in the instruction sheet. Find the steam holes in the gasket and drill the head accordingly using a .125-inch drill. The holes are located on the spark plug side of the head between the cylinder bores. Drill straight into the head (90 degrees from the deck) until the drill breaks through into the water jacket (about 9/16 inch). The coolant holes absolutely must not overlap into the head gasket sealing ring area. When you are finished use an air hose to blow out the debris.

If you are working on a 350-ci engine, drilling the heads is not necessary.

Place Heads on Block

6 Place the heads on the block using the dowel pins for alignment. Thread in two bolts on each head to anchor them to the block and prevent them from slipping off. This allows the heads to stay in place while the rest of the bolts are being installed.

Coat Head Bolts with Silicone

7 Because these bolts go into the block and into the water jackets, apply silicone on the threads to seal the bolts and prevent coolant from seeping out of the cylinder heads. Place a dab at the end of the bolt. As the bolt is torqued, the silicone works its way up the threads. (Big-block Chevy engine bolts must be coated with silicone or sealer to prevent water leaks because all the bolts pass into the water jackets.)

Lubricate Head Bolts

8 Lubricate the head side of the bolt so it can be torqued down to the block smoothly and more accurately. The bolts can be lubricated with camshaft assembly lube, anti-seize, or even a heavy oil such as STP.

Torque Head Bolts

9 The center bolt between the springs doesn't fit properly without some modification, so use a grinding wheel to remove material from the ARP-supplied washer. All others fit fine, but the center one needs to be modified by grinding the sides of the washer flat enough to fit between the springs.

Modify Center Washer

10 Tighten head bolts with a socket wrench prior to following the cylinder head torque sequence. (I used these special Edelbrock-supplied ARP bolts to fasten the heads.) In most, but not all, cases, torqueing the bolts begins in the center of the head in pairs. Then alternate to fore and aft of each head, working your way to the outside. While this procedure is typical, you must refer to specific instructions from your manufacturer.

I started by tightening them to 40 ft-lbs, following the torque sequence, then to 55 ft-lbs, and finally to 65 ft-lbs. It is always a good idea to go back over the bolts to make sure all are torqued to the correct spec to make sure you didn't miss one.

11 Grind the washer on each side to clear the valve-springs. Use either a small hand sander or a bench grinder as seen here. The washers become hot when grinding, so it is a good idea to use a pair of Vise-Grips or pliers to safely hold them.

Torque Engine Bolts Again

12 After the engine is fired up and runs for a while, check the torque of head bolts and tighten them one more time because they generally loosen after the engine expands and contracts. Typically, the torque sequence starts from the middle of the heads and works outward to the ends.

ENGINE PERFORMANCE

Using these heads with 64-cc combustion chambers and flat-top pistons, this engine has 10:1 compression. With the intake manifold, carburetor, and camshaft that I am using, the horsepower is more than 400, according to dyno-test figures on a similar engine that Edelbrock built.

Before the spark plugs are installed, gap them. All of the spark plugs in this set were gapped at .35 inch from the factory, which is correct for this engine. Edelbrock heads require a special deep spark plug such as this Champion RC12YC. If you install standard plugs for a 1972 Chevy 350 the engine won't operate properly.

When installing spark plugs in an aluminum head, coat the threads with anti-seize lubricant. If you do not use anti-seize, the heat cycling from combustion heating and cooling can fuse the spark plugs to the aluminum heads. As a result, when you try to remove the plugs that haven't been coated with anti-seize, you either strip the spark plug hole or are unable to remove the plugs. Anti-seize also prevents corrosion.

Here is the head after it is installed on the block following the proper procedure. The heads flow much more air than stock heads and, therefore, produce much more horsepower. They also look nice on the orange Chevy block. Now that the heads are installed, the intake manifold and carburetor can be installed.

CHAPTER 3

Selecting and Installing a Camshaft

A camshaft is a crucial component in the high-performance top-end equation. In other words, the camshaft serves as the mechanical brain of the engine, actuating vital timing events for the valvetrain. As the brain, it's an integral component of the top end, so it needs to be matched to the heads, pushrods, intake, carb, and other components. The correct-profile camshaft flows the right amount of air and fuel through the heads' intake ports and into the combustion chambers.

Most OEM top-end engine parts for this generation of Camaros and Firebirds are restrictive as well as antiquated. Over the course of three decades, the aftermarket has developed much better high-performance equipment than General Motors had when the cars were built.

When building an engine, most select heads with larger ports and a far more efficient combustion chamber design. These heads require more air and fuel, and therefore, you typically select a longer duration, higher lift, and larger LCA (lobe centerline angle) cam than stock, to get a larger fuel charge into the engine. When you do that, you typically get a larger carburetor and more efficient manifold.

There are four basic camshaft designs: hydraulic, solid lifter, hydraulic roller, and roller. The hydraulic and hydraulic roller camshafts are designed for street performance and mild drag racing or track use. The solid-lifter and roller camshafts are designed to produce high-RPM power and are best suited for drag racing, circle track racing, and other off-road uses.

There are two hydraulic roller camshaft designs for Chevy engines: one used for engines up to 1986 and the other for Chevy engines built after 1987.

Emission and Mileage Standards

In the 1970s all auto manufacturers had to meet emissions regulations and fuel mileage mandates. They were partially able to do that with camshaft designs, along with other emissions-related parts. Many cars were equipped with camshafts that were designed in a retarded position, as opposed to a standard or advanced design, and the duration and valve lifts were small when compared to a performance cam. When you look at the horsepower figures of the small-block Chevy engines from the mid 1970s you can see how camshaft design altered the power of the engine. Along with camshaft design, manufacturers also changed the head designs and intake manifold designs to meet emissions standards.

In 1970, the Camaro's 350 LT-1 engines produced 360 hp, but in 1971 the LT-1 was rated at 255 net hp. But keep in mind, the industry changed the ratings from gross horsepower (measured at the crank) to net horsepower (measured at the rear wheels). Certainly, this move lowered horsepower by approximately 20 to 25 percent. But as we all know, the culmination of certain events, including the oil crisis, rising insurance rates, increased emissions standards, and political concerns, led to the demise of the muscle car era.

In 1972, compression ratios dropped substantially, emissions equipment was installed, and horsepower production was seriously stifled. By 1974, the muscle car era had

SELECTING AND INSTALLING A CAMSHAFT

effectively ended, and in 1975, General Motors offered three different 350 engines, which produced 125, 145, and 155 hp, respectively. Altering the camshaft, head, and intake manifold design increased horsepower, and performance changes. In particular, installing a new hydraulic roller or other high-performance cam and complementing it with the right engine parts produced serious horsepower gains.

Fundamentally these are legitimate high-performance V-8 engines, but these engine equipment packages seriously hindered performance. Hence, mid to late 1970s Pontiac and Chevy V-8 architecture supports high-performance cams, pistons, cranks, rods, heads, intakes, and other pieces. It's just that these stock components are mild in order to meet emissions and mileage standards and need to be replaced with suitable aftermarket components. As a result, you can build a reliable street engine with 400 to 500 hp, and in some cases, even more.

Hydraulic Lifters

The main difference among the four styles of camshaft is the lifter design. Hydraulic lifters and hydraulic roller lifters are generally adequate up to 6,500 rpm, and that should be plenty for street-driven cars. Solid lifters and solid roller lifters can be revved above 6,500 rpm and with all of the other necessary hardware to go along with the camshaft design they can be revved to 9,000 rpm or more in many drag race uses.

When you consider a camshaft for your car, be aware of how you intend to use the car. All manufacturers list these specifications: lift, duration, and where the design makes power. The big mistake many enthusiasts make is thinking that the bigger the cam, the better the engine runs, but that's not necessarily the case. If you plan on using the car on the street and will limit the RPM to 6,500 or less you should select a camshaft that is listed in the cam specifications as a cam that builds power between 1,500 to 6,000 or 2,000 to 6,500 rpm. It would be ridiculous to order a cam that delivers power from 3,500 to 8,500 rpm just because it's bigger. The opposite is also true: If you are building a drag race engine that will spin at a high-RPM range you want a cam that is designed for high-RPM power.

The valve lash gaps of a hydraulic lifter or hydraulic roller lifter are typically already set and stay in adjustment for quite a long time. A solid lifter or solid roller lifter requires regular valve lash adjustment with hard use or prolonged daily driving. Today, setting the valve lash isn't done as much as it was in the past on a street-driven car, but racers check the lash after a few runs just to make sure the settings remain accurate.

Solid Lifters

Solid lifter engines are noisier than hydraulic lifter engines, so it is a personal decision if you want an engine that's quieter or one that has a definite ticking noise. Some enthusiasts like a solid lifter engine because to them the ticking of the rockers sounds intimidating. It is quite possible to get a solid lifter engine that builds power in the 2,500- to 6,500-rpm range, so they certainly can be used on the street if desired.

Chevrolet's use of solid lifters in its highest horsepower engines is proof that a solid lifter engine can be used on the street. Chevrolet used solid lifters in the 375-hp 327 Corvette engines, Z28 302 engines, and high-horsepower (435 and L88) 427 Corvette engines in the 1950s and 1960s. If you have ever owned a Chevy with solid lifters, you know the valve lash had to be set regularly. If you do not plan to rev your engine above 6,500 rpm, a hydraulic camshaft for street applications is suitable.

Roller Cams

A standard hydraulic lifter or a flat-tappet cam can be installed in a high-performance engine and be used to make excellent horsepower. They are also less expensive than the roller designs. The standard lifters of both variations are designed for a cam that has a simple lobe design that provides a lift and duration for increasing horsepower. In the late 1970s and early 1980s, the factory started to use the hydraulic roller camshaft because the camshaft lobe design could be changed with not only convex lift surfaces but also with concave lift surfaces, so that cam profile could be used to meet emissions and fuel mandates. Since the roller has a very small contact point, lobe designs could be used that the flat-tappet couldn't take advantage of. When the factory started using hydraulic roller designs the aftermarket followed, and today we have some high-performance roller camshafts available for street use.

The late-model engines were designed with provisions for roller camshafts, so when you order a camshaft be sure to order the correct one for your application. The early engines can still take advantage of the roller camshaft but they don't have the same provisions.

In the past, camshaft designs varied, so it was very important to degree a cam to make sure it was cut properly. Today that isn't as important because most cams are made on computer numerically controlled (CNC) machines, and they are dead accurate. I did degree the cam in this installation just to verify timing, but it was right on the money and wasn't really necessary.

Project 1: Hydraulic Roller Camshaft Installation

To properly install a cam in an engine that's installed in a vehicle, you need to remove all the components in front of the cam tunnel so you have access. This means removing the radiator, all accessories, and timing cover. This is a much easier process if the engine has been removed from the car as in this project.

The performance cam here is an Edelbrock Performer RPM Roller Hydraulic camshaft (PN 2201). It is designed for all 283- to 400-ci small-block Chevy engines made from 1957 to 1986. This camshaft's optimal operating range is 1,500 to 6,500 rpm, and it should only be used with standard 1.5:1 rocker arms. This cam features an intake duration of 296 degrees and an exhaust duration of 300 degrees. The intake valve lift is 0.539 inch while the exhaust lift is 0.548. All of the important cam specifications can be found on the cam card that comes with a camshaft. This cam is designed for use with Edelbrock's Performer RPM heads and Performer RPM intake manifold.

In order to properly install this cam and cams like it, you must buy compatible parts for the cam system. They include roller lifters, hardened pushrods, camshaft thrust button, intake manifold gaskets or equivalent, timing chain set, pipe plugs, and RTV silicone sealer.

Before installing a roller cam, remove the timing cover and timing chain and gears. Once the cam gear has been removed, unbolt the cam locking plate and carefully remove the existing cam from the cam tunnel.

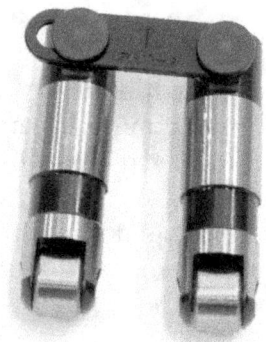

High-performance hydraulic roller lifters come in pairs for the small-block Chevy engine. The link bar keeps the lifters straight in the bores so they don't rotate and alignment is maintained at high RPM. These strong Edelbrock lifters are made of 86L20 steel, and the heat-treated case has a 50- to 52-c hardness with a depth range of .010 to .015 inch. Unless you're an accomplished engine builder, don't mix and match valvetrain parts from various manufacturers because design and material differences among these parts may make them incompatible over the long haul. You get an integrated system if you buy a complete cam kit from one manufacturer. Therefore, if you're installing a Comp cam, use Comp lifters, pushrods, and related parts, which come as a complete kit.

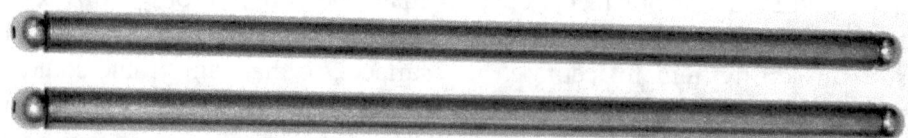

Hardened chrome-moly pushrods are designed for use with a roller cam. All aftermarket camshaft manufacturers offer high-strength pushrods in various diameters and lengths. Many sets come in 5/16-inch diameter. The particular cam manufacturer supplies the correct pushrods for an application when you purchase a cam in a kit combination. If you're running a non-stock rocker arm ratio or altered rocker arm geometry, a custom pushrod length is often needed. This is just one factor that affects rocker arm length. Others include valvestem length, pushrod seat height, lifter design, cam base circle, block, and head deck height.

Remember that each pushrod manufacturer has a different way of measuring pushrods, so coordinate with the particular pushrod manufacturer to determine the correct method for measuring pushrods. Comp Cams offers a simple way to measure pushrod length using the company's pushrod length checker that has a standard length stamped in it. With the two halves fastened together, use the length of the gauge to measure .140 inch. For cylinder number-1, rotate the cam so the gauge length is .050 inch. For example, a pushrod that's screwed one rotation open measures 7.800 + .050 for a 7.850-inch gauge length. As a result, you select the length of the pushrod that matches this specification.

SELECTING AND INSTALLING A CAMSHAFT

Before the engine is assembled, you can dip the lifters in Valvoline 20W-50 racing motor oil for lubrication. But in most cases, that doesn't fully prime the hydraulic lifters. Instead, use an oil pump priming tool to fully prime the lifters before initial start-up. When it comes to soaking the lifters, Edelbrock doesn't recommend keeping the lifters in oil for very long. I soaked them for about five minutes.

Remove Stock Cam

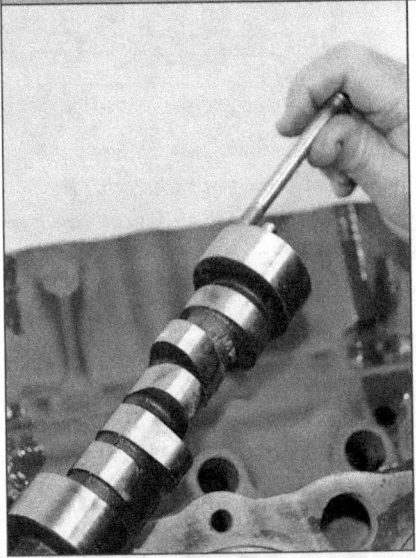

1 Remove the old cam sprocket. To remove the old cam, thread in a cam installation handle (from Goodson or another company) or a bolt to the end of the cam. Turn the cam from side to side and slide it straight out of the tunnel, taking care not to nick the lobes on the cam saddles.

Coat New Cam with Lube

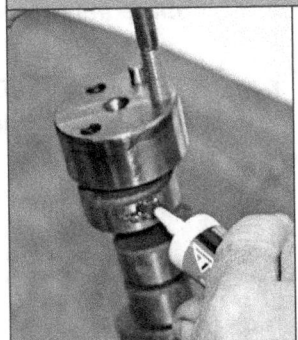

2 Coat the new cam with assembly lube before installing it in the engine. This lube is supplied with the camshaft. Spread the lube oil over the cam lobes and journals, and use your finger to make sure the entire circumference is coated. Adequate lubrication is necessary to prevent premature wear when the engine is broken in—you don't want to ruin your cam at initial start-up because you didn't apply enough assembly lube.

Appling enough lube is important on a flat-tappet or hydraulic tappet camshaft, but less so with a roller cam because the roller doesn't wear out the lobes.

Install Cam in Cam Tunnel

3 Firmly grasp and steadily guide the cam into the cam tunnel to make sure the cam bearings aren't being nicked or scratched. Here I am balancing the cam as it is being installed to make sure it is seating properly in the cam bearings.

4 Install the camshaft into the last cam bearing journal using a bolt or a cam installation handle. When the camshaft has been seated properly, the bolt can be removed. Make sure the cam spins easily in the cam journals before proceeding.

Install Timing Chain Set

5 For this project, an Edelbrock double-roller timing chain (PN 7802) is fitted to the engine. Turn the camshaft and the crankshaft until the dots on the upper and lower sprockets face each other. When correctly installed, the dots on the cam sprocket and crank sprocket align perfectly in the middle as seen here. Route the chain under the crank sprocket, and place the cam sprocket onto the cam dowel pin. Ensure that the timing marks are properly aligned and the chain and/or sprockets properly align. The crankshaft sprocket is torqued to 20 ft-lbs.

Install Cam Sprocket

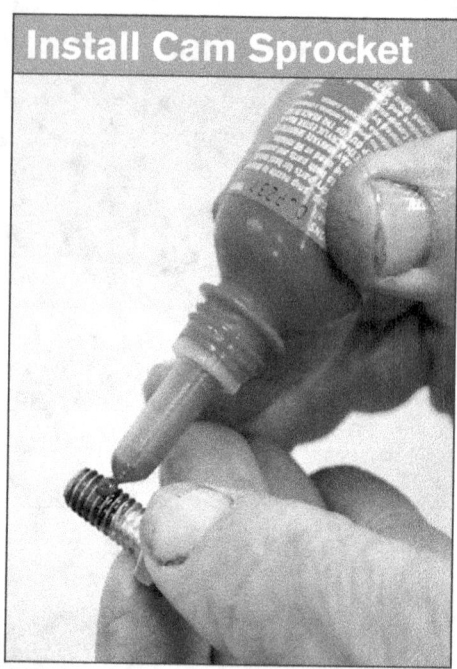

6 Coat the cam bolts with Red Loctite and then install the cam sprocket on the camshaft. Tighten sprocket bolts to 20 ft-lbs.

Verify Timing Set Alignment

7 If the dot on the camshaft is pointing down while the dot on the crankshaft is pointing up, the timing set has been installed properly. The camshaft bolts are 5/16 inch long with a 1/2-inch head; the torque specification is 20 ft-lbs, so use a small 3/8-inch torque wrench.

Install Cam Button

8 This camshaft came with a cam button. This button may have to be modified to work with certain timing chain covers, but it may work as is with others. Put the aluminum cover on. If it hits against the cam button it must be shortened. If you are using a thin steel cover, for example, it might work fine as is. There should be enough clearance so that the cam can be checked with a dial indicator when you move the cam forward or backward. If the button does fit under the cover it is a good idea to check the clearance to make sure it is correct.

Degree Cam

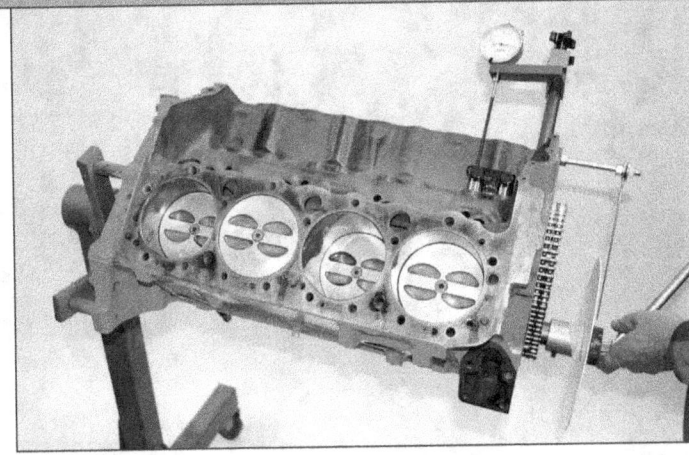

9 In the past several years, computer numerically controled (CNC) machines have manufactured camshafts, so the cam specs printed on a cam card are extremely accurate. Left, a degree wheel is connected to the crank and a pointer is connected to the block. The piston is brought up to top dead center (TDC) and then the pointer is set at TDC on the degree wheel.

To determine TDC (right), turn the crank clockwise, bringing the piston down the cylinder about 1 inch. Turn the center bolt on the bar to touch the piston. Make a mark on the degree wheel then turn the crank in the opposite direction until the piston stops at the bolt. Note this degree position on the wheel. Count the number of degrees between the two spots on the wheel. Then divide the number by two, and the result specifies the true position of TDC. Now turn the degree wheel to TDC.

10 Remove the bumpstop and attach a dial indicator to the block. Move the piston until the maximum lift of the number-1 piston is achieved. Set the dial indicator to 0. Turn the crank clockwise until the dial indicator reads .050, which is a typical lift for many engine setups. Mark the degree wheel where the spot lines up with the pointer.

11 Reverse the procedure and continue to .050 on the other side. Count the number of degrees between the two marks. Divide the resulting number in half, and mark it on the degree wheel. That number should be exactly the same as the number on the cam card (here, 107 degrees at TDC).

Degree Cam (Continued)

12 Repeat the procedure on the exhaust lobe.

Trim Cam Button

13 The button can be trimmed on a lathe, but if you don't have access to one, trim the button with a small hand sander as seen here. Do this very carefully a little at a time until you reach the desired clearance. I recommend using a medium grit, such as 100, so only a small amount of material is removed at a time. The button has to be sanded evenly so one side isn't longer than the other. If you want it to be perfect, you can design and make a small fixture.

Install Timing Cover

14 After the cam is degreed, the timing chain cover can be installed. I selected an aluminum Milodon cover for this engine.

15 Set the timing chain cover on the engine. If the cam button touches the inside of the cover but it doesn't fit flush, the button needs to be shortened to allow .050- to .100-inch clearance.

Check Clearance of Cam Button

16 Use a screwdriver to snug the camshaft forward so you can check the shortened button's end clearance. Use a dial indicator at the back of the block to get a measurement. If the measurement is .15, for example, the clearance on each end is .075.

Install Roller Lifters

17 After you have adjusted the cam button, install the roller lifters. Dip the lifters into the 20W-50 motor oil again for a few minutes just before they are installed. Align the lifters so that the balance bar can be installed. The balance bar faces the inside of the engine. (The balance bar is used to keep the rollers going in the correct direction over the cam lobes.) Apply Joe Gibbs Racing or other assembly grease into the lifter pushrod cups. Roller lifters also get a dose of oil on the roller, tie-bar pivot points, and lifter body.

Install Pushrods

18 Here, I am installing Edelbrock high-quality hardened pushrods. I made sure the ends were properly resting inside the lifters. I lubricated both ends of the pushrods with assembly lube before they were installed. As a precaution, always check the trueness of new pushrods, even though they should be true and have no deflection. Mistakes in manufacturing or quality-control slipups can produce flawed pushrods.

Roll the pushrods across a piece of glass. If they do not roll perfectly straight, you have a bent one. Put the cam on the base circle, adjust the pushrod outward (including your lash setting at the valve), or pre-load on the lifter (generally .030 inch to .060 inch). Rotate the camshaft and watch the rocker tip; it should never roll off the tip of the valve. It should always favor the center of the valve tip through its travel. For long guide and seal life, you are looking for the shortest travel on the valve tip.

Inspect Rocker Arms

19 Note that the center of a rocker arm has one flat side and one round side. The flat side should be on the top where the lock nut will be installed.

CHAPTER 3

Install Rocker Arms

20 Dip the rockers in oil before installing them on the screw-in studs. Align the fulcrum inside of the rocker until the flat side is facing up, and then install the hole in the fulcrum over the screw-in stud. One end of the rocker rests on the valvespring while the other rests on the pushrod. Make sure the pushrod is installed properly in the rocker's pushrod receptacle. Also ensure that the pushrod is installed properly in the pushrod cup in the lifter.

Install Locknuts

21 Install the locknuts. Set all roller rockers when the valves are fully closed. Set the rockers at 0 lash to start with. While tightening the rocker nut, spin the pushrod. When you feel resistance, 0 lash has been achieved. When the rockers are at 0 lash, tighten the rocker nut three-quarters to one full turn past 0 lash. Tighten the Allen-head stop bolt to keep the nut in place. Adjust the lifter preload one cylinder at a time.

Tips for Newer Engines

If you are building a 1987-or-newer Chevy engine, you use a different-style roller lifter. These engines use a cast-aluminum balance bar, which connects to the flattened end of each roller rocker.

A steel plate that attaches to the inside of the block keeps the aluminum balance bars in place on newer Chevy engine blocks.

CHAPTER 4

INTAKE MANIFOLDS AND CARBURETION

When you're building a high-performance Camaro or Firebird, selecting the best carburetor and intake for your particular setup is crucial. But as I said before, you need to ensure the carb and intake correctly meter fuel for the cam, heads, and other engine components. If your carb and intake are not suitable or calibrated for your engine, performance suffers dramatically. Specifically, if your carb is incorrectly set up or too small for the heads and cam, an engine typically accelerates well enough from low-end to mid-range throttle but it runs out of fuel on the top end, and acceleration and top-end speed are limited.

On the other hand, if you select a carb and intake that provide too much fuel, the engine stumbles and coughs on the low end and runs stronger on mid-range to top-end throttle. But the engine doesn't reach peak performance because it is essentially drowning in fuel, and the fuel isn't being adequately burned.

Various OEM carbs appeared on the small-block and big-block engines during the production run of the second-generation cars. General Motors primarily installed the Rochester 2- and 4-barrel carbs on the 305 and 350 V-8s and the Holley 780 4-barrel on the LT-1 Camaro Z28s. The 4-barrel Rochester Quadrajet (or Q-jet) carbs provided respectable performance for stock and mildly modified engines, but many have not used the Q-Jet for high-performance applications. The goal for most owners is to build a 400- to 600-hp, high-performance engine.

When the second-generation Camaros were released in mid year 1970, the small-block Chevy and the new LT-1 were equipped with different componentry. The LT-1 was brand new and featured high-end componentry, such as a solid lifter cam, 11:1 compression ratio, a special aluminum intake, and a 780 Holley carb. The 375-hp 402 big-block in the Super Sport model was also equipped with a Holley.

Rochester Quadrajet carbs supplied the fuel to the small-block Chevy engines, such as the 300-hp 350. Unfortunately, only a small number of high-performance engines powered Camaros from 1970 through 1981, so there was plenty of room for improvement for the standard 350 engines. During the later 1970s, many Firebirds were also available with 305 and 350 Chevy engines, now called corporate engines, so these engines can also be upgraded.

It is important to improve the power potential of the small-block and big-block Chevy engines with aftermarket parts, particularly the carburetors and intake manifolds, to vastly improve performance. All of the improvements made on the small-block engine can also be made to the big-block Chevy engine. The small-blocks greatly benefit from installing an aftermarket aluminum intake and a larger carburetor, especially if you're installing high-performance aftermarket heads.

Intake Manifolds

Intake manifolds come in two basic designs, dual-plane and single-plane, and they have different uses. A dual-plane intake manifold is a great street manifold because it helps to produce low-end torque and horsepower up to 6,500 rpm. Some drag race enthusiasts run dual-plane intake manifolds for engines that are built for lower RPM ranges, but the hardcore drag enthusiasts who rev their engines in the high-RPM range prefer a single-plane intake because it works better above the 6,500-rpm range.

If you have a street-driven car, the single-plane intakes look mean but you sacrifice low-end power and driveability. The manifold you choose to improve your engine's horsepower has to work with the camshaft you are using and how you plan to use the car. Street-driven cars work better when they are equipped with a dual-plane intake, such as one from Edelbrock, Holley/Weiand, Air Flow Research, or World Products.

Edelbrock Corporation

Several intake manifold suppliers are building aluminum intakes for small-block Chevy engines. Edelbrock Corporation is a pioneer intake manifold supplier and offers a large variety of intakes for both small- and big-block Chevy engines. Edelbrock makes intakes that work with heads with small intake ports and others that work with heads with larger racing-size intake ports, so it is important to select a manifold that works with the engine you are building. If you are working on a Camaro that was originally equipped with a low-horsepower 305- or 350-ci small-block Chevy you have to select the appropriate intake to work with those heads, or you can improve the heads that are being used.

Holley and Weiand

Holley is another company that offers top-quality intake manifolds under the Holley and Weiand names. Weiand offers a variety of excellent dual-plane street manifolds and many really effective single plane race intake manifolds. Holley offers a few street manifolds and a wide

The Rochester Quadrajet

The majority of Quadrajets feature a vacuum-operated piston that actuates the primary fuel-metering rods. Therefore, the amount of vacuum dictates the air/fuel ratio, and as a result, the carb delivers a lean mixture under low-load conditions and a rich ratio under high-load conditions. According to Q-jet design, a progressive throttle linkage actuates the primary throttle plates first and then opens secondaries, but on-demand air valves are also used.

The air valves are depressed when airflow increases through the secondary bores, and consequently, the secondary metering rods are activated. When that happens, the larger holes in the fuel rods are exposed to deliver more fuel. In turn, the air valves modulate both fuel flow and airflow of the secondaries, and that's plainly evident when the secondary throttle plates are fully opened.

General Motors installed the Quadrajet on many models from each make from 1967 to 1974. In 1975, the Q-jet was completely redesigned to meet the new emissions standards, and this included new metering rods. The Q-jet kept pace with the times and it remained in GM's lineup of cars until 1988. The spread-bore design was different than many of its competitors, such as the Holley, which has a square-bore design. The Q-jet's secondary venturis are much larger than the primary venturis. At maximum flow, the earlier Quadrajets were rated at 750 cfm, but many are rated at 800 cfm.

Opinions vary on the Q-jet's high-performance capabilities, and it must be noted that General Motors often equipped its high-performance 396 and 454 big-blocks with a Holley double pumper. However, the Quadrajet is a capable design and can be set up to run with its competition. While some have not used the Q-jet for high-performance applications, the carbs have been successfully used in NHRA and IHRA Stock and Super Stock competition. If you're building a 500-hp engine, or above, you'd be better served to select a brand-new aftermarket carb from Holley, Edelbrock, Demon, or another that's calibrated to your engine setup.

The Q-jet carbs from 1975 and on are set up to meet emissions standards and are essentially detuned, and therefore not your best choice when building a high-performance engine. While you can rebuild the carb with larger jets and different fuel rods, it's far easier to select a suitable aftermarket carb. As an alternative you could scrounge swap meets and online listings to find an earlier Q-jet, manufactured between 1965 and 1971, which provides ample air/fuel flow and is not detuned. However, it's not necessary if you're building a high-performance non-original engine.

variety of race manifolds for both the small-and big-block Chevy engines. Holley has spent time testing the manifolds on dynameters and on the track to make sure they work well.

World Products

In 1987, World Products began producing steel performance heads for small- and big-block Chevy engines and because they worked well the business succeeded. The

World Products specializes in large-displacement engines, so the company developed intake manifolds that produce maximum horsepower from big-block Chevy engines. The Merlin 4150 intake manifold is designed to accommodate a 4150-style carburetor and operates efficiently in the 2,500- to 7,500-rpm range. The intake is designed for use on 454 and larger big-block Chevy engines. (Photo Courtesy World Products)

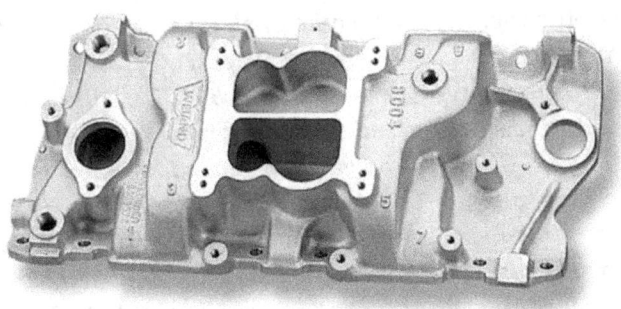

One of Weiand's most popular street-performance intake manifolds is the Action Plus (PN 8024), which is suitable for a variety of small-block Chevy engines. This low-rise, dual-plane design features a universal carburetor mounting flange and no EGR provisions. The effective powerband is from idle to 6,000 rpm. (Photo Courtesy Weiand)

If your Camaro or Firebird is equipped with a big-block Chevy engine, installing a Weiand Stealth intake manifold (PN 8018) provides far greater flow than stock. Designed for use with high-performance, rectangular-port heads, it features a high-rise, dual-plane design with a square-bore mounting flange and is compatible with an HEI ignition system. This intake has a powerband from idle to 6,800 rpm. A similar intake is available for engines with oval-port heads. (Photo Courtesy Weiand)

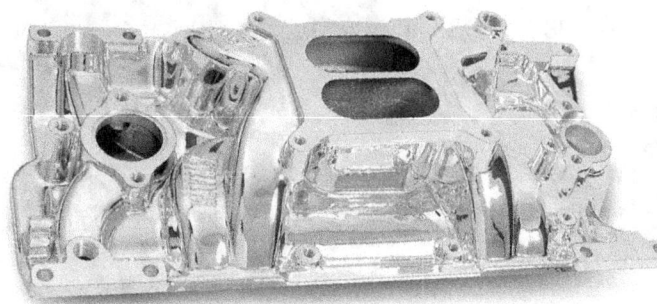

A Stealth intake manifold (PN 8151C) with Weiand's Everbrite finish is an excellent choice if you are building a show-quality Camaro and want a strong-running and attractive engine. Featuring a high-rise, dual-plane design with a square-bore mounting flange, this intake delivers the best flow for a 1,500- to 6,700-rpm powerband. This intake has provisions for a late-model alternator, an air-conditioning bracket, and an additional vacuum tap off an intake runner. This is a really nice street-performance intake. (Photo Courtesy Weiand)

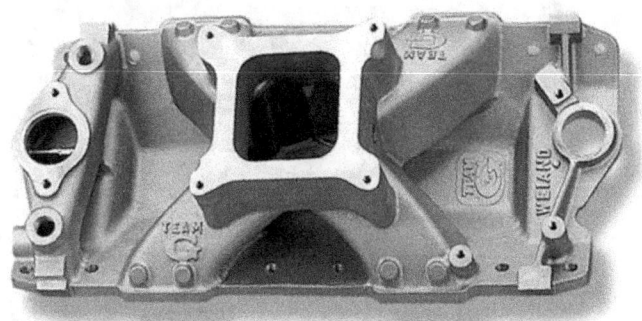

Chevy small-blocks built for drag racing can increase performance with a Weiand Team G intake manifold (PN 7531). Designed for use with carburetors with a square flange, this manifold provides its best performance from 3,000 to 8,200 rpm. This single-plane intake with an isolated plenum is raised 2 inches higher than the 7530 intake. This intake is designed for all 262- to 400-ci engines and 1987-and-later engines with aluminum heads. (Photo Courtesy Weiand)

CHAPTER 4

World Products designed this manifold for large-cubic-inch engines to provide an ample volume of air and fuel while maintaining good velocity. The Merlin X 4500 combines excellent throttle response with top-end power. This intake is designed exclusively for 4500-series carburetors and is one of the best single-plane manifolds for big-block Chevy engines. This intake develops power in the 3,500- to 8,500-rpm range. (Photo Courtesy World Products)

A favorite of street enthusiasts and racers is Holley's 750-cfm 4-barrel carburetor (PN 3310C). This dual-feed carburetor has a manual choke and vacuum secondaries. It is the perfect carburetor for modified Chevy small-block engines and can also be used on most mildly modified big-block Chevy engines. (Photo Courtesy Holley)

company then started producing intake manifolds, which also became a standard in the industry.

Selecting a Carburetor

One of the biggest challenges performance enthusiasts face when building a really strong engine is selecting the right carburetor. Many think bigger is better, so if a 600-cfm carburetor is good, a 1,000-cfm carburetor is better. That is not the case because a carb that's too big delivers too much fuel, and that actually slows down the car, not speeds it up, because the fuel-to-air mixture is not the recommended 14:1. It essentially floods the engine and it does not have a strong, clean combustion cycle.

Remember: The carburetor needs to be the correct size for the engine and related internal engine parts. If you have a nice, small-block Chevy engine built for high-performance street use with a moderate street cam your 350-ci engine can probably be equipped with a 650- to 800-cfm carburetor. When Chevrolet released the Z28 Camaro, it was equipped with a 780-cfm Holley carburetor, and that was a little 302 with a hot cam, excellent heads, and a high-rise intake manifold.

A high-horsepower race engine with a large cam and high-RPM

The Holley 600-cfm (PN 0-80450) carburetor has been engineered to improve performance and keep car emissions legal. This carburetor is a perfect addition for a mildly modified small-block Chevy engine. It features a single-feed fuel inlet and vacuum secondaries. (Photo Courtesy Holley)

Edelbrock manufactures a variety of AFB-style carburetors in 500-, 600-, 750-, and 800-cfm styles for street and race use. All are 50-state legal. This 600-cfm square-flange carburetor with a manual choke (PN 1405) is perfect for a high-performance street engine. (Photo Courtesy Edelbrock)

INTAKE MANIFOLDS AND CARBURETION

Removing an Intake Manifold

Installing an intake manifold on a Chevy engine is pretty straightforward if the engine is out of the car (see Project 1 on page 36). If, however, the engine is still in the car, there are several things you have to do first:

You have to drain the coolant out of the engine. Your radiator should have a petcock at the bottom so the coolant can be drained into a pan. If the pan is clean the coolant can be reused after the new intake is installed, but I recommend the use of new coolant because it's not that expensive. If you remove the radiator cap, the radiator drains faster.

After the coolant is drained you have to remove the upper radiator hose from the thermostat housing and the heater hose if it is connected to a fitting in the manifold. It is also a good idea to take a digital photo of the smog- and accessory-related vacuum hoses so that they can be connected properly when the new intake is installed. You generally have one connected to the power brake booster, one to the vacuum modulator, and one that feeds vacuum into the interior of the car that works with the heater and air conditioning controls. Camaros in the later 1970s have a large variety of vacuum hoses dealing with the emission system but if you live in a state that is not affected by emissions laws you may be able to delete some of those hoses.

When all of the hoses have been disconnected, you can start removing the intake manifold bolts with an open-end 9/16-inch wrench. It is also advisable to remove the carburetor at this point because sometimes the intake bolts are easier to reach when the carburetor is removed. You can remove the carburetor with an open-end 1/2-inch wrench.

After all of the bolts are removed the original manifold has to be broken loose by prying a screwdriver between the head and intake. A few hammer taps on the screwdriver should do the job. If it doesn't break loose quickly, check to make sure you have all of the bolts out. When the intake breaks loose, there is a good chance that chunks of the intake manifold gasket will remain on the heads or fall into the engine valley.

The manifold gasket residue needs to be removed, but before you attack the head-sealing area with a scraper you should install a few paper towels inside the engine valley and intake ports so that the residue can be removed from the engine. If some gets into the valley you can vacuum it out with a wet/dry shop vacuum.

Now you can proceed with the installation, as described in Project 1 (page 36).

The Ultra Street Avenger 4-barrel carburetor (PN 0-86670BK) has a 670-cfm rating and is another carburetor designed for high-performance street use and track action. This carburetor features light aluminum construction that saves 5 pounds, shiny tumble-polished finish, billet metering blocks and base plates, black (or red or blue) anodized billet aluminum metering blocks and base plates, built-in sight window for simple float adjustment, and high-performance fuel curves. (Photo Courtesy Holley)

potential requires a larger carburetor. Big-block race engines can be equipped with one or even two 1,200-cfm Holley Dominator carburetors. If you install a Dominator carburetor with 1,200 cfm on a mildly built 350 engine, it would run terrible because the fuel/air ratio would be off target. The car would run extremely rich and there would be less power than if a 600-cfm carburetor were used.

Most of the Chevy engines with one horsepower per cubic inch that I have built were equipped with 780-cfm Holley or Edelbrock carburetors, and they worked fine. I have also used dual-quad intakes that were equipped with 500-cfm carburetors. Most of the time the engine is only using the single carburetor. Both carburetors are only used at full throttle.

Starting in 1957, Pontiac and Oldsmobile used triple 2-barrel carburetion on maximum-performance engines. That top-of-the-line engine option was available from the mid 1950s to the mid 1960s. General Motors came down with a ruling in 1966 that stated that all of the company's performance engines in 1967, excluding the Corvette, could only use a single carburetor.

Edelbrock and Holley are still the leaders in carburetor availability. Another carburetor manufacturer is Quick-Fuel, and all of the carburetors the company builds are designed for maximum performance.

Project 1: Intake Manifold and Carburetor Installation

Early on, performance enthusiasts realized that improving the fuel delivery system increased engine horsepower. In the 1950s, companies developed multiple carburetion systems for the early flathead engines. The Stromberg two- and three- carburetor intakes were turning cars into record setters on the dry lakes and on the drag strip. In 1955, when Chevrolet introduced the 265-ci small-block, it quickly became a favorite of performance enthusiasts. Edelbrock was one of the first companies to develop improved intake manifolds for the small-block Chevy. Edelbrock has also spent time designing parts that work together to maximize the horsepower available by bolting on the company's performance parts.

This is the installation of a Performer RPM high-rise intake manifold and an 800-cfm Edelbrock carburetor on a small-block Chevy engine. This engine is a 1972 Camaro four-bolt main 350 engine that has been recently updated with new rings and bearings. It is also equipped with Edelbrock Performer RPM aluminum heads that are designed to work with the Performer RPM intake manifold. This installation features Edelbrock intake manifold gaskets and can be accomplished in a few hours.

Edelbrock was one of the first companies to develop high-rise intake manifolds for small-block Chevy engines. Over the years, it has improved the design, and today the Performer RPM dual-plane intake (PN 7101) is one of the best manifolds available for street-performance use. From the time the first one was released, Edelbrock has improved the internal flow design and has dyno tested the manifold until the optimum has been achieved. The current intake is one of the best manifolds I have used, both on the street and on the track. (Photo Courtesy Edelbrock)

Inspect Manifold Gasket Kit

1 The intake manifold is going to be installed on the heads using an Edelbrock gasket set (PN 7361). This set includes gaskets for the intake manifold and the valve covers. (Photo Courtesy Edelbrock)

Install Manifold Gaskets

2 Place a few dabs of weatherstrip adhesive on the intake manifold gaskets and place the gaskets on top of the heads. I let the adhesive dry, so the gaskets are securely in place and don't move when the intake is carefully placed.

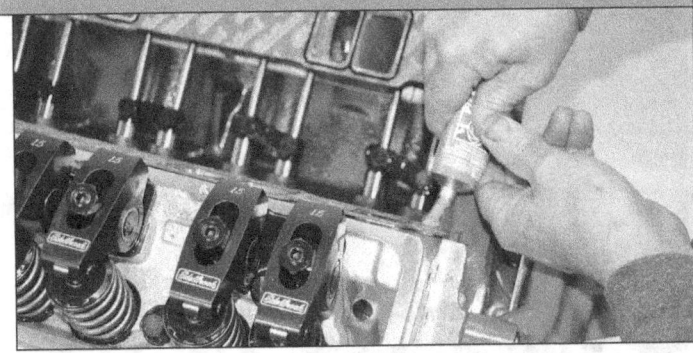

3 Some gasket sets are available with rubber end seals, but the Edelbrock intake gaskets use silicone instead. Place a few dabs around the perimeter of the gasket to hold it in place. I used gray silicone because it matches the color of the intake and won't stand out like red, copper, or blue silicone after the intake is in place. I recommend using a new tube so that you can apply it in a very thick bead all the way across the opening.

Apply Silicone to Water Ports

4 Place a light coat of silicone around the water ports to make sure they don't leak. Keep the silicone far enough away from the openings so it doesn't squeeze into the ports.

Place Manifold on Heads

5 Gently place the intake on the heads, making sure that all of the holes are perfectly aligned. Even though the aluminum manifold is light, it is a good idea to have a friend help you place the manifold squarely over the ports, making sure to align the holes in the manifold over the holes in the head.

Place Silicone on Manifold Bolts

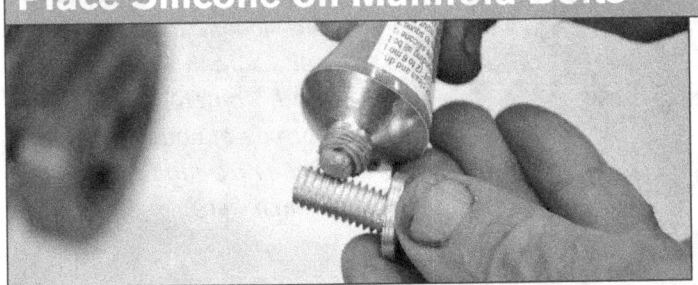

6 Dab a little silicone on the bolts that are adjacent to the water jackets. The silicone helps prevent the coolant from seeping around the bolts. This intake was installed with top-quality Edelbrock intake manifold bolts.

Thread In Manifold Bolts

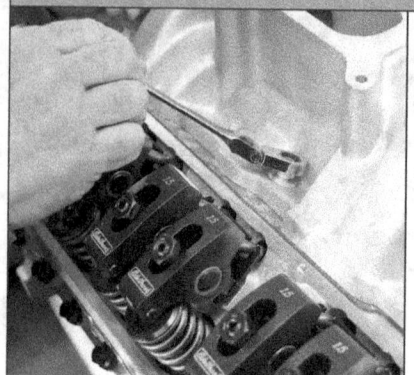

7 Thread in the center manifold bolts and then tighten them from side to side. Following the torque sequence on the intake manifold instruction sheet, snug the bolts with a box-end wrench.

Torque Manifold Bolts

8 After snugging down the bolts, tighten them again to 25 ft-lbs using a torque wrench. Follow the torque sequence shown on the instruction sheet. Tighten from the middle working side to side and toward the ends of the manifold.

Install Carburetor Studs

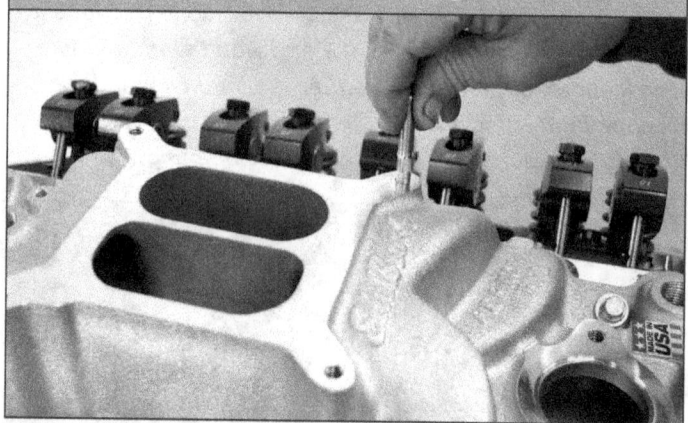

9 Install the carburetor studs into the manifold as seen here. The manifold side accepts coarse-thread bolts while the carburetor side accepts fine-thread bolts. Screw in the bolts by hand most of the way; to get them tight, screw two nuts on the threads and tighten them together until the stud turns. Use a 1/2-inch wrench to tighten the stud. After the stud is tight, separate the nuts with two 1/2-inch wrenches and then remove the nuts.

Place Thermostat on Manifold

10 Some cars may require a thermostat that opens at a higher temperature, but a 160-degree thermostat works fine with any car that is not computer controlled and some that are computer controlled. The thermostat rests in a relief in the intake manifold as seen here. Find the arrow on the thermostat and place it in the correct position for installation, so it functions properly. If the thermostat is not correctly installed, the thermostat does not correctly open and close, and as a result, the engine often runs hot.

Install Thermostat Housing

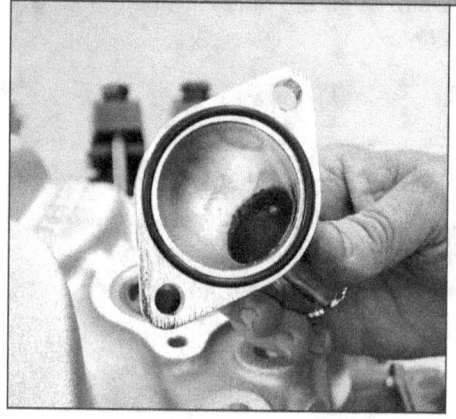 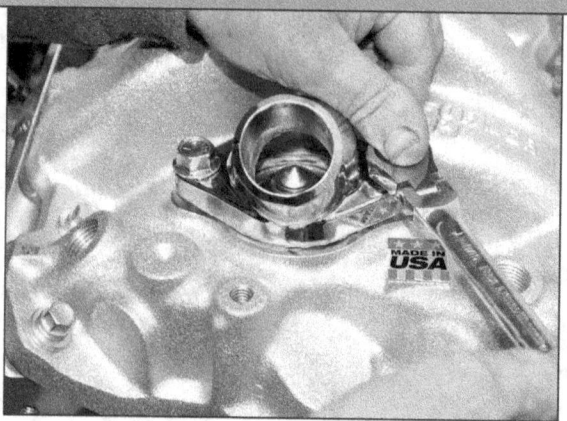

11 Install the thermostat housing with a large O-ring for sealing (far left). Add silicone to the bottom to make sure the seal is really good. Tighten the 9/16-inch thermostat housing bolts with a box-end ratchet wrench (left).

INTAKE MANIFOLDS AND CARBURETION

Install Carburetor Gasket

12 Slip the carburetor gasket over the manifold studs and make sure it sits flat on the mating surface of the manifold. The Edelbrock carburetor comes with a thick carburetor gasket.

Place Carburetor on Gasket

13 Place the carburetor over the mounting studs and make sure the carburetor is facing in the correct position when installed. The throttle cable and linkage align with the throttle lever on the left side.

Mount Carburetor on Intake Manifold

14 Position the carburetor correctly on the manifold studs, and then thread the stud nuts down to the carburetor casting. At this stage, torque the stud nuts and complete installation. No torque sequence is used, so just work front to back and make sure all nuts are torqued to spec. After the engine has been started and warmed up, check the nuts again to make sure the proper torque spec has been maintained.

Finish Carburetor Installation

15 Install the throttle ball as seen here. The carb has several vacuum openings—depending on the car, some openings are used and others are plugged. The carburetor comes with a small variety of vacuum plugs.

CAMARO & FIREBIRD PERFORMANCE PROJECTS: 1970–1981

CHAPTER 5

IGNITION SYSTEM

A strong ignition system that ignites the fuel/air mixture from idle to the high-RPM ranges is vital to attaining top performance. You can have aftermarket aluminum heads with improved flow, an improved intake manifold, and a carburetor that complements them. You also can have a camshaft that works with the other parts to maximize the fuel and air mixture that is delivered into the cylinders. But to improve the horsepower potential of the engine and make everything work properly there has to be an ignition source. To maximize horsepower the ignition system can't miss a beat, and that is where the aftermarket comes in. The electronic ignition systems that were used in the 1970s worked well and today the engineers have even better ignition systems, but it was not always so.

Early engines in Camaros and Firebirds were originally equipped with a breaker-point-style distributor. Many owners have converted to full electronic ignition systems, so if your project engine has a breaker-point distributor, you need to convert to modern electronic ignition because the old system cannot provide the necessary timing and spark for a high-performance engine setup.

Essentially, the early ignition systems worked fine for typical street use on engines that had a 5,000-rpm redline, but high-performance factory engines, as well as modified engines, required an improved ignition system to get the maximum horsepower in the higher RPM ranges. In extreme use, the points in a stock distributor can float, and that can cause the engine to misfire and run terrible. Points can also burn, and that can cause misfire problems. That was somewhat common with factory resistance wires that didn't always work properly, allowing the points to burn prematurely.

General Motors saw the need for an improved ignition system and introduced HEI electronic units, which were a huge improvement over the earlier systems. Most 1970- and-newer Camaros and Firebirds were equipped with HEI ignition systems because they worked well and actually improved fuel economy and emissions, which was important in the 1970s.

The only problem with the HEI system was the large cap that didn't work well in many high-performance Camaros and Firebirds with modified firewalls. The coil was part of the distributor cap, and that was what increased the size of the cap. The distributors were fine in a car with a stock firewall and they can be used and upgraded with an assortment of aftermarket parts that are available from many of the leading ignition manufacturers.

The aftermarket began producing improved ignition systems in the 1950s, starting with dual-point distributors for flatheads and early V-8 engines, and in the 1970s some of the first electronic ignition systems were introduced. Today the leading manufacturers include Mallory, MSD, PerTronix, and Proform. They also offer improved coils and electronic control units that improve and control the spark in the engine's combustion chamber.

Engine performance is increased when the air/fuel mixture in the cylinder is ignited and burned completely. The hotter the spark is, the better the combustion mixture is

IGNITION SYSTEM

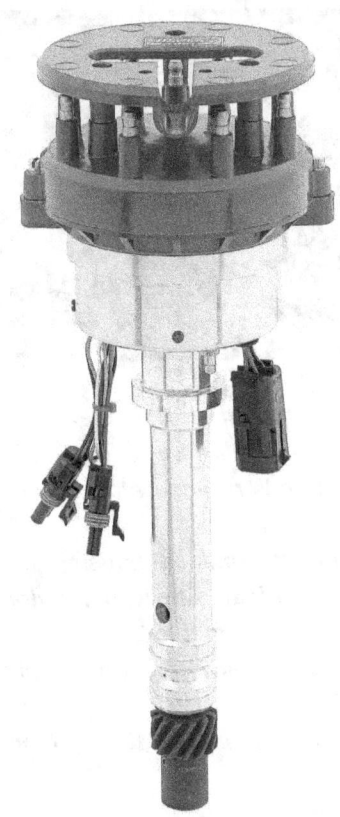

If the engine butts up to the firewall and there isn't much room for the distributor, Mallory has a solution. It offers this smaller Max-Fire distributor that includes all the features of a modern digital CDI with a state-of-the-art electronic advance distributor. This distributor fires multiple sparks for 20 or more degrees at low engine speeds for better throttle response, quicker acceleration, and cleaner burning plugs. (Photo Courtesy Mallory Ignition)

The Mallory Max-Fire distributor combines all the features of a modern digital CDI ignition with a state-of-the-art electronic advance distributor. This distributor fires multiple sparks for 20 degrees or more at low engine speeds for better throttle response, quicker acceleration, and cleaner burning spark plugs. (Photo Courtesy Mallory Ignition)

PerTronix Performance Products has just released its Flame-Thrower HEI performance distributors for Chevy, Olds, and Pontiac engine applications, which are all found in Camaros and Firebirds. These units use new components and feature a specially engineered module and coil combination that operates without misfires up to a minimum of 7,500 rpm, which is 3,000 rpm higher than most enthusiasts report with original HEI systems. (Photo Courtesy PerTronix Performance Products)

One of Mallory's best-selling distributors is the Unilite, which is triggered by a photo-optic infrared LED system. This unit offers improved combustion efficiency and economy, increased spark plug life, and cold-weather starting. This unit is also popular due to its small-diameter distributor cap that fits in the tightest spaces. (Photo Courtesy Mallory Ignition)

CHAPTER 5

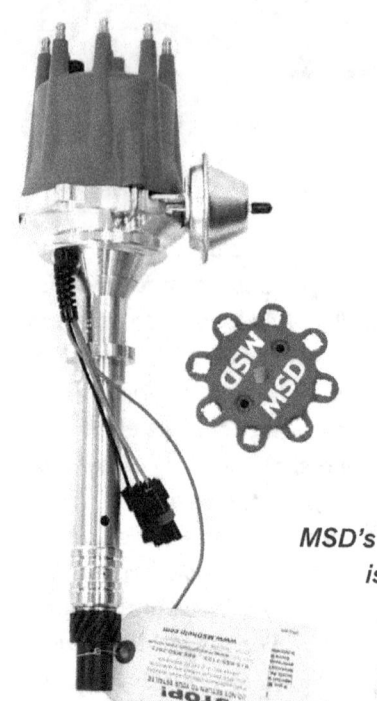
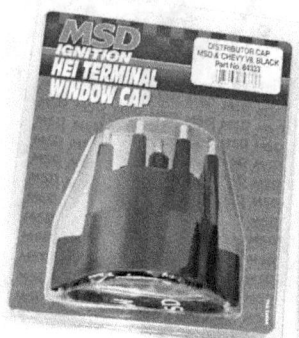

This engine features a variety of black accent parts, so I thought it would look the best with a black distributor cap (PN 84333) and black spark plug wires (PN 31233). In order to keep the wires in order, I also ordered Pro-Clamp Wire Separators (PN 8843).

MSD's Pro-Billet small-diameter distributor features a CNC-machined aluminum housing that is 3/8 inch smaller in diameter and 7/8 inch shorter than conventional Chevy distributors. A maintenance-free magnetic pickup and precision reluctor create stable trigger signals through the RPM range. It also has an easy-to-adjust mechanical advance with supplied springs and stop bushings. I ordered an MSD Pro-Billet distributor (PN 8360) with an internal module, which is a standalone distributor that doesn't require an MSD ignition box. However, it certainly can be used with a box if desired.

ignited. Some of the ignition control units actually provide a multiple spark cycle in the combustion chamber, so all of the air/fuel mixture is ignited to provide maximum power. A side benefit is that the air/fuel mixture is ignited so completely that it also improves the engine's emissions.

Many years ago PerTronix released electronic conversion units that fit into original distributors so restoration enthusiasts can improve the ignition of their original cars and still maintain the factory appearance of the engine. Most companies also recognized that the HEI ignition was an intelligent system that works well, so the aftermarket started making improved parts for the factory HEI ignition systems that improved street and track performance.

Project 1: Distributor, Spark Plug Wires and Coil Installation

One of the most important parts you can install in your engine is a high-quality electronic distributor. You need a strong spark to efficiently ignite the mixture when the carburetor delivers the fuel/air mixture through the free-flowing intake manifold; it travels through the big port and valve heads and finally ends up in the combustion chamber. The fuel needs to be ignited at 800 rpm when the engine is idling, and as high as 6,500 rpm when it is crossing the finish line in the quarter-mile. Igniting the air/fuel mixture under all conditions can be done by installing a top-of-the-line electronic distributor, a high-powered coil, and spark plug wires.

In this project I use an MSD distributor, spark plug wires, and a coil because I know through experience that the parts work terrific together. If you had auto shop in high school or built a few engines over the years it is easy to install a distributor in an engine, but if you have never done it before you may not know where to start. This project takes you through all the steps.

This project also shows you how to install the spark plug wires because they are a little tricky if you have never installed a cut-to-fit wire set. I recommend that if you plan to install spark plug wires in a variety of cars in the future you should purchase a spark plug wire crimping-tool, such as one from MSD.

You also learn how to install a complete ignition system using a ready-to-install, stand-alone distributor. MSD also makes some great ignition boxes, and they have become a favorite of drag racers.

IGNITION SYSTEM

Rotate Crankshaft to TDC

1 In order to install the distributor, rotate the crankshaft so the number-1 piston is at the TDC position. In order to find the correct position I removed the number-1 spark plug for a compression test.

Identify Compression Stroke

2 Have a friend help by holding a finger over the spark plug hole. Then turn the engine over and feel for the pressure rise in the cylinder. Once you feel this, you have identified the compression stroke.

Set Timing Gauge for TDC

3 Turn the engine over, find the compression stroke, and set the timing mark at 0. This is the TDC of the number-1 stroke, and from there you can install the distributor. A Chevy engine turns clockwise, so put the number-1 wire in the cap in the location found in the Chevy engine manual. Although the distributor has 8 holes instead of 12, install the wire at the 7:00 o'clock position (looking at the distributor from the front of the engine).

Remove Distributor Cap

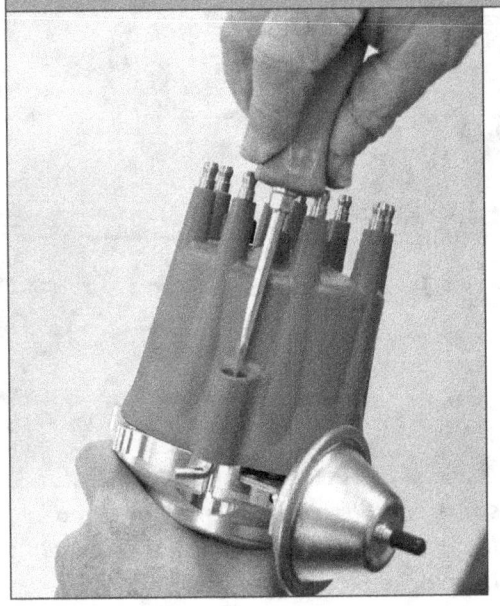

4 Before installing the distributor, remove the distributor cap to see the rotor. The rotor has to be turned to the wire location position. It must point to the number-1 cylinder position.

CAMARO & FIREBIRD PERFORMANCE PROJECTS: 1970–1981

CHAPTER 5

Coat Distributor Shaft and Gear with Assembly Lube

5 Before installing the distributor, coat the gear and shaft with the assembly lube supplied with the distributor. In particular, coat the gear at the bottom of the shaft, so there's no unnecessary friction and wear as it seats into the oil pump.

Install Distributor Gasket

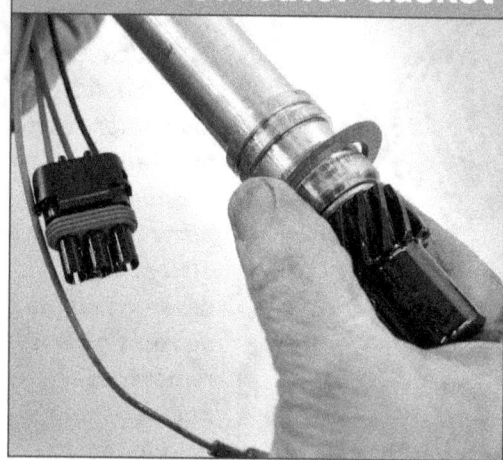

6 Install the distributor gasket over the shaft so oil does not leak from the back of the engine.

Install Distributor

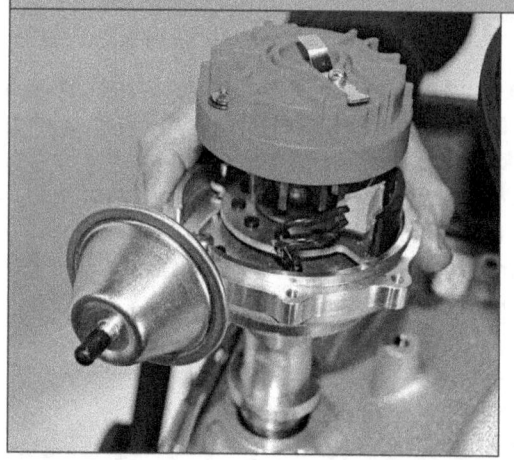

7 Insert the distributor shaft into the block with the vacuum module facing the passenger's side of the engine. If you look closely at the bottom of the gear on the shaft you find a slot that must align with a depression in the oil pump gear driveshaft.

Correctly Orient Rotor

8 Orient the rotor so it's facing the rear carburetor bolt on the passenger's side. I generally call it the 7:00 o'clock position, as seen here. At this stage, it can get a bit challenging. Install and position the striker on the rotor in the 6:30 to 7:00 o'clock position. At the same time align the shaft key to the oil pump driveshaft, and get it seated in that position.

Install Distributor Cap

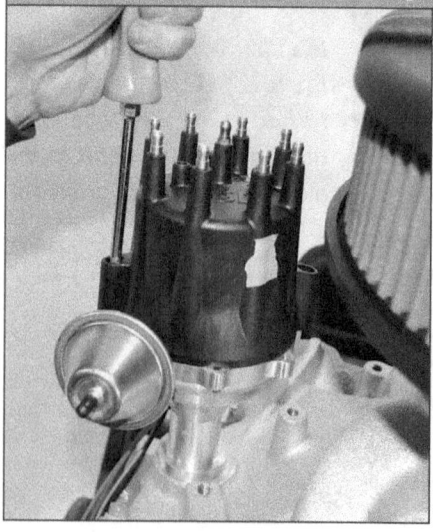

9 After properly seating the distributor, verify the number-1 piston is still in the correct firing position. Once checked, install the new black cap. Use a piece of tape to mark the number-1 position where the rotor is facing.

Install Spark Plug in Number-1 Cylinder

10 Coat the spark plug threads with anti-seize and reinstall the spark plug in the cylinder. Thread it in and tighten it with a socket wrench.

CAMARO & FIREBIRD PERFORMANCE PROJECTS: 1970–1981

IGNITION SYSTEM

Verify Position of Distributor Cap

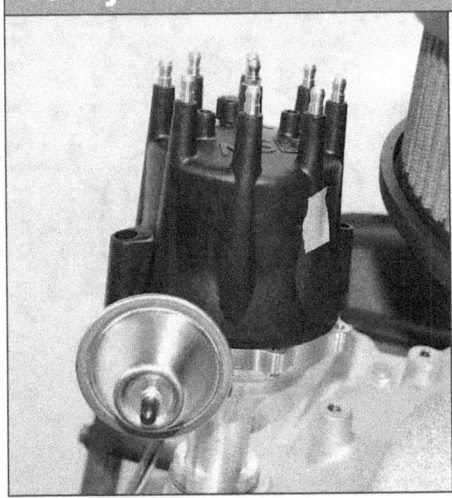

11 Here is another look at the cap. You can see the relationship between the number-1 cylinder and the vacuum module.

Make Bracket Separators

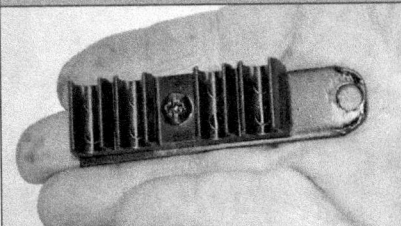

12 Using Pro-Clamp Wire Separators, make small brackets for the four-wire and two-wire separators to attach to. The brackets can be made out of flat strap steel that can be purchased at any hardware store. Cut the strap steel to size using a 3-inch cut-off wheel and then round off the end. Drill a hole in the rounded-off end so it can be mounted to the valve cover bolts. Paint the bracket (optional) semi-gloss black and then screw the separator to it. Simple, and it works great.

Gather Spark Plug Wires

13 Spark plug wires come in various lengths. The longest ones are used for the number-1 and number-2 cylinder spark plugs; the shortest ones go to the number-7 and number-8 cylinder spark plugs. From the front of the engine on the driver's side, the cylinder order is 1-3-5-7, while from the front of the engine on the passenger's side, the cylinder order is 2-4-6-8.

Install Spark Plug Wire Separators

14 Here is a close look at the brackets after they were connected to the valve covers. The separators keep the wires neatly in place.

Crimp Spark Plug Wire Ends

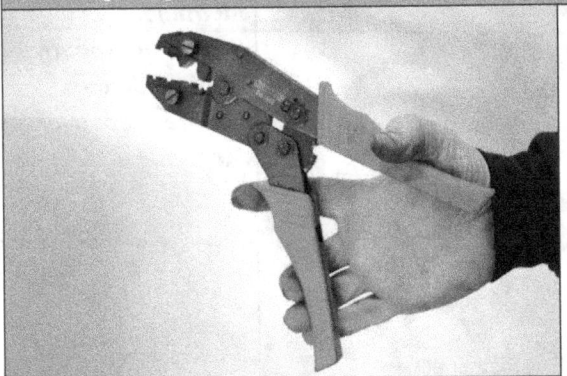

15 Use the aluminum crimping tool included with the wires to crimp the wire ends properly. Be patient because this takes some time. Since I install spark plug wires frequently, I use an MSD crimping tool. This tool cuts the wire properly, and it also crimps the metal spark plug ends.

CHAPTER 5

Coat Wire Ends with Lubricant

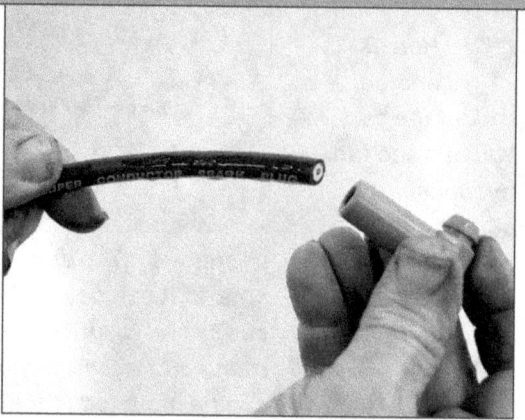

16 *After the wire is cut to length, coat the end with a good lubricant; liquid Tide laundry detergent works well (left). Slip on the rubber boot (middle) and move it back until it is about 2 inches from the end (right). Determine the length of the wire needed by running the wire through the separators and to the distributor, allowing enough wire for the distributor to be turned when the timing is set.*

Cut Spark Plug Wires to Length

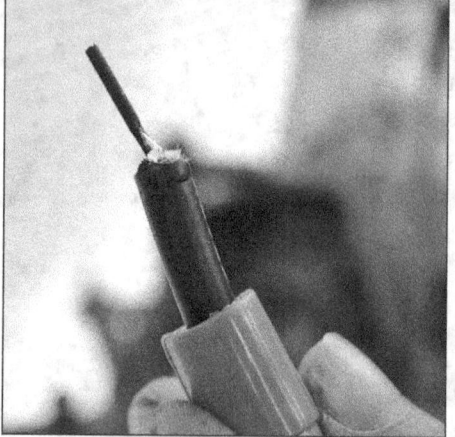

17 *Cut the wire in a way to expose the core as seen here. Notice that the boot is about an inch from the end at this point.*

Install Spark Plug Terminals

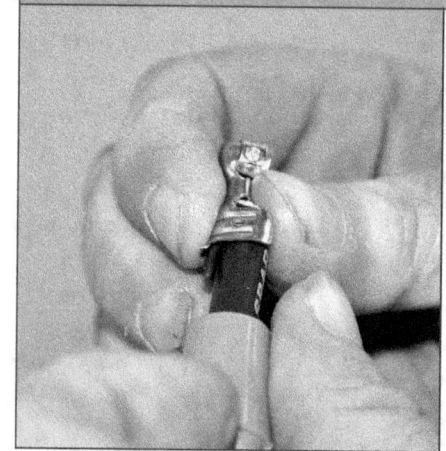

18 *Fold the core over, install the spark plug terminal, and tighten slightly with a small pliers. This readies the terminal for crimping.*

Crimp Spark Plug Terminals

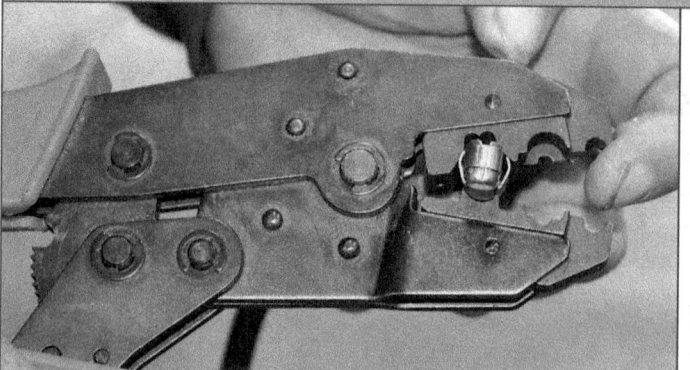

19 *Install the wire in the crimping tool and crimp the terminal to the wire. This provides a tight professional crimp.*

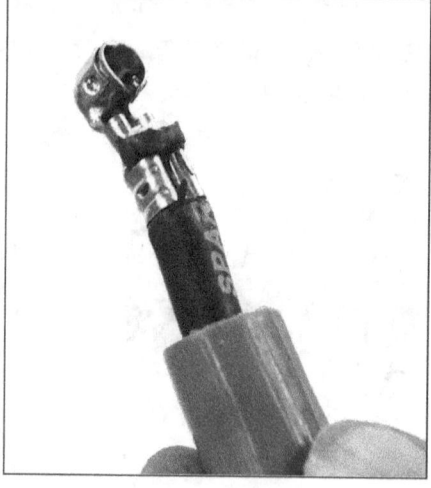

20 *Here is the wire after the terminal was crimped properly. Now slide the rubber boot over the terminal end.*

CAMARO & FIREBIRD PERFORMANCE PROJECTS: 1970–1981

IGNITION SYSTEM

Install Spark Plug Wires

21 One by one, cut the wires to length and install according to engine firing order. The cylinder firing order for the Chevy 350 engine is 1-8-4-3-6-5-7-2, and the distributor is adjusted in a clockwise rotation. Follow the firing order and install the wires in the distributor. Notice how the wires are neatly held in place by the separators. The big-block firing order is the same.

Install Distributor Clamp

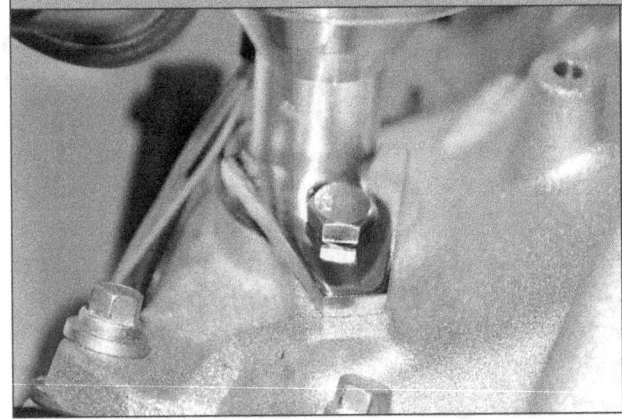

22 After the wires have been installed, connect the distributor clamp. It should be snug, but do not overtighten it to the point where the distributor doesn't turn. It has to be turned slightly one way or the other for the engine to fire up, and then the timing has to be set with a timing light.

Install Coil Bracket

23 Install the MSD coil bracket (PN 8213) on the coil, and then tighten down the screw to secure the coil (PN 8200) into the bracket.

Inspect Coil and Bracket

24 Here is the coil and bracket fastened to the Edelbrock intake manifold. The chrome coil and bracket is an attractive addition to the engine.

CAMARO & FIREBIRD PERFORMANCE PROJECTS: 1970–1981

CHAPTER 6

Exhaust System

If you get the fuel delivery system working properly with improved heads, a high-flowing intake manifold, a superior carburetor, and a well-designed camshaft fire the mixture with a performance ignition system, the exhaust gases have to be managed effectively. If a car is running a restrictive exhaust, it is not running up to expectations.

The final part of this performance improvement is installing a good exhaust system, either factory header-style exhaust manifolds or tubular headers. The headers should flow into a non-restrictive exhaust system with free-flowing mufflers. Generally 2½-inch exhaust tubing works fine for most high-performance engines. Some enthusiasts with really powerful big-block engines use 3-inch exhaust tubing, but remember that with a lowered car there is always a chance of bottoming out.

The second-generation Camaros and Firebirds were equipped with many different exhaust systems, depending on the engines that were used and the year they were built. It should be obvious to a car enthusiast that a Camaro outfitted with a six-cylinder engine wasn't equipped with the same exhaust system that a 396-powered Camaro was. Chevrolet and Pontiac were aware of an exhaust system's potential for increasing horsepower as early as the 1950s and the top-of-the-line engines such as the 375-hp 396 Chevy engine. The Pontiac Ram Air engines were equipped with header-style exhaust manifolds and dual exhaust.

Several design features of the exhaust can improve horsepower, such as the size of the exhaust tubing and the design of the muffler itself. Chevrolet was well aware of the restrictive exhaust manifolds used on the early Z28 Camaros, so the cars were sold with headers in the trunk that the owner could switch to if desired. The change from exhaust manifolds to factory-included headers really improved a car's overall power on the street and, especially, at the track. The Z28 engine was a high-revving engine, so the power potential of the headers could be realized when the engine was spinning over 3,000 rpm.

All early high-performance Camaros and Firebirds were equipped with well-designed exhaust systems, but there always remained plenty of room for improvement. The factory had to meet federally mandated exhaust noise requirements, so it did the best it could under the circumstances and restrictions. Some cars had mufflers and resonators, and that restricted exhaust so they were quiet, but that also lowered the engine's horsepower. Enthusiasts were given the opportunity to make improvements without worrying about the noise levels, and the resonators could be found on shop shelves. Before long cars were being equipped with glass-pack muffler systems, and many aftermarket muffler companies started building high-performance mufflers.

Many cars in the 1940s and 1950s were equipped with single-exhaust systems, so in this early period a performance gain was accomplished by installing dual exhaust. Then, as today, the cars were outfitted with glass-pack mufflers and they were and still remain a good performance improvement over factory muffler systems.

EXHAUST SYSTEM

Since then many companies have released mufflers of other designs that sound great and have been performance tested to verify the horsepower improvement they provide. Today there are exhaust and muffler systems that allow your car to run as good as one with open exhaust, which has been in drag racing test runs.

The early second-generation Camaros and Firebirds had exhaust systems that remained relatively unrestricted until 1975, when all cars had to be outfitted with catalytic converters to meet emissions mandates. Gone were the days of true dual exhaust. The GM converters were large, so using two of them was not possible; Ford used two small units and managed to have real dual exhaust. The floorpan of the Camaros and Firebirds had to be modified to make room for the converters and that took room away from the passenger's floorboard.

The Camaros and Firebirds needed a new exhaust system that directed exhaust from the driver's side of the engine to the passenger's side, and then exhaust from both sides could be directed through the catalytic converter. The exhaust then ran through one pipe to the muffler; it was split into two exhaust exits on the performance models. This system was extremely restrictive and the horsepower numbers of the engines reflected the power loss. The catalytic converter system used for the second-generation Camaros and Firebirds remained the same from 1975 to 1981. Unfortunately, not only did the catalytic converter restrict horsepower, it also reduced fuel efficiency

To improve exhaust performance, you need to start by ditching the restrictive stock manifolds and installing a lighter, more efficient set of headers. Headers are an integral part of an engine package, and just like the rest of the components on the engine, the headers need to be matched to the heads, cam, and intake. If your high-performance engine is stuffing more fuel into the engine, it needs to evacuate more exhaust gases efficiently. If a set of headers doesn't suit the setup or the production of horsepower, torque will be hindered. Keep in mind that a set of headers is also designed to produce the best power within a certain RPM range. A set of road-race headers, for example, typically don't produce torque like a set of street headers. So a word to the wise: You need to select the proper set of headers for a particular application.

Header Selection Tips

When selecting a set of headers, you need to take the following factors into account: head size, compression ratio, camshaft timing, intake and carb size, and others. I don't have the space to explain the interdependence and all the variables associated with these factors. But I can offer you some guidelines about the length of the tube, the diameter of the tube, and the collector size.

In general terms, you need to find a good balance of tube diameter, tube length, and collector size. The system with ideal dimensions to match your setup is the system you want to buy.

Tube Diameter

A small-diameter tube effectively scavenges and redirects gases back into the combustion chamber for better low- to mid-range power. Conversely, a large-diameter tube flows more exhaust at higher RPM to increase top-end power.

Therefore, for a street header you need to select one that's a good compromise between tube diameter and power. Since torque is essential on the street, a smaller diameter header of 1⅝ or 1¾ inches is suitable for many engine setups, while 1⅞ inches are often better for high-RPM competition engines.

Test Results

In tests I made for an early magazine article, I installed Ram Air III exhaust manifolds on a Pontiac-powered 1979 Trans Am with dual exhaust using DynoMax mufflers. First, the car was run on a rear-wheel dyno to get a base figure. After the work was completed the horsepower increase was slightly more than 50 rear wheel horsepower. The car was noticeably faster and the gas mileage also increased.

The car was also taken to the drags and it turned consistent low-15-second quarter-mile passes, which was good when you consider its high rear-end gears. With lower gears the car was easily in the high-14-second range. This improvement was done using nicely designed factory exhaust manifolds but an even greater improvement could have been achieved with full-length, tuned headers.

CHAPTER 6

Tube Length

Long-tube headers of 30 inches or more are preferable for a street application because they provide a strong exhaust pulse for improved low- to mid-range power. When you shorten the exhaust tube, such as with shorty headers, the exhaust signal is reduced and low- to mid-range power won't be as strong, but top-end power is stronger than with long-tube headers. There are certain clearance issues with certain cars, so you may need to go with shorty headers. Unless your ride height is particularly low, you should be able to run long-tube headers in a second-generation Camaro.

Collector Length

The place where two pipes merge into a combined single pipe is the collector area. A long collector area essentially functions as longer primary tubes. When pipe diameter rises to 1⅞ inches, these wide pipes are already flowing a lot of air and do not have a collector area, which is common in many systems.

This 400-ci Pontiac engine is equipped with a set of Doug's headers are designed for use in a Firebird chassis. The headers have a thick steel flange to avoid warping and sturdy tubes that are tuned in length. The headers are designed to improve horsepower from 2,500 rpm on up. (Photo Courtesy Doug's Headers)

Emissions Standards

If you are building a second-generation Camaro or Firebird, you can raise horsepower with a well-designed exhaust system matched to the engine. A big-block engine may need an exhaust with larger diameter exhaust tubing than a hot small-block engine. Free-flowing factory exhaust manifolds or aftermarket headers can also increase horsepower, especially in the higher RPM ranges. If you have an early Camaro or Firebird, there will be no problem to make the necessary improvement, but if you have a car built after 1975, you can improve the exhaust; but make sure it is legal according to your particular state's requirements.

Many of the emissions laws are restrictive, but unnecessarily so, because a free-flowing exhaust system actually improves a car's combustion, making the engine run cleaner. When you combine a high-performance ignition system and a free-flowing exhaust system, you can actually improve the car's emissions and fuel economy to the point where a catalytic converter is no longer needed.

Another factor when considering the emissions rules is your ability to find the smog-related parts the engine is required to use. Many of the original valves and parts are no longer available, so you cannot make the car smog legal. For clean exhaust the use of aftermarket parts can bring about a cleaner burning engine and at the same time improve fuel economy. Today there are several companies that make small catalytic converters, so it is also quite easy to build a true dual-exhaust system that is completely emissions legal.

When you are shopping for speed parts for a 1975-or-newer car, keep in mind that many have gone through testing and are legal for use in even the most stringent states. Many states are looking at changing their laws to allow cars 1981 and older to be smog exempt because there are only a miniscule number of cars that are still; the cars that remain are generally not driven daily. They are the next wave

EXHAUST SYSTEM

of collector cars that will be taken to shows or placed in museums.

A large number of companies make good high-performance headers and mufflers for both street and competition use. Patriot Exhaust Products is one that makes excellent headers for a wide variety of American performance cars, including Camaros and Firebirds as well as Firebirds that are equipped with Oldsmobile engines.

Glass-pack mufflers have been an enthusiast favorite for years because they don't restrict exhaust flow as much as some competing muffler designs, plus they sound awesome. If you are building a show-quality Camaro or Firebird, another advantage is the glass-pack mufflers look terrific when constructed out of stainless steel. This muffler is designed for use in a completely polished stainless-steel exhaust system. (Photo Courtesy Smithy/Petronix)

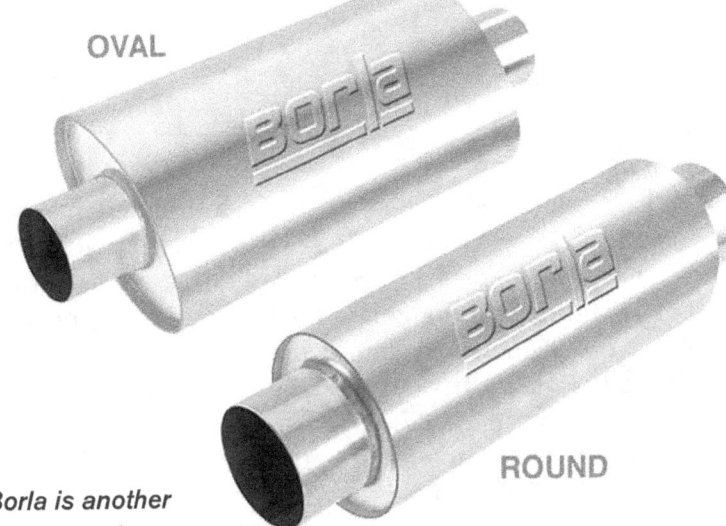

Borla is another manufacturer of many models of high-performance mufflers, offering both individual mufflers (pictured here) and complete exhaust systems. The company offers Turbo, Turbo XL, and Boomer universal mufflers that are suitable for street applications of the second-generation Camaro and Firebird. Borla mufflers are stainless steel and completely welded; the company warrantees them for one million miles. Pictured here are the XR-1 Sportsman mufflers for racing. As a racing muffler, this is a straight-through design for maximum performance. But according to Borla, these mufflers reduce noise by 10 decibels for the 3½-inch-and-larger mufflers. (Photo Courtesy Borla)

The 40 Series Flowmaster mufflers feature a dual-chamber design called Delta Flow Technology. These mufflers deliver a throaty, muscle car sound and free-flowing design for an excellent combination of performance and sound. Even if your car is not equipped with headers, the Flowmaster mufflers provide a muscular sound similar to headers. If you are running headers, they sound even better. Some of the Flowmaster mufflers designed for racing are so free flowing that the cars run equally fast with or without them. These mufflers are constructed with a 2-inch-offset inlet, 2-inch-offset outlet, 4-inch-thick x 9.75-inch-wide x 13-inch case length, and 19-inch overall length. (Photo Courtesy Flowmaster)

CHAPTER 7

INSTALLING A CRATE ENGINE

Today, buying a crate engine is popular because enthusiasts figured out that some crate engines cost less than fixing up an original small-block or big-block engine when you add up the parts cost and the machining expenses. But if you do have the money to perform a high-performance engine build, there are other factors to consider. You need the time, facilities, tools, and the skill set to perform a professional caliber rebuild. Selecting a crate engine is, therefore, a viable option and in many cases is the path to higher performance.

Manufacturers recognized the rise in crate engine sales, so they started building some strong engines that could be sold in crate form. In 1970 the top-of-the-line Chevy engine was an LS6 454 that was rated at 450 hp. Some LS7 engines were also produced for drag racers, but they were too radical for street use. Today, Chevrolet not only sells 427 and 454 Chevy big-block engines, it also offers 502 engines and 572 big-block Chevy engines that deliver unreal horsepower figures.

When the new LS engines were introduced in Corvettes, they became popular with enthusiasts because they were lightweight and offered enormous horsepower. It seems enthusiasts are willing to invest more money on engines than in the past, and when you go to a car show today you see plenty of 502 and LS engines. Chevrolet sells many of these engines but aftermarket suppliers are also selling crate engines. When you purchase a crate engine, you get instant gratification, typically a warranty, and peace of mind because you don't

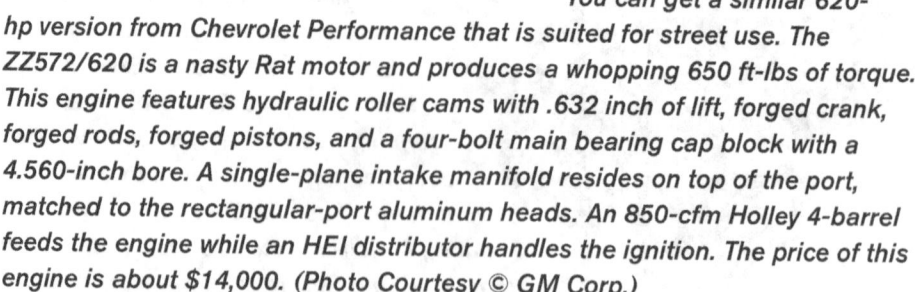

Chevrolet Performance offers a radical big-block Rat engine for track use. If money is no object, this engine easily slots into the frame rails of a second-generation F-Body car. This ultimate big-block Chevy engine is a 720-hp 572-ci race engine. While this engine is not recommended for street use, many performance enthusiasts do put them into street-driven Camaros.

You can get a similar 620-hp version from Chevrolet Performance that is suited for street use. The ZZ572/620 is a nasty Rat motor and produces a whopping 650 ft-lbs of torque. This engine features hydraulic roller cams with .632 inch of lift, forged crank, forged rods, forged pistons, and a four-bolt main bearing cap block with a 4.560-inch bore. A single-plane intake manifold resides on top of the port, matched to the rectangular-port aluminum heads. An 850-cfm Holley 4-barrel feeds the engine while an HEI distributor handles the ignition. The price of this engine is about $14,000. (Photo Courtesy © GM Corp.)

INSTALLING A CRATE ENGINE

have to go through the entire process of rebuilding an engine.

If you have one of the prime and highly collectible second-generation F-Body cars, such as a Z28 with an LT-1 350 or a SS396 Camaro or a 400 or 455 Pontiac-powered Firebird, you should keep the engine and chassis together to maintain its collector value. However, sometimes owners opt to pull the engine and/or transmission, place them safely in storage, and then install a high-performance Chevy or LS crate engine, along with a modern 5- or 6-speed transmission or an automatic overdrive (AOD) transmission. Common six-cylinder, 305, and 350 Camaros do not command high-collector values and, therefore, are excellent cars for LS engine swaps.

In the 1970s car manufacturers limited engine power for safety and liability reasons, but the potential was there for much higher horsepower and torque figures. Many performance aftermarket companies such as Edelbrock, Holley, Dart, Competition Cams, Crane Cams, and others offered parts for the OEM engines. Unfortunately, as the 1970s rolled on, the horsepower was emasculated by the emissions and fuel economy requirements, so many of the later Camaros and Firebirds can definitely use a power upgrade.

Although the original low-horsepower engines can be turned into performance engines, it's often a more cost-effective and time-saving route to select one of the many crate engines available. These modern crate engines offer more horsepower than any of the engines available in the 1970s. Some are available from Chevrolet Performance while others are available from aftermarket sources.

To Crate or Not to Crate

If you are going to buy an engine for your Pro Touring muscle machine there are a variety of things to think about before you make the final decision. First of all, how much money are you willing to spend on the engine of choice? Sure, you could hit the wrecking yard and pull an engine out of an old hulk and drop it into your muscle machine for a few hundred bucks, but that engine is an unknown, and it would be a good idea to rebuild it. The only time that is no longer a problem is when the wrecking yard can show you the car the engine came out of and it has very low mileage. I've seen some auto wrecking establishments that specialize in Chevy LS engines and can show you the source car's mileage. I know of one auto wrecking establishment that buys wrecked Corvettes and it either rebuilds the car or, if it is beyond repair, sells the parts. If you want reliability coupled with excellent performance, you can consider purchasing a crate engine. If you are a skilled mechanic, you may prefer to rebuild your own engine. The choice is yours but the easier of the two methods for novice enthusiasts (and probably the less expensive) is to purchase a crate engine.

If you are building a Pontiac and want an original-type Super Duty or Pontiac V-8 engine, the aftermarket does not offer inexpensive crate engines. If you are not a purist you can certainly install a hot Chevy engine into a Pontiac because Pontiac shared the big-block Chevy engine in racing endeavors after the originally designed Pontiac engine was discontinued in 1979. The late-model Pontiac GTO was equipped with an LS2 engine, which is considered a corporate engine, so that could also be a good transplant.

Crate engines are available in a wide range of performance levels and similarly associated prices. A Goodwrench 350-ci engine can cost you as little as $1,600 for a low-performance 350-ci engine, but on the other end of the spectrum, a top-of-the-line LS7 Corvette or ZZ572 big-block Chevy

Another rendition of the Rat motor is the Ram Jet fuel-injected 502-ci engine that delivers awesome performance on the street. With 565 ft-lbs and 502 hp, this Rat spools out gobs of torque for stoplight-to-stoplight acceleration contests. This engine produces 500 ft-lbs of torque at 2,200 rpm and up, and that's what makes this such a tractable and ideal street engine. It features a roller cam, forged rods, 4-inch forged crankshaft, 4.47-inch forged aluminum pistons, and has the necessary high-performance hardware. The aluminum oval-port heads have 2.25-inch intake and 1.88-inch exhaust valves. The price of this engine is about $10,400. (Photo Courtesy © GM Corp.)

engine lists at $12,995 and $13,800, respectively. If you want to purchase a fully detailed engine, it can be even more expensive.

Before an engine selection is made, you should also think about how the car will be used. If you're building a bad-to-the-bone trailer queen that will never see the highway and will seldom see the back roads to the fairground, you can install a high-compression racing engine or even a blown alcohol engine. Sure, everyone will be awestruck as you cruise in, but on the way home, as you pull your trailer along, you'll probably be jealous of all the fun the people in their Pro Touring cars are having as they zoom by you.

There are plenty of engines that provide excellent acceleration combined with reliability and dependability. There are also engines for drag race enthusiasts such as the ZZ572 that turn your drag car into a bullet without any other alterations.

Remember, every summer the price of gasoline rises, so you may want to select an engine and transmission that deliver excellent fuel economy as well as performance. If you plan to drive your Pro Touring car, especially on long-distance runs to events, a performance engine backed by an overdrive transmission would serve you better. Now, I'm not saying that you shouldn't purchase a strong-running engine because there are plenty or excellent ones that offer you the best of both worlds.

A recommendation that could be made is to install an engine that provides one horsepower per cubic inch. A good example is a ZZ4 Chevy 350 engine that is rated at 355 hp. Coupled with a 700R4 overdrive automatic transmission you have an engine that can deliver 20 mpg on the highway and pin you into the seat from a standing start. The best feature here is the complete aluminum-headed engine, less carburetor, only costs about $3,995. Rebuilding a wrecking yard engine with comparable horsepower could cost you about the same.

When you select an engine, you need to think about what kind of car you're building. If you want an ultimate handling machine, you might want to install a powerful engine that is lightweight because a cast-iron big-block makes a car nose heavy. If straight-line performance, such as drag racing, is a higher priority than going around corners, the new 502 or ZZ572 engine might be the right choice for your car. If you want a lightweight engine that offers excellent straight-line performance and cornering ability you might want to consider a new LS1, LS2, LS6, LS7, or LS9 aluminum Corvette engine.

Chevrolet Performance Small-Block and Big-Block

A number of reasons may have dictated why you aren't rebuilding the engine in your second-generation F-Body car. The engine may be a pedestrian six-cylinder or 305. Maybe the car didn't come with an engine. Perhaps your car came with a rare LT-1 or Super Duty engine, and you just need a reliable high-performance engine for driving it. Whatever the reason, a wide range of Gen-I small-block and Mark IV Rat motors are available through Chevrolet Performance. A full line of eight small-block Gen-I–derived engines are also available. Specifically, Chevrolet Performance offers five 350 engines and three 383 engines, so you are certain to find a small-block with a particular head, cam, and intake options that best suit your application and budget.

At the top of the crate 350 pyramid is the ZZ4 350 engine. This engine carries aluminum heads with

Chevrolet Performance offers a wide variety of small-block Chevy engines in many horsepower configurations. A very popular small-block is the Fast Burn 385 that combines a high-lift cam with the latest cylinder technology. This Fast Burn 385 resides in Mary Pozzi's Pro Touring 1973 Camaro. The Fast Burn heads are some of the best flowing heads and have a closed-chamber design for efficiently burning the fuel charge and maximizing torque and horsepower. This high-performance small-block offers 385 ft-lbs of torque and 385 hp to provide the ideal balance of acceleration and top-end speed for street applications. It's equipped with a steel hydraulic roller cam, forged-steel crankshaft, and hypereutectic pistons. The turnkey engine retails for about $5,700. (Photo Courtesy Tony Huntimer)

INSTALLING A CRATE ENGINE

The classic small-block and Rat motors are certainly viable options for any Camaro or Firebird high-performance project car, but certainly not the only options. The modern lineup of LS engines provides more horsepower per cube than almost any other modern pushrod V-8 engine. But that's not all; these engines are lighter and more compact than their small-block Chevy predecessors. Shown is the LS376, a hot rendition of the LS3, which is an established powerplant in the LS lineup and standard equipment for the Camaro SS. The LS376 takes the stock performance of an LS3 one step further, and it's a bargain for horsepower per dollar. This LS engine features a hot cam and fuel injection in a high-revving package. It features efficient rectangular-port cylinder heads that post a 50-hp improvement over the stock LS3. A more aggressive camshaft is an essential ingredient of the package at .525-inch intake and exhaust valve lift . Duration is 219 degrees intake and 228 degrees exhaust. Other key features are 10.7:1 pistons, heavy-duty rods, nodular crankshaft, and six-bolt aluminum block. This Chevrolet Performance engine retails for about $7,600. (Photo Courtesy © GM Corp.)

D-shaped exhaust ports, hydraulic roller cam, forged-steel crankshaft, and hypereutectic pistons. The high-velocity intake runners and exhaust port design provide efficient combustion and help produce 355 hp and 405 ft-lbs of torque.

On the big-block side, Chevrolet Performance has a stable of ten big-block engines to choose from. Nothing matches a big-block for visceral acceleration and street appeal, but very few early-1970s SS Camaros fitted with big-blocks were made. Another factor is that many small-block stroker and LS engines can produce similar horsepower and torque to Rat-motor big-blocks.

To replicate the big-block experience in a Camaro, you can get the 454 HO crate engine. It features a four-bolt main bearing block, forged rotating assembly, and a roller cam with .510/.540-inch lift. Cast-iron heads with a 8.75:1 compression ratio allow it to easily run on pump gas. With this package, the engine cranks out 425 hp and 500 ft-lbs of torque. And the classic big-block attracts attention when the hood is popped.

LS Crate Engine Sources

Cube per cube, the Chevrolet LS engines offer more performance than about any modern pushrod V-8 on the market. In addition, they also easily swap into an F-Body chassis. Manufacturers, including Holley, Street & Performance, ATS, and Dirty Dingo, offer motor-mount plates, so it's a relatively easy swap. If you need to replace your current engine or are looking to take a big leap in performance and you do not want to perform a rebuild, then an LS engine is certainly one of the best options.

Crate engines are available from a wide variety of sources, starting with original corporate engines from Chevrolet Performance. Chevrolet Performance offers the engines through car dealerships but they are

This large-displacement, lightweight LS7 engine delivers awesome power. The LS7-equipped 2006 Corvette Z06 tops out at 198 mph, runs the quarter-mile in 11.5 seconds at 127 mph, and accelerates from 0-60 mph in 3.5 seconds. The LS7 features a 7.0-liter, aluminum dry-sump block; CNC-ported cylinder heads; and titanium rods and valves to pump out 505 hp and 470 ft-lbs of torque. Installed in the 2006 Corvette Z06, the LS7 attained more than 28 mpg and was the fastest Corvette of its time. Chevrolet Performance offers the legendary LS7 as a complete crate engine for about $13,600. (Photo Courtesy © GM Corp.)

CHAPTER 7

Several aftermarket engine builders offer strong-running engines for street machines at prices comparable to those of Chevrolet Performance offerings. This is a Smeding Diesel economical small-block engine. (Photo Courtesy Smeding Diesel)

also available from many aftermarket speed parts dealers and even restoration shops, including Summit, Classic Industries, Hawaii Racing, Service Center, Friesen Chevrolet, Street and Performance, and many others. Other engine sources are machine shops, such as Lingenfelter, Arias, Dart, FH Dailey, and Smeding Diesel.

There are so many LS crate engine options that I simply can't cover them all in this chapter, so I highlight the most prominent ones.

Chevrolet Performance

Formerly known as GM Performance Parts, Chevrolet Performance offers a large number of LS engines to suit almost any high-performance street application and budget. In fact, Chevrolet Performance offers ten LS engines for street applications, but many of these are also suitable for competition applications. The lineup includes the LS327, LS1, LS6, LS3, LS376/480, LS376/515, LS376/525, LS7, LSA, and LS9.

The LS3 and LS376 engines are some of the most popular LS engines. The LS3 engine has powered the Corvette and the Camaro SS. The aluminum 6.2-liter engine produces 430 hp and 424 ft-lbs of torque to make it a very quick street engine. This Gen-IV engine caries rectangular-port heads, 63-cc combustion chambers, 2.16-inch intake valves, and 1.59-inch exhaust valves. This stellar engine package propels the new Corvette to 190 mph.

If you want to take a step beyond the stock LS engines, Chevrolet Performance also offers the LSX line, which is essentially designed for street and strip. The LSX376 cranks out 450 hp and 444 ft-lbs of torque while the LSX454 and LSX454R spool out 620 hp and 590 ft-lbs of torque.

Mast Motorsports

Mast Motorports offers a full line of specially enhanced LS crate engines that fit virtually every application. Mast offers 18 different models of Gen-IV drop-in motors. The line-up starts with a 416-ci stroker LS3 that pumps out 575 hp and goes all the way up to an RHS 427 that delivers 800 hp. Mast can also build an LS crate engine to your precise specifications and application needs.

Mast also sells its Black Label line of engines that elevate performance above the standard line-up of crate engines. These hand-built engines are intended for competition use but still retain good idle and low-end acceleration for excellent street driving. The LS3 416-ci engine features a 4-inch

Chevy offers a base engine, so you can choose your own intake, carb, and heads. It includes block, crank, pistons, cam, heads, and valve covers. This is the 290-hp, 350-ci engine. (Photo Courtesy © GM Corp.)

One of Smeding's most popular engines is the aluminum-head 383. This one features polished heads, custom valve covers, a chrome-plated timing chain cover, and oil pan. It also features a polished-aluminum intake manifold and a Holley carburetor. (Photo Courtesy Smeding Diesel)

INSTALLING A CRATE ENGINE

This engine features the LS7 with a six-bolt pattern, titanium valves, and high-lift camshaft. On the lower end, it carries forged LSX pistons, rods, and crankshaft. A suitable engine for the street, you can build the engine with an 11:1 compression ratio and run it on pump gas. (Photo Courtesy © GM Corp.)

Lingenfelter

Lingenfelter's line of specially prepared high-performance LS engines that are suitable for nearly any second-generation F-Body. The company offers nine LS engines that provide a wide range of performance levels. The LS3 378-ci engine features the full array of GM high-performance equipment. It also carries Callies crank, forged Mahle pistons, LS3/L92 heads, LS intake, and many other parts. The aggressive performance package cranks out 630 hp.

the Lingenfelter GT11 hydraulic roller cam, special CNC porting, and head polishing. At 11.5:1 compression it runs on 93-octane pump gas. It also carries Comp Cams valvesprings, titanium retainers, and heavy-duty pushrods. With all the equipment in this package, the engine spools out 550 hp.

Everyone knows about the LS engines used in the Corvettes but not that much is known about the Cadillac version LSA. This engine is very similar to the Corvette LS9 engine but it features hypereutectic pistons instead of the forged pistons in the LS9 engine and a smaller 1.9-liter supercharger. The LSA engine is rated at 556 hp and has a different charge-cooler design on top of the supercharger. This engine isn't a cheap date, but it would be an awesome addition to a Camaro or Firebird.

While the LS9 tops the list of high-performance stock Chevrolet LS crate engines, it also comes with a serious price tag. An LS9, stock engine for Corvette ZR1, is the most powerful production engine that Detroit has ever made. The 6.2-liter engine produces 638 hp at 6,500 rpm and a maximum torque of 604 ft-lbs at 3,800 rpm. Key features include all-new Gen-IV small-block V-8 for Chevrolet Corvette ZR1, Gen-VI supercharger with twin four-lobe rotors, dual brick air-to-liquid intercooler, forged pistons with oil-spray cooling, titanium connection rods, refined low-overlap cam, center-feed fuel system, direct-mount ignition coils, and stainless-steel exhaust manifolds. It is the ultimate engine for any Pro Touring car and typically sells for about $21,100. (Photo Courtesy © GM Corp.)

CHAPTER 8

Performance Transmission

It's equally important to select a transmission that works effectively with the engine. The transmission options from General Motors ranged from very good to mediocre. On the high end, the Turbo 400 and Borg-Warner T10s delivered excellent performance but the PowerGlide was past its prime.

Camaros built from 1970 to 1973 were equipped with the Turbo 350 (small-block applications), Turbo 400 (big-block applications), antiquated PowerGlide automatic, Muncie or Saginaw 3-speed, or Muncie or Saginaw 4-speed manual gearboxes. Often the Muncie was used with higher horsepower engines. The 4-speed Muncies are definitely worth rebuilding and often are suitable for a 400- or 500-hp engine build. The Turbo 350 as well as the 400 are automatics worth using in many high-performance applications. But I never recommend using the 2-speed PowerGlide.

In the years following, the Super T-10 and the Turbo 350 continued to be extensively used in the Camaro line-up. And it's generally accepted that the Super T-10 is a stronger transmission than the Muncie 4-speeds because of its internal spline design. In 1980, General Motors used the TH200 with the V-6, but it is not suitable for high-horsepower V-8s.

The vast majority of 1970s Camaros and Firebirds were outfitted with the reliable Turbo 350 transmissions and there is nothing wrong with them behind an engine with moderate horsepower. In fact, with performance improvements, the transmission will live comfortably behind a big-block engine if the car is driven on the street and not for all-out drag racing. If you want to modernize your car and get improved gas mileage an overdrive automatic 200R4 is exactly the same size as a Turbo 350, so this is an easy transmission swap to perform. The 200R4 transmissions were used in a wide

If you install a high-performance automatic transmission in your Camaro or Firebird you need a high-stall torque converter, a transmission cooler, and transmission fluid. This is a Chevy 700R4 automatic overdrive transmission built by TCI and should be able to stand up to many high-performance Chevy engines.

variety of GM cars but they are not as strong as the big 700R4. The 200R4 works fine in moderate performance use and is easy to find.

During the muscle car years many Camaros and Firebirds were delivered with 4-speed transmissions, so if you prefer a stick you can find a variety of 4-speeds from the 1960s and early 1970s. In the 1960s Chevy and Pontiac used the Muncie M20, M21, and M22 transmissions; they were strong enough to handle big-block Chevy and large displacement Pontiac engines.

If your Camaro or Firebird is currently equipped with an automatic transmission and you want to upgrade it with a 4-speed you can get all of the change-over parts from your restoration supplier. Starting in the 1970s the later model Camaros and Firebirds, including the Z28 and Trans Am, were offered with optional Super T-10 4-speed transmissions. In the early 1980s some Camaros and Firebirds were offered with T-5 5-speed transmissions and they were designed for use behind V-8 engines of moderate horsepower. Although not a direct replacement, the later T-5 transmissions can be installed in the earlier Camaros and Firebirds. Today, it would probably be easier to find a 5-speed than it would be to find an earlier 4-speed in your local wrecking yards.

The Corvette was one of the first performance cars to offer a 6-speed transmission, so you should be able to find one in a salvage yard, although most prefer to sell the engine and transmission as a packaged deal. If price isn't a concern or if you have a very high-powered engine you can order a Tremec 6-speed transmission that can handle an engine that is delivering a lot of horsepower. If you outfit your car with a 5- or 6-speed transmission the top gear is overdrive, so it allows better high-speed cruising and improves mileage by keeping the RPM at a lower level.

Second-Generation OEM Options

Second-generation Camaros and Firebirds were outfitted with several possible transmission choices. In the early years the high-horsepower engines were backed by a Turbo 400 automatic or a Muncie 4-speed transmission. The smaller horsepower engines were backed by a Turbo 350 automatic transmission or a Muncie or Saginaw 4-speed transmission. General Motors also equipped many Z28 and Trans Am cars with a Super T-10 4-speed in all states except California. Camaros and Firebirds in California were limited to automatic transmissions because there was an untrue and unproven belief that 4-speed cars emitted more emissions than automatic-equipped cars.

The Turbo 400 transmission was a rugged transmission that could be built to handle even the highest horsepower engines and it is still a popular choice by hot rodders and drag racers. They are more difficult to find today because they were built in limited numbers in the 1960s. The most popular transmission used by General Motors in a wide variety of cars (including the second-generation Camaros and Firebirds) was the Turbo 350. It was a smaller, lighter transmission that was built to handle the power of most moderate-horsepower engines, including the lower horsepower 400 and 403 Olds engines found in the Trans Am Firebirds. They were also used behind the stronger 350 engines in Z28 Camaros. The Turbo

If you install a 5-speed transmission in your Camaro or Firebird you need a bellhousing, flywheel, and clutch and pressure plate as shown here.

If you are building a restored Camaro or Firebird and want a top-quality 4-speed transmission, new M22 units are available from the Autogear Company. The transmissions have been upgraded and are capable of being used behind a 700-hp engine.

CHAPTER 8

The Tremec T-5 5-speed transmission was developed for a broad range of vehicles. It features advanced synchronizer technology with powdered steel core blocker rings, engineered friction materials for improved durability, double-cone design for lower shift effort, and a patented strut-type design for improved durability. This transmission should hold up to a moderate performance Chevy engine.

350 transmission was lighter than the Turbo 400, so it actually worked well to improve the handling ability and fuel economy of the mid to late 1970 Trans Am Firebirds and the later 1977-and-newer Z28 Camaros.

As time went on, lower emissions and improved gas mileage were important to auto manufacturers, they decided to design new 5-speed manual transmissions that provided an overdrive fifth gear. The most popular 5-speed was the Borg-Warner T-5 transmission that was strong enough to handle the engine selections that were available in the 1980s. General Motors also designed two overdrive automatic transmissions, the 200R4 and the stronger 700R4 automatic. Both could be improved to handle more horsepower and are still popular with enthusiasts who want an overdrive transmission.

The 200R4 is exactly the same size as the Turbo 350 and swaps right into a 1970–1981 Camaro or Firebird without any modifications.

The Tremec T-56 6-speed transmission was developed for adaptation to a wide range of vehicle requirements, such as the Z06 Corvette and Dodge Viper. Obviously this transmission can stand up to engines producing large amounts of horsepower and torque.

In a performance-improved condition it holds up to a moderately built, street-driven 350 Chevy engine without a problem. The 700R4 transmission is much stronger but it is larger and longer than a Turbo 350, so some modification is necessary if you plan to install one in a second-generation Camaro or Firebird.

During the 1980s, General Motors installed a 6-speed transmission in Corvettes, which improved the car's acceleration and gas mileage. Other companies, such as Tremec and Richmond, started building high-performance 5- and 6-speed transmissions, both of which are popular with builders today. The 6-speeds are not for the weak of wallet because you will spend more than $6,000 for a transmission and bellhousing. General Motors and other companies have also started building multiple-gear automatic overdrive transmissions that are used behind the modern computer-controlled high-horsepower engines. These newer transmissions offer excellent acceleration, and because of the overdrive gear selections, they also provide excellent gas mileage. For example, a 400-hp, LS2 Corvette turns the quarter-mile in 12.5 seconds, but it also provides 26 mpg on the highway. You can get the same results when you install one in your Camaro or Firebird.

Transmission Sources

If you are building a second-generation Camaro or Firebird, many high-performance transmissions are available. A well-built and maintained standard Turbo 350 or 400 transmissions can handle plenty of horsepower. If you want to move into the new millennium you may want an overdrive manual or automatic transmission. The following are a few of the options available today.

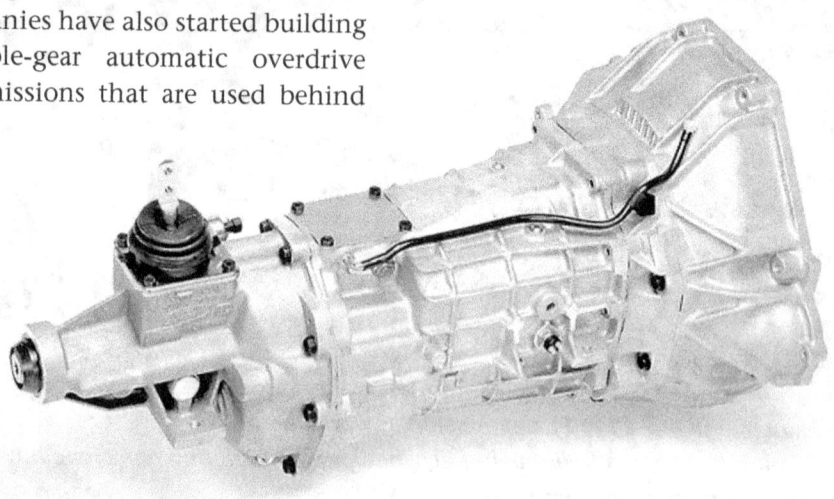

60 CAMARO & FIREBIRD PERFORMANCE PROJECTS: 1970–1981

PERFORMANCE TRANSMISSION

If your car is equipped with a Turbo 350 transmission you can update it with a 200R4 automatic overdrive transmission. Both transmissions are the same length so the new transmission bolts into the car with only small linkage changes.

Tremec

Tremec has been the industry leader for decades. The T-56 has become a top choice for muscle car and Pro Touring car owners because of the strength and shifting precision of the gearboxes. This 6-speed transmission and its T-56 Magnum sibling can handle the torque of the highest horsepower V-8 engines. In fact, the T-56 first appeared in the V-12 Dodge Viper and has been used in a number of OEM supercars.

If you install the T-56 in your second-generation F-Body, the Classic Chevy 6-Speed Elite T-56 kit is an ideal option. This kit contains the hydraulic clutch assembly and all the parts back to the driveshaft, which include McLeod clutch components, Inland Empire Driveline driveshafts, and all required GM parts. With the sixth gear, you definitely save money on gas when freeway cruising to events.

The T-5 is another viable option for second-generation F-Body owners. The compact and durable T-5 has been used in Ford Mustangs and many other high-performance applications. And it's currently being used in many OEM muscle car and high-performance car applications. The transmission transmits up to 300 ft-lbs of torque, and it is one of the best values in the high-performance manual transmission market.

Chevrolet Performance

General Motors makes a number of transmissions that are suitable for the second-generation Camaro. In particular, if you're looking for a high-performance automatic overdrive transmission, the 4L60 is a mechanically controlled transmission. If you're installing a GM LS engine in your second-generation F-Body, you can certainly opt for the computer-controlled version, which is the 4L60E. These transmissions are tough enough in most cases to handle nearly 600 hp.

B&M Racing

In the mid 1960s General Motors released two 3-speed automatic transmissions, the Turbo Hydramatic 350 for small-block-equipped cars and the Turbo Hydramatic 400 for big-block-equipped cars. Since there were so many more small-block-equipped cars manufactured in the 1960s and 1970s, the Turbo 350 quickly became the most abundant transmission. They were used in Chevrolets, Pontiacs, Oldsmobiles, Buicks, and a wide variety of Chevrolet and GMC pickup trucks. The Turbo 350 transmissions came with two different aluminum cases, one for Chevy vehicles and another for Buick, Oldsmobile, and Pontiac (BOP) vehicles.

The Turbo 350 was smaller and lighter than the Turbo 400 transmission. With performance improvements, the Turbo 350 transmission could live behind many high-performance small- and big-block engines, especially in cars designed for street use. Throughout the 1970s the Turbo 350 became the staple of the GM fleet because the big-block engine's horsepower was greatly reduced to meet fuel efficiency and emissions standards.

B&M Racing started building high-performance transmissions for race cars in the 1950s and early 1960s with racing versions of the Hydramatic transmissions found in Pontiacs, Cadillacs, and Oldsmobiles. The company soon became well known in the early Gas class race cars. When the Turbo 350 and Turbo

If you have plenty of room under your car, you can hook the engine up to a 4L80E automatic transmission. This large transmission is designed for use with high-horsepower engines in GM cars and trucks.

CHAPTER 8

If you are looking for a very strong 5-speed transmission for your Pro Touring Camaro or Firebird you can hook up a Richmond transmission and it can be purchased in two styles: one for street use and one for road racing.

400 transmissions replaced the earlier Hydramatic transmissions, B&M Racing started developing parts to make the new transmissions, stronger and shift faster.

I once found a Trans Am with 68,000 miles on the odometer, powered by a 403 Olds engine producing 190 hp, and backed by a Turbo 350 transmission. The transmission was an unknown since the car hadn't been running for the past 20 years and the engine and transmission were removed from the car. The transmission was very dirty on the outside so it probably was never rebuilt in the past. I contacted B&M Racing and wanted to have the transmission rebuilt and strengthened for high-performance street use. (B&M offers several types of rebuilding such as for towing, off-road racing, and drag racing.) This one had been built for high-performance street use.

B&M also offers a rebuild kit (PN 30229) that you can use to duplicate the B&M-prepared transmission at home following the detailed instruction sheet. Or, if you like instant gratification you can order a transmission that was already rebuilt by a B&M technician. In either case it is a good idea to purchase a new B&M Hole Shot torque converter.

TCI Automotive

Another legend in the industry is TCI. This company offers a 6-speed automatic transmission that can be used fully automatic or shifted manually. This new, innovative transmission is built around the strong GM 4L80E transmission case, but the internal design is 100-percent TCI engineering and is so different than anything available that the technology is currently patent pending. The transmission is designed to handle 850 hp and comes with a limited lifetime warranty. If you are looking for a fantastic overdrive transmission this is definitely one of the best available.

Bowtie Overdrives

Another company that specializes in late-model automatic overdrive transmissions is Bowtie Overdrives. It has been a leading transmission shop for more than 16 years. The company specializes in rebuilding 200R4, 700R4, 4L65E, 4L80E, and their exclusive 765R4 automatic overdrive transmission. The company offers complete bolt-in kits for any GM vehicle from 1955 to 1981. This company can work with you to install a high-performance automatic overdrive transmission into your 1970–1981 Camaro or Firebird. The company also offers transmissions that work with LS engines.

SW Performance Transmissions

This company specializes in performance transmissions for muscle cars, street machines, Pro Touring cars, and street rods. It rebuilds transmissions for all brands, with GM transmissions being the most popular. This company can work with you when you want to upgrade your second-generation Camaro or Firebird.

FB Performance Transmissions

FB Performance Transmissions specializes in automatic overdrive transmissions. This shop builds transmissions that are rated from 900 to 1,400 hp so the transmissions it builds hold up to just about any engine you put in front of it. The GM performance transmissions it builds feature gear ratios of 2.40, 1.47, 1.00, and 0.67:1. The company also has optional ratios of 2.84, 1.56, 1.00, and 0.70:1.

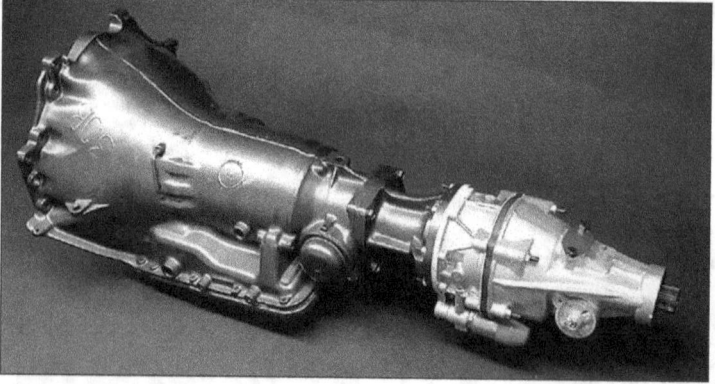

If you have a standard automatic transmission, such as a Turbo 350 or Turbo 400, and want overdrive you can back up the transmission with a Gear Vendors overdrive unit. This unit can be used automatically or manually, so your 3-speed transmission can effectively be turned into a 6-speed.

CHAPTER 9

CHASSIS UPGRADES

By the latter half of the 1960s, Detroit's prevailing philosophy was to build a muscle car with jaw dropping acceleration and top speed, with chassis performance relegated to second-tier priority or lower. Hence, handling, road holding, and brake performance suffered. As we know, this was an era of bias-ply tires, small-diameter wheels, drum brakes, and worm-gear steering boxes. This technology became antiquated and was replaced over the succeeding years.

Today, we have sticky-compound radial tires, 18-inch wheels, 14-inch brake rotors, tubular A-arms, rack-and-pinion steering, and much more. For more than a decade, the muscle car industry and enthusiast market have recognized the enormous benefits of upgrading chassis, suspension, brake, and steering components on classic muscle cars, and in particular, the second-generation Camaro, one of the most affordable classics. The aftermarket continues to offer a wide range of parts to enhance chassis rigidity and performance.

The Pro Touring segment of second-generation owners is squarely focused on extracting maximum chassis performance from their cars. With the right combination of products and professional-caliber installation, well-modified Camaros now rival the performance of late-model sports cars. In essence, performance is now attainable that just a few years ago was never thought possible.

While the Pro Touring movement is very popular at the moment, this isn't the first time muscle cars were made to handle like sports cars. Detroit manufacturers showed that muscle cars could be made to quickly negotiate corners in SCCA Trans-Am road racing series during the late 1960s and early 1970s. When the Camaro was released, SCCA Trans-Am road racing was a very popular form of racing.

General Motors brass and its engineers were interested in sedan racing and saw that as a good venue to introduce the new car. The car also received handling improvements to allow it to compete successfully with Mustangs. This was showroom stock racing, so in order for the car to homologate to racing standards, a similar production car had to be sold to the public. It took a while for enthusiasts to catch on to what Chevrolet was doing. Ford didn't like it because the Mustangs could not compete with the new Camaros. The Z28 was the start of the handling movement. Enthusiasts who drove the Z28 Camaros saw the potential of the car, and they liked it.

When the muscle-car-buying public realized the benefits of a road-racing-inspired Z28, sales increased. A new emphasis was placed on suspension design when the new second-generation Camaros and Firebirds were created. Pontiac wasn't as successful as Chevrolet when it came to Trans-Am racing because the company didn't have an engine it could successfully downsize to less than 305 ci with a competitive weight. The engineers worked on several variations but none of the block and head combinations worked well enough to be both competitive and be sold to customers.

Herb Adams, a young engineer, was chiefly responsible for the development of the 1969 Trans Am, and he was in charge of the suspension end of the product. He experimented with many spring and sway bar improvements and ended up with a Firebird that really handled well. When the 1970 Firebird was getting close to production Adams started working on the new Trans Am. Using ideas he learned on the previous car he developed a suspension system that made the Trans Am a fantastic handling car. Apparently, what he learned wasn't shared with the Camaro engineers because the divisions were still competing.

Due to production problems, the second-generation Camaro and Firebird had a late release date. When the cars were released both were well received by the automotive press and the public. The Trans Am was very impressive when it came to handling. The Z28 Camaro handled well, too, so Z28 sales were very impressive. The Trans Am was a great car but it was very expensive compared to the Camaro, so Trans Am sales were low in comparison.

As engine performance and demand was on the decline Chevrolet discontinued the Z28 Camaro but Pontiac forged ahead with the Trans Am, knowing it was one of the best performance cars available. Pontiac turned it into a luxury performance model that featured excellent handling. Enthusiasts who purchased the car were aware of its handling prowess, and that became one of the features that created the car's high demand. The movie *Smokey and the Bandit* also helped the car's success story.

When engine performance was limited by emissions and mileage concerns in the mid 1970s, engineers were looking for ways to make Camaros and Firebirds more exciting to drive. Pontiac had been improving the Firebird suspension all along while the management at Chevrolet moved away from performance and toward luxury by discontinuing the Z28 package. The Firebird took advantage of the new radial tire technology when the engineers released Pontiac's Radial Tuned Suspension package that improved the Firebird's handling.

After a few years Chevrolet saw the success Pontiac was having with the Trans Am, so it re-released the Z28 package in 1977 with improved handling, but Pontiac had a head start. In 1978, Pontiac also went one better with the WS6 suspension package that included heavier sway bars, an improved steering box with a tighter ratio, and 8-inch-wide wheels with top-of-the-line Goodyear radial tires. In many respects Pontiac actually started the Pro Touring movement with a Trans Am that turned out to be the best handling American passenger car in 1978, even beating the Corvette.

Improving a car's handling with aftermarket components was really popular in the late 1970s and early 1980s. But it wasn't long before the car manufacturers caught on and started their own suspension improvements that went above and beyond what the average enthusiast could take advantage of.

In the late 1970s, magazine editors were doing stories about autocross racing Z28 Camaros and Trans Am Pontiacs, but the sport never caught on to any great extent. Today, autocross racing is conducted at tracks and Goodguys events, and it has caught on with a larger number of car enthusiasts than it did in the late 1970s. Similar to what happened then, a number of hardcore performance and suspension improvement companies display their suspension products at autocross events.

Today there are many aftermarket suspension components that can vastly improve the handling of second-generation Camaros and Firebirds, which were good-handling cars to start with. Similar to what was happening in the 1970s, enthusiasts are adding suspension improvements to their cars for improved handling on the street and on the track. When owners spend a small fortune turning a second-generation F-Body into a wild Pro Touring–style show car it is unlikely that they will autocross the car every weekend on a course where the car can be damaged physically or mechanically, but they will improve it for fun cruising through the canyons. On the other hand, if a car competes for the Street Machine of the Year competition at the Goodguys Nationals, it has to run the autocross course to make sure that it can actually be driven.

Suspension Component Sources

If you want to improve your Camaro or Firebird suspension, there are many companies building components that can help you out. Suspension improvements include everything from simple and easy-to-install spring and shock modifications to complete new front clips with lightweight A-arms and coil-over shocks.

The following are just a few of the companies that have become involved with suspension improvements. Some shops build individual components to be used with the original subframe; others offer complete new subframes that improve a Camaro's or Firebird's ride and handling. All of the subframes are designed for Camaros with mounts for big- and small-block Chevy engines. Pontiac enthusiasts with early Firebirds have to do some fabrication to install a Pontiac or Olds engine into an aftermarket subframe because the engines mount differently and the oil pans are wider.

Energy Suspension, Inc.

Energy Suspension started specializing in polyurethane parts more than 25 years ago, and it is currently the leader in the industry. The company's in-house experience in innovating, engineering, and formulating a wide selection of polyurethane components for many different industries has qualified it as a premier manufacturer of the highest quality polyurethane products available today.

The company has a state-of-the-art, on-site, new product development program that carefully analyzes various reactions of vehicles equipped with Energy's Performance Polyurethane technology. Today the company offers the largest product line in the industry for both import and domestic vehicles. It offers replacement Performance Polyurethane automotive control arm bushings containing outer metal shells. It also sells the Hyper-Flex System, which offers a complete Performance Polyurethane suspension bushing set for front to rear coverage of many popular domestic vehicles. Energy Suspension also offers greaseable anti-sway bar bushings that feature easily greaseable zerk fittings as well as Performance Polyurethane ball joint and tie rod dust boots.

Energy Suspension offers a wide selection of polyurethane bushings and suspension parts to improve the ride and handling of 1970–1981 Camaros and Firebirds. When you order parts you have to know several things about your car, such as sway bar size and the engine that will be used. The parts are easy to install and a complete upgrade can be done over a weekend.

If you want to improve your 1970–1981 Camaro or Firebird's ride and handling it can be done with Energy Suspension's high-quality polyurethane parts. I ordered a complete set for a Firebird Trans Am to improve the car's performance without making extreme alterations so the car can have a restored appearance. The parts are available in red (for a nice performance appearance) or black (for a stealth appearance that is not noticeable until you look close).

Schwartz Performance

Schwartz Performance makes the G-Machine Chassis, which is a full-perimeter chassis that increases rigidity several fold. The Camaro or Firebird body simply fits over the chassis so it does not require cutting or welding of the floorboards, just some simple attachment of chassis brackets. The integration of the frame to an F-Body car provides exceptional torsional chassis rigidity, so the suspension performance and ride quality are optimized. The body and stock frame rails are given exceptional support, so the body is not subjected to excessive torsional twisting that could lead to fatigue and body/frame cracks. This frame comes with a choice of QA1 coil-over shocks or RideTech (Air Ride) Shockwaves. Narrowed rear frame rails accommodate mini-tubbing and 15-inch-wide rear tires in most cases. All Schwartz chassis feature a 1.08G skidpad handling capability. With the g-Machine Chassis, you can run up to 345-mm-wide rear tires with installed minitubs in the wheel wells. In addition, the chassis readily accepts a Moser full-floating 9-inch rear axle.

Jim Meyer Racing Products

Jim Meyer Racing Products makes a variety of chassis upgrades for street rods, classic cars, trucks, and muscle cars. The company released a second-generation F-Body aftermarket front subframe that's precision built on a jig to exacting standards. Like other subframes, it features tubular 1-inch upper and 1¼-inch lower A-arms. The front spindles accept GM, Baer, and Wilwood disc brake kits. The frame comes with 11-inch GM discs, but you can select optional upgrades, which include Baer 13- or 14-inch discs or Wilwood 12.19- or 13-inch discs, 2-inch drop spindles, power rack-and-pinion steering, RideTech's (formerly Air Ride Technologies) ShockWave suspension system, and nickel-plated components. It comes with AirRide Tech ShockWave bags or QA1 adjustable coil-over shocks. The ultra-strong frame is made of 2x4-inch box tubing.

The fully adjustable bolt-in subframe features 3 to 4 inches of stance adjustment, has adjustable upper tubular A-arms with stock replacement or drop spindles, and comes complete with a pre-drilled transmission crossmember for all popular GM and aftermarket transmissions. The Meyer subframe is extremely strong but it weighs less than the original, and that allows it to improve the handling of the second-generation cars. The frame has a 60-inch front track and has provisions to accept big-block or small-block engines.

Chris Alston's Chassisworks

Chris Alston's Chassisworks has been a respected name in the aftermarket chassis industry for more than 35 years. The company has gained its reputation through building tube drag race chassis, but it now has a full line of aftermarket subframes for GM vehicles, including the 1970–1981 F-Body cars. Specifically, it offers a bolt-on complete front subframe, called the g-Machine Front Subframe, for both the 1970–1976 and the 1977–1981 F-Body cars. Both front subframes offer similar equipment and exceptional affordability.

Chassisworks calls these value systems for limited budgets; they include A-arm clip, upper and lower arms with ball joints, spindles, manual rack, tie rods, and billet coil-over shocks with springs. Along with kits for many cars Chassisworks released a modular three-section frame system for 1970–1981 Camaros and Firebirds. The chassis features a g-Machine front subframe, a frame connector, and a g-Bar rear suspension system.

The heart of the system is the direct fit, fabricated, g-Machine Camaro front subframe, a high-performance suspension and steering solution that was engineered from the ground up to give F-Bodies the broadest selection of performance configurations available. Control arm, shock absorber, spindle, brake, and steering options allow custom configurations suitable for show-dropped air suspensions, competitive road handling, lightweight drag racing, and everything in between.

The g-Street system package includes tubular upper and lower control arms with bonded-rubber or poly bushings, depending on vehicle application. The g-Street lower control arms feature a true coil-over-style ear mount. To keep the installation simple and maximize compatibility, control arms utilize the factory chassis mounts and bolt directly to stock or aftermarket dropped spindles. The arms feature a gray hammertone powdercoated finish. The g-Street systems are available with single or double adjustable, billet-aluminum VariShock coil-over shocks or Shock-Wave air suspension.

Each style features a pivot-ball lower mount with ball-stud upper mount that bolts directly to the factory mounting location. The exclusive greaseable ball-stud mount provides more positive control of the suspension while still allowing free pivoting movement. Anti-roll bars are available for each of the g-Street suspension applications. Premium polyurethane bushings and direct-fit hardware are included with each kit. Bushing housings can also be upgraded to billet-aluminum housings.

In order to bridge the unsupported distance between the front subframe and the rear suspension, multiple styles of mandrel-bent 2x2-inch subframe connectors are available for bolt-in installation with factory or Chassisworks' front subframes. A bolt-in, factory-welded, center support with optional driveshaft loop can also be added to further stiffen the chassis and strengthen the lower suspension mounting area.

Chassiswork's g-Bar and g-Link systems represent the current state-of-the-art in retrofit, canted four-bar suspension design. Following suit with the configuration options of the g-Machine front subframe system, the g-Bar and g-Link air spring and coil-over systems feature multiple styles of suspension links, shock absorbers, anti-roll bars, and installation brackets. The system can be installed with factory 10- or 12-bolt rear end housings, or Chassisworks' FAB9 Ford 9-inch-conversion, fabricated housings. To accommodate multiple levels of vehicle customizing and performance goals, rear frame brackets can be ordered as bolt-in, weld-supported brackets, or as short 2x3-inch front rail and full-length 2x3-inch frame rails to dramatically increase rear tire clearance.

The Roadster Shop

The Roadster Shop has been a source for street rod chassis for many years and the quality is considered one of the best in the industry. Street rods continue to be a mainstay of the business, but the owners knew they would have to expand the business to include newer cars similar to what many other chassis manufacturers did. Today, The Roadster Shop offers chassis for a variety of street rods and muscle cars, and the facility also builds turn-key cars for customers. The company built a beautiful Nova that competed in the 2011 Goodguys Street Machine of the Year awards and won the competition.

The Roadster Shop saw a need for a better Pro Touring-style chassis for 1970–1981 Camaros and Firebirds, and through extensive tests with the new chassis the F-Body cars handle much better than those with the original front subframe. The new chassis features tubular upper and lower A-arms suspended with coil-over shocks. The front suspension also features a large sway bar and plenty of adjustability for camber, caster, and toe-in. The original rear leaf springs are eliminated and the rear end features traction bars and a Panhard bar, and it is suspended on coil-over shocks.

This new F-Body chassis is also a full chassis that adds structural stiffness, which also improves the handling ability of the car. Pro Touring enthusiasts who want to build the ultimate show machine also notice

CHASSIS UPGRADES

the quality of the chassis construction and the attractive appearance of the frame.

Detroit Speed, Inc.

Detroit Speed and Engineering manufactures several performance suspension upgrades for second-generation Camaros and Firebirds. The Camaro/Firebird/Nova chassis design was created in the 1960s. It featured a unibody with a separate front suspension that was bolted on with four large bolts and rubber pads between the body and subframe. It was unique at the time, and without a doubt, it worked terrific. The rubber pads insulated the body from harsh road conditions and engine vibrations. The design worked so well that second-generation Camaros used a similar, improved design with a change in the location of the steering box for improved handling.

When the Camaro was designed, it wasn't intended to be a road racer, although it did do well in Trans-Am racing. That racing endeavor showed the kind of improvements that could and should be made to make Camaros and Firebirds handle even better.

The Detroit Speed front and rear suspension system is a major improvement over original parts, and the subframe is bolted to the body with aluminum mounts to provide the ultimate in handling. Even with the aluminum subframe mounts, there is some body flexing under hard cornering, so the company designed a subframe connector kit that eliminates the flexing and improves the overall handling of the car.

Heidts Hot Rod & Muscle Car Parts

Gary Heidt was an engineer and a hot rodder in the 1970s who was always looking for a better way to build a nice-handling and comfortable-riding street rod. He became interested in the Shay replica Model A Ford and the Mustang II suspension the cars were using.

In original form the suspensions didn't look that nice but the cars did offer a soft ride and positive steering from the rack-and-pinion steering system. A universal installation kit was offered for street rods.

A friend of Gary suggested that if someone could design easy-to-install kits tailored to Model A Fords, Deuces, 1933 and 1934 Fords, and 1935-and-newer Fords he would make a lot of money. Gary thought about that and started designing kits for the cars using Mustang II parts.

In the process of designing the parts, Gary realized that if he made triangular upper and lower A-arms, he could eliminate the strut rods from the original suspension plus improve the appearance of the suspension. Using his engineering talent, he designed suspension systems that used the original Ford geometry with an attractive appearance. In terms of how the suspension works I can verify that the suspension provides an exceptional ride and positive steering far superior to the original suspension systems.

Ford, Chevrolet, and other manufacturers still used antiquated I-beam suspension systems. The industry needed a much improved suspension; Heidts superior suspension filled a market need and the business thrived.

Gary also saw that some of the 1960s cars, such as Mustangs and Novas, also had suspension systems that could be improved with regard to handling, steering, and engine compartment room. He expanded into those areas and started to build kits for Novas and Mustangs that opened up the engine compartment by eliminating the spring towers.

With growth in the new Pro Touring movement, the company started designing suspension systems that could improve the handling of Camaros and other performance models. Today the company is a performance suspension leader in the muscle car market and it offers several improvements for 1970–1981 Camaros and Firebirds.

For second-generation F-Bodies, Heidts makes replacement A-arms for improved handling, which offer improved geometry and are much lighter than the factory A-arms. Heidts also offers complete front subframes that are a direct bolt-on that feature tubular A-arms and coil-over suspension. Heidts' rear suspension upgrades include tubular control arms with coil-over shocks and a fully independent rear suspension that improve the ride and handling of any post-1970 F-Body.

Project 1: Subframe Connectors Installation

One way to turn a Camaro into an ultimate canyon carver is to install Detroit Speed's subframe connectors.

When the front subframe is linked to the rear suspension via subframe connectors, the torsional rigidity of the chassis increases, thus greatly improving handling. Made of heavy-gauge rectangular steel tubing, subframe connectors feature brackets and install inconspicuously on the

CAMARO & FIREBIRD PERFORMANCE PROJECTS: 1970–1981

frame. Installed correctly, these form a strong weld joint.

Safety is paramount so be sure that the chassis of a second-generation F-Body car is safely supported. Shops securely suspend the chassis on a lift and have full and easy access to the entire underside of the car, so the floorpans can be easily cut and the subframe connectors welded-in.

Most enthusiasts do not have access to a lift, so you have to support the chassis on jack stands. The load has to be evenly distributed, or your chassis will deflect in some area. Do not install subframe connectors when the chassis is twisted because the connectors anchor the chassis in that twisted position. Therefore, be absolutely sure to put the jack stands under the rear axle in back and under the lower control arms up front.

And never crawl under a vehicle that is not safely supported. Installing subframe connectors is not worth risking your life. When performing this type of work, always use the appropriate safety gear and clothing, including eye protection and gloves.

Identify and Measure Subframe Connectors

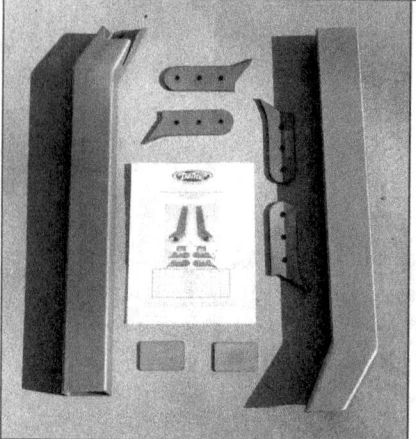
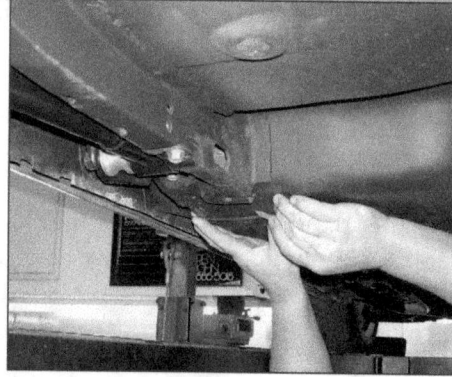

1 *The Detroit Speed kit includes formed, rectangular-tube subframe connectors; inside and outside brackets; and end caps for the connectors. The subframe connectors are not the same, so they are labeled left (LH) and right (RH) for your convenience (far left).*

Position the angled end of the subframe connector toward the rear of the vehicle and pointing outward. Start the installation by measuring inward from the pinch weld along the bottom of the rocker panel. Mark all measurements on the undercarriage (left).

Mark Subframe Connector Cut Lines

2 *Once the measurements have been made, use a wide-tip Sharpie to mark the subframe connectors' cut lines on the floorpan. Use a pneumatic rotary tool with a 3-inch cut-off wheel to cut the pan. A plasma cutter can be used to cut the pan, but remember that it cuts so quickly it's easy to make a mistake.*

Templates are provided for marking the floorpan. Cut the templates from the provided sheet and transfer them to a piece of poster board. Once transferred to the poster board, you have a sturdy template for making the precise cutout lines for the floorpan.

Mark Floorpan

3 *Place the floorpan template on the floorpan near the rear frame rail and use a silver Sharpie, scratch awl, or another suitable utensil to outline the cuts. The template can be used on both sides of the car by simply turning it over. This is a critical step, so I recommend double-checking your marks before cutting the pan. Once you cut the sheet metal it requires welding to fix any mistakes.*

CHASSIS UPGRADES

Cut Floorpan

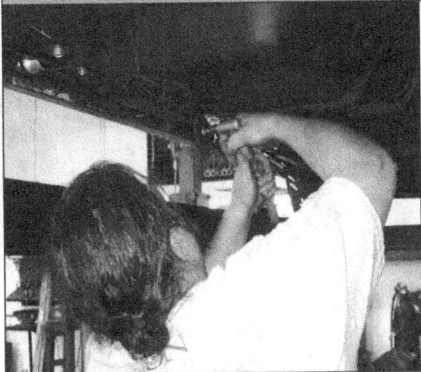

4 Once the cut lines have been accurately marked on the floorpan, cut and remove the sheet metal. You have just one chance to get it right. If you've never used a cut-off wheel mounted to pneumatic angle grinder, get an old junk sheet-metal panel, mark some cut lines, and practice making cuts.

A huge range of cut-off wheels is available. You have made a sizable investment in upgrading your Camaro so invest in the best materials. For example the 3M Green Corps premium 3-inch cut-off wheels are 1/32 inch wide to precisely and easily cut through sheet metal and frame rails. Remember to use a 3-inch cut-off wheel that is as close to 1/32 inch wide as possible to provide the best cuts.

Guide the cut-off disc to the inside of the marks, so the cutouts are not too large. If the fit is too tight, remove more sheet metal, but remember that it's far more difficult to add material back onto the floorpan. Your goal is to achieve a tight fit with minimal gaps between the connectors and the floorpan. You need a pneumatic grinding tool and an air compressor that can supply a consistent 80 psi to complete the job.

Body work involves extensive use of air tools, and if you're going to do bodywork, you need a large-capacity, high-quality air compressor with a 25-gallon tank, or larger.

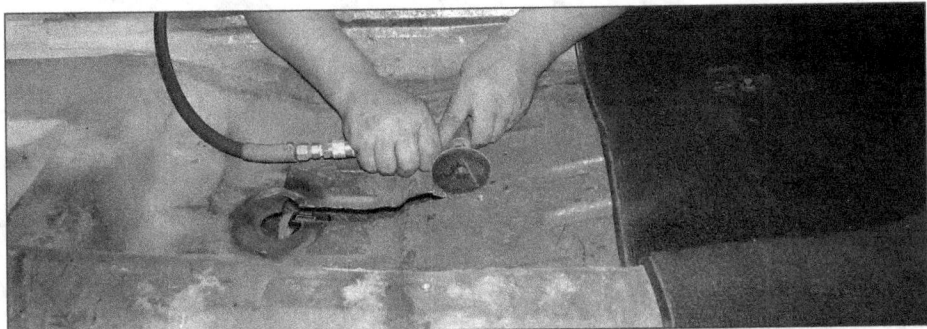

5 Cut out some of the floorpan from inside of the car. For most enthusiasts, it's best to use a 3-inch cut-off disc on an angle grinder. Keep a fresh cut-off wheel on your angle grinder. These are abrasive discs and continue to wear as they are used. A plasma cutter can be used to cut out floorpan sheet metal but it takes some expertise and experience to use it well. A plasma cutter becomes hot very quickly and you can inadvertently cut off more sheet metal than you intended. It is necessary to take care when cutting along the line so that the disc stays inside the line.

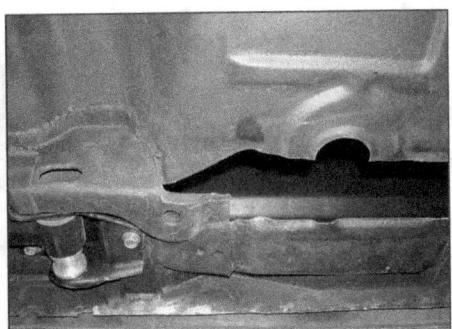

6 With a steady hand, patience, and a good cut-off wheel you can create fine cuts such as these around the lines of a template. Some grinding may be necessary for a perfect fit. This metal was removed to make way for the installation of the subframe connector.

Install Subframe Connector

7 Insert the subframe connector into the rear of the floorpan by starting with the slotted end of the subframe connector. The lower portion of the connector butts against the front of the rear frame rail.

CHAPTER 9

Install Subframe Connector (Continued)

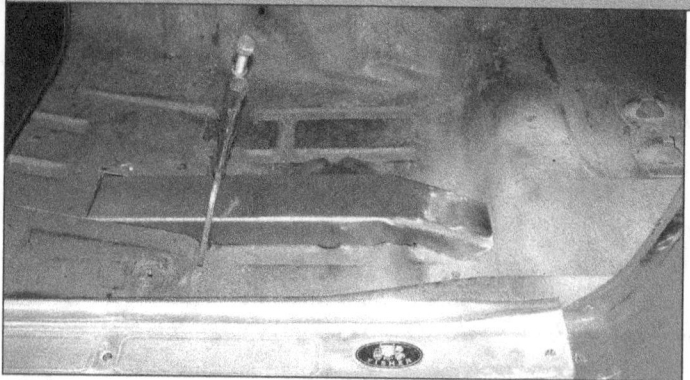

8 The subframe connector is held in place with a large clamp and is seen here from the inside of the car. Check the frame alignment and fit with the floorpan to see if more trimming is necessary.

9 Line up the front of the subframe connector with the end of the front subframe. Linking the front suspension to the rear suspension adds substantial strength to the chassis. Ensure that the subframe connectors align with the front subframe for the ultimate strength. When connected, the subframe connectors add strength to the body to substantially reduce flexing.

Connect Bracket to Subframe

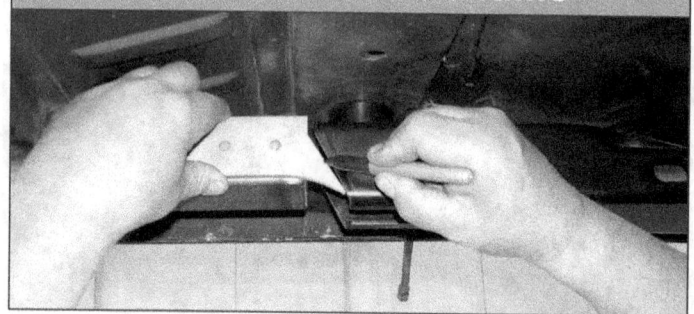

10 Connect the brackets to the subframe connectors and the front subframe. Align the brackets and mark for minor trimming. Every car is a little different so you have to judge how much alteration is necessary.

Fit Bracket to Subframe Connector

11 Use a 5-inch angle sander to grind the brackets down to size. (Both of these brackets required trimming to match the shape of the front subframe). Sand the ends until the desired length is reached.

Drill Holes in Bracket

12 Before welding the brackets to the subframe connectors, place each one in a bench vise to securely hold it. Drill the initial hole to 3/8 inch and use a 1/2-inch bit to countersink it. Place spot welds through the bracket and onto the subframe connector and frame member. Countersink the hole to promote a larger welding surface. This makes the welding pattern of the rosette weld larger and stronger.

CHASSIS UPGRADES

Tack Weld Bracket to Subframe Connector

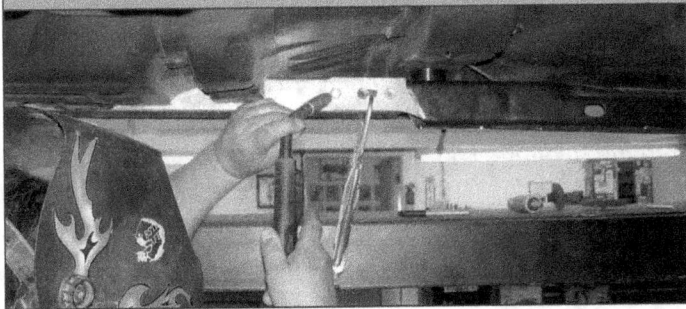

13 Hold the bracket up against the front subframe and clamp it to the subframe connector using a Vise-Grips or similar clamp. After placing it in the correct position, use a MIG welder to tack weld the bracket to the subframe connector. Place three tack welds on each side to secure the connection. Also, place a weld along the curved back edge of the bracket.

Perimeter Weld Entire Bracket

14 Remove the subframe connector and complete the welding. Carefully use a MIG welder to perimeter weld around the entire bracket. When perimeter welding, be sure not to overheat the pieces being welded. Lay down part of the bead, allow it to cool, switch to the opposite end of the piece, and continue welding. Avoid applying too much heat from the welder and causing the piece to warp. Allow the piece to cool, or quench if necessary.

Box Weld End of Bracket

Reinstall Subframe Connector

15 Use an 80-grit 3- to 4½-inch grinding wheel to make the connector welds smooth for an attractive appearance. Box weld the end for added strength to the subframe and a better look.

16 Make sure the subframe connector is properly aligned with the front subframe and within the floorpan cut-out. If additional trimming is required for a proper fit, do it now. Then make sure the connector butts up against the end of the front subframe rail member. Use a wire brush or sanding wheel to remove the paint from the end of the front subframe. You need bare metal-to-metal contact to promote welding adhesion. Once the subframe connector has been properly aligned, use Vise-Grips to clamp it into the desired position.

Tack Weld Subframe Connector to Chassis

17 Place three tack welds between the subframe connector and the front subframe. Examine your work. Use a straightedge if necessary to check alignment of the subframe connector. Don't fully weld on the connector unless it's completely aligned. Once alignment has been verified for the last time, lay a bead of weld around the entire bracket and the front subframe for more strength. Weld 2 to 3 inches at a time and then switch to the opposite side. This way you are spreading heat around the work area and preventing warping the components.

Tack Weld Entire Subframe Connector

18 After the front end is connected, tack weld the entire subframe connector to the floorpan and rear frame section. Place a tack weld about every 3 to 4 inches around the floor support and rear frame member. Floorpans are made of 18- to 24-gauge sheet metal, so make sure not to apply too much heat with the MIG welder. If you apply too much heat, the floorpan warps.

Weld Subframe Connector to Top of Floorpan

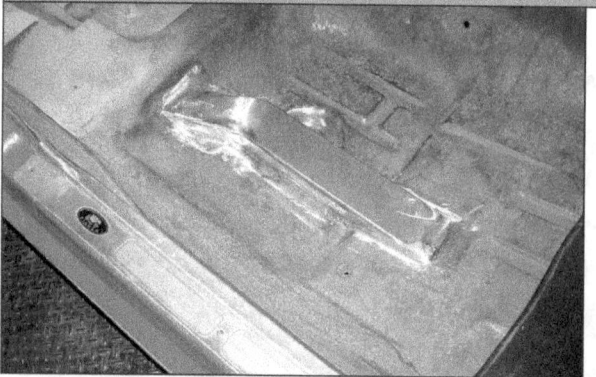

19 For full connection to the chassis, weld the subframe connector at the top side from inside the passenger compartment. Use a medium-grit sanding pad to remove paint from the floorpan surrounding the connector. Tack weld the subframe connector every 3 to 4 inches, making sure not to apply too much heat to any one area. Tack weld and alternate welds from one side to another.

Once all the tack welds have been placed, lay down small beads to connect the tack welds together. Once again, alternate from side to side and make sure not to apply too much heat in one area. Use compressed air or water to cool the welded area. This is not a race, and high-caliber or quality work isn't accomplished at a break-neck speed.

Once all the beads have been placed, use a medium-grit sanding pad to clean up the welds. After all of the welding has been completed the subframe is ready for paint.

Weld Subframe Connector to Bottom of Floorpan

20 Place a bead of weld around the entire perimeter of the subframe connector. Similar to the top side, weld in three 4-inch beads connecting the tack welds together. Manage heat distribution over the thin sheet metal. Weld small sections at a time and from side to side to spread out the heat to prevent warping. Shown here is the floor and subframe connector after welding is complete.

Weld Filler Plate to Subframe Connector

21 Many small steps are required for a professional-looking subframe connector installation. If necessary, tack weld a small filler panel between the subframe connector and the front subframe to make the connection stronger and to also make it more attractive. Tack weld the small rectangular plate at each corner to the subframe connector.

Finish Weld Filler Plate to Subframe Connector

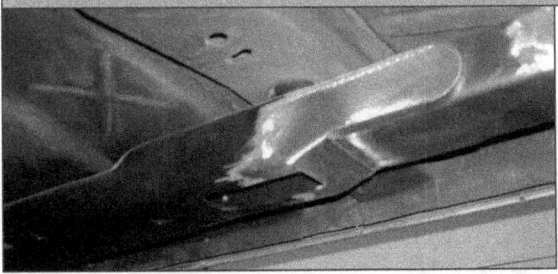

22 Once the filler plate has been tack welded to the end of the subframe connector, lay down a bead of weld between the tack welds. As before, don't apply too much heat to any one area, alternate from side to side, and quench the welds when needed. Once the welding has been completed, use a medium-grit sanding disc to clean up the welds and welded area. Here is the front subframe-to-subframe connector after the filler panel was welded in and sanded smooth.

Weld in Subframe Connectors

23 Here, the subframe connectors have been welded in. The subframe connectors tie the rear of the car to the front of the car to add strength to the unibody construction. This keeps the chassis from flexing under hard cornering and uneven track conditions.

Complete Subframe Installation

24 Use a medium-grit sanding disc to clean up spatter or weld. Smooth off the subframe connector welding to improve the appearance of the installation. Bare steel or sheet metal starts rusting almost immediately unless it's treated with rust inhibitor. Take the opportunity to coat it with primer to keep it from rusting. Apply primer and then flat-black floorpan paint, so the floorpan has a factory appearance. While the subframe connectors are clearly evident, they look like an integrated piece and are done so well it looks as if the car was constructed like this.

Project 2: Rear Wheel Tubs Installation

A 1970 Camaro is equipped with large-diameter wheels with wide tires for superb handling. When Camaros and Firebirds were developed, they were equipped with 70-series tires. Many enthusiasts were able to squeeze 60-series under the fenders without any problems. Today enthusiasts want to use extremely wide tires on the cars and that is only possible with inner fender-well modifications, so Detroit Speed developed a kit to increase the rear wheel well width that maintains an original appearance.

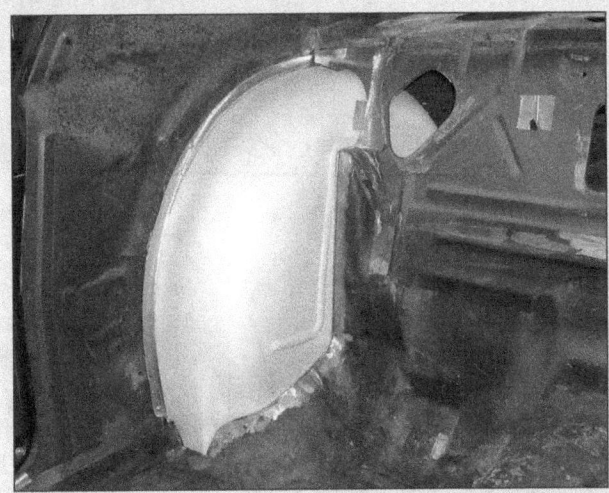

The Detroit Speed wheel tub has been installed in this second-generation Camaro.

CHAPTER 9

OEM Rear Wheel Well Removal

Inspect Wheel Tub Kit

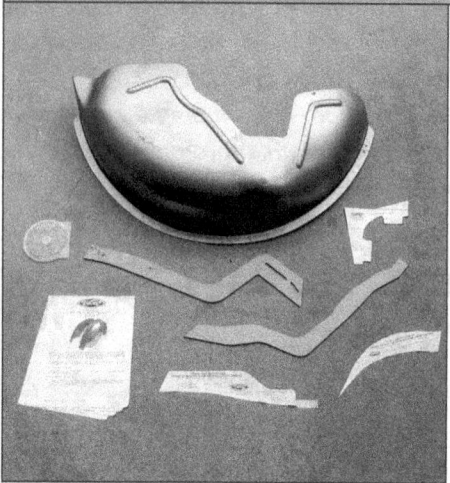

1 The Detroit Speed rear wheel tub kit comes with an original-appearing wide wheel tub, trim pieces, and some instructions. All of the parts and templates are required in order to install the larger tubs.

Strip Undercoating from Wheel Well Area

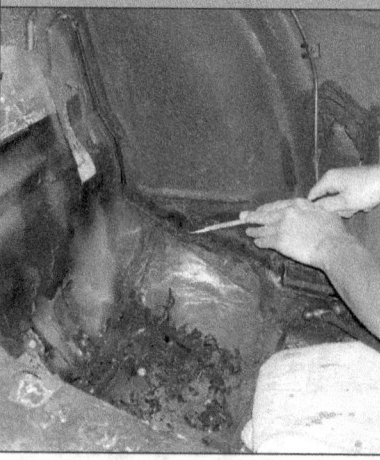

2 Use a wire wheel with a pneumatic grinder or electric drill to remove the undercoating. Before any welding can be done, the flammable undercoating has to be removed to eliminate the chance of catching fire and contaminating the welding.

Remove Spot Welds

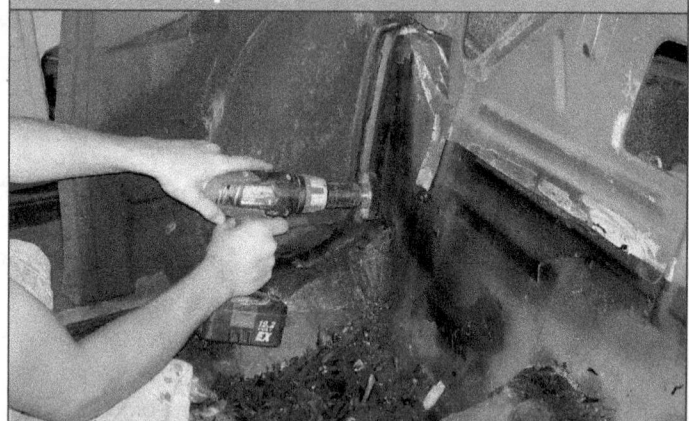

3 Drill out the spot welds with a 1/4-inch bit. On the passenger's side of the car, drill out the spot welds with a 1/4-inch spot-weld cutter so this section of metal can be removed. This can also be done with a regular 1/4-inch drill bit if you don't have a spot-weld cutter.

Mark Cut-Out Line for Tub

4 With a T-square as a guide, use a Sharpie to draw a line where the metal has to be cut for fitment of the wheel tub. Follow the measurements provided by Detroit Speed.

Drill Out Spot Welds

5 Moving to the driver's side of the car, drill out the spot welds in preparation for removing the panel. Be patient; drilling out several spot welds takes time. Also, factory technicians laid down the spot welds by hand, so each car is welded a little differently.

CHASSIS UPGRADES

Cut Interior Wheel Well Panel

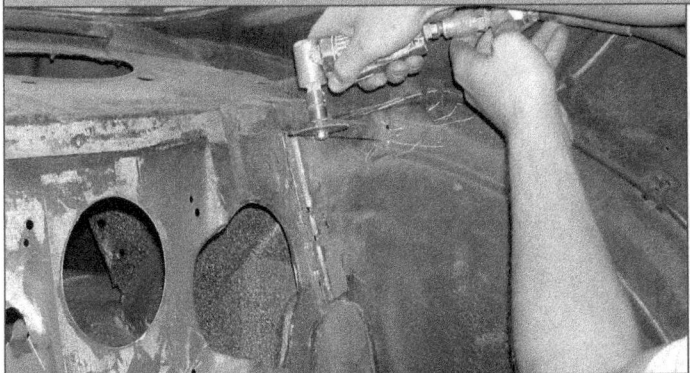

6 Use a flat-blade screwdriver between the two panels to lightly pry them apart. This adds separation of the two sections of metal so the panel comes out easily when the rest of the cuts are made. Use a high-quality 3-inch cut-off wheel with a pneumatic angle grinder. Closely follow your cut line and use a steady hand. The cut-off wheel is equipped with extra-thin blades so it cuts very effectively and quickly.

7 Cut along the line at the top, and then cut the panel along the side following the shape of the wheel tub. Use a cut-off blade and a thin carbide wheel and be careful. It is also possible to cut this section with a plasma cutter but the line is not as crisp.

8 Here is a close look at a panel being cut with an angle grinder equipped with a cut-off wheel.

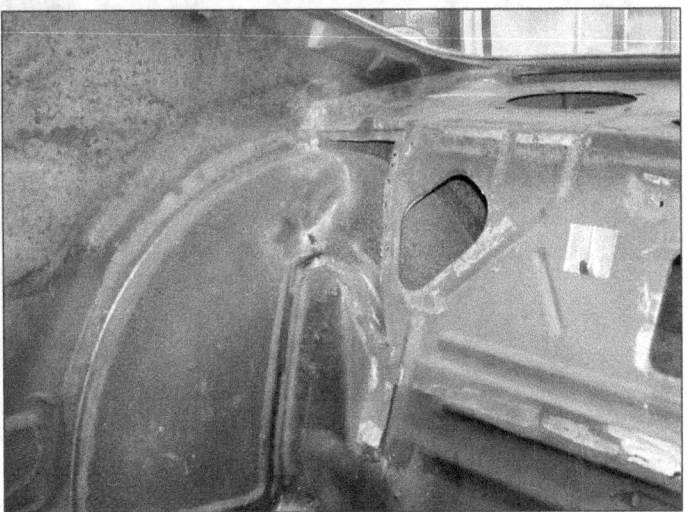

9 After the panel has been completely cut out around the wheel well remove the steel panel to allow additional space for the wider wheel tub.

10 Repeat the process on the other side and remove the panel.

CAMARO & FIREBIRD PERFORMANCE PROJECTS: 1970–1981

CHAPTER 9

Remove Rear Suspension and Axle

11 The rear axle and the suspension must be removed in order to install the wheel tubs. The rear end receives new coil-over shocks along with new brackets for the springs and the four-bar Detroit Speed Quadralink rear suspension. Looking from the underside, this Camaro is in excellent condition with the body pan undercoated and the rear chassis rails painted shiny black.

Aftermarket Wheel Well Installation

Apply Template to Cut Rear Wheel Well

1 The Detroit Speed rear tub kit comes with templates for cutting areas to conform to the tub installation. Lay the templates on the floor and mark for the cuts necessary with an indelible marker. You can also transfer the templates to cardboard to make them stronger.

Mark Hole for Seat Belt Mount

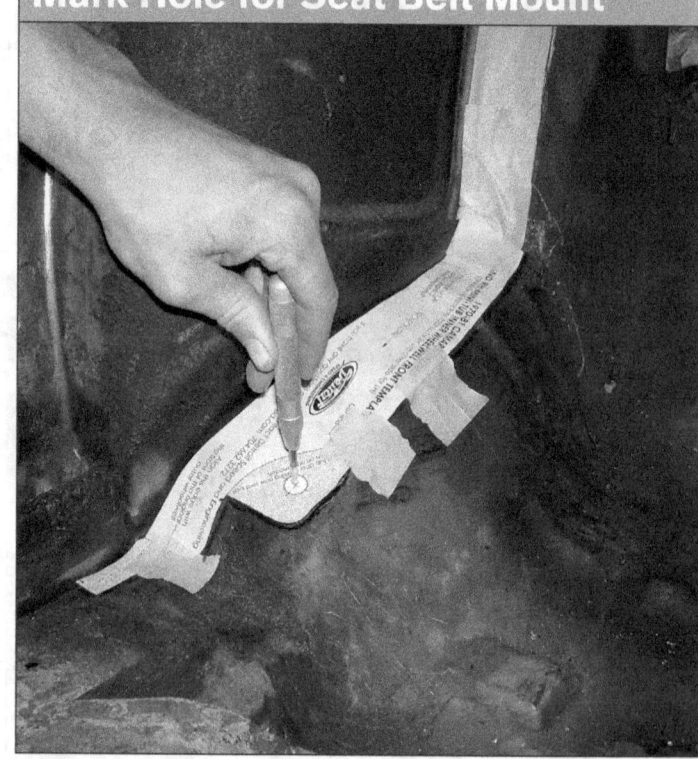

2 Use the template as a guide, and mark the pan accordingly. Mark the floor for a hole that has to be drilled for the new mounting position of the seat belts. Simply lay the template down in the correct position and the template has the position for the seat belt location. Make the mark and drill the hole to the desired size.

CHASSIS UPGRADES

Mark Cut Line on Wheel Well

3 Using the template and a silver Sharpie pen, carefully mark the cut line. Make sure it follows the shape of the original wheel tub.

Mark Trunk Floor for Cutting

4 Use another template to mark the trunk floor for cutting, and use a silver Sharpie marker or similar marker so the line can be clearly seen.

Prepare Template

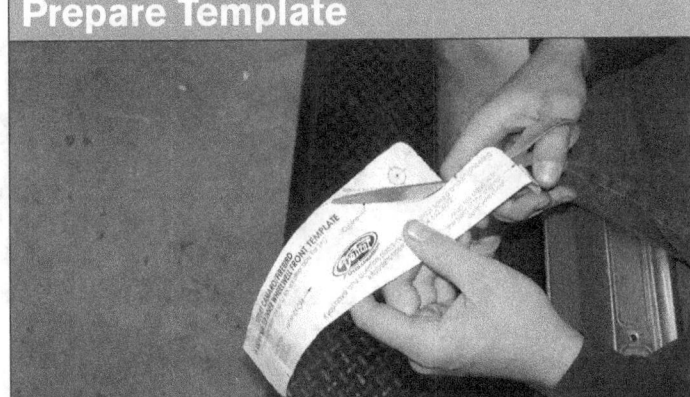

5 Trim the template with scissors following the supplied instructions. Use the paper template supplied or transfer it to a thicker and stronger piece of cardboard.

Place Template and Mark Floor

6 After one side of the car floor is marked with a silver Sharpie pen, flip over the template and mark the other side.

Cut Tub Along Marked Line

7 Use a 3-inch cut-off wheel and cut the tub along the line previously marked. Also cut the floor where indicated. The 3-inch cut-off wheel is easy to use, and once it cuts through the metal, it follows easily along the line.

CHAPTER 9

Cut Tub Along Marked Line (Continued)

8 Use the 3-inch cut-off tool to cut the trunk floor by following the cut marks. A plasma cutter cannot provide accurate enough cuts for fitment of these body panels. When cutting multiple body panels like this, the more precise the cuts, the better. The panels are going to fit better and you will not have to install any patches. These tubs are exposed to the elements, and you want strong weld beads to join well-installed panels; therefore, you do not want rust to form.

Remove Wheel Tub

Clean Up Cut Line

9 After the sections are cut, remove the original wheel tub as seen here. Now there is plenty of room for the new wheel tubs. The same was done on the other side of the car. You can see the large opening that allows the installation of a new wheel tub for wider rear tires.

10 Here is the trunk after one of the original wheel tubs has been removed. After the section is cut out of the floor, smooth out this cut line with a small angle sander. Slowly and carefully sand the edge of the metal until it is completely flat and smooth. Wear safety glasses to guard against debris.

Shape Trim Piece to Contour of Floor

11 The metal panel supplied with the kit is flat for shipping. You need to stretch the piece into the necessary shape so that it fits the floor. This can be done in a sheet-metal break, by hammer and dolly, or by using a vise and a piece of wood.

CHASSIS UPGRADES

Mark Section to Cut

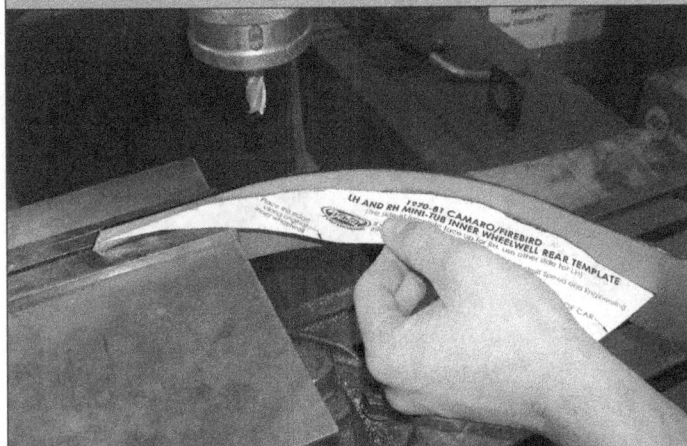

12 Using the detailed template supplied with the kit, mark the metal section for cutting with a black Sharpie. Use the correct template to achieve the proper shape.

Bend Metal Strap into Shape

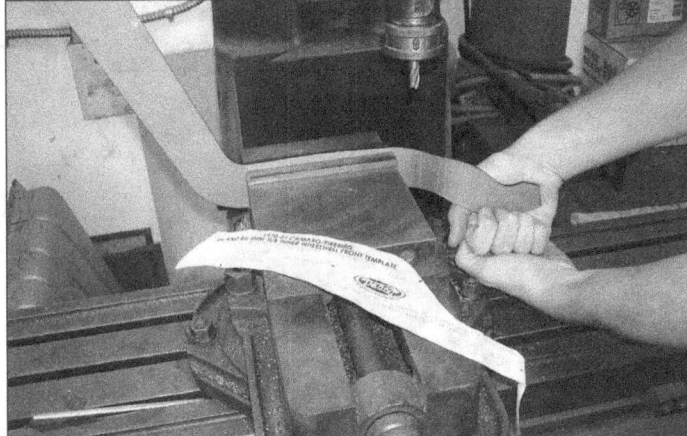

13 Choose one of the provided templates (left) to modify the metal strap. Install the strap in a vise (right) to make the necessary bends following the instructions in the kit.

Tack Weld Metal Strap

14 Now that the strap has been formed to fit the profile of the tube you can install it with tack welds according to the instructions.

Apply Primer to Wheel Well

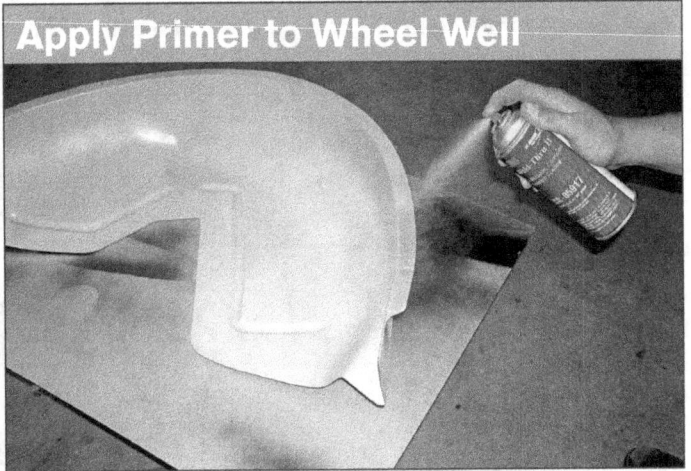

15 Paint the new wheel well with a weld-through, spray-can primer to keep the part from rusting. Notice that the supplied wheel well panel looks similar to the original.

CAMARO & FIREBIRD PERFORMANCE PROJECTS: 1970–1981

CHAPTER 9

Install Wheel Tub in Chassis

Drill Wheel Tub for Trial Fit

16 You need to test fit the wheel tubs to the quarter panel and trunk area to ensure correct fit. The lip of the tub should overlap the truck and inner wheel well sheet metal. Once you have lined up the tub, clamp the wheel tub in the trunk area using locking pliers.

17 Position the wheel tub by drilling several holes around the perimeter of the wheel tub and through the existing sheet metal of the wheel well for installation of self-tapping sheet-metal screws. Make sure you're drilling through the tub and the overlapping sheet metal from the wheel well.

Fasten Wheel Tub into Position

Mark Metal Straps

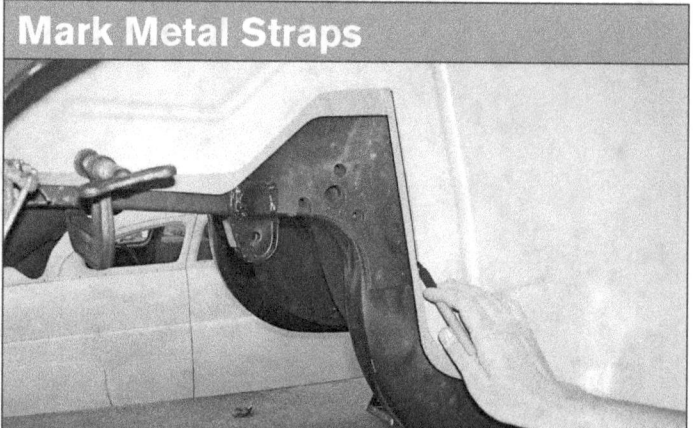

18 Use several screws to correctly position the wheel tub on the car. Install one screw at the leading edge of the tub toward the top and install one screw at the trailing edge toward the rear. You want the wheel tub to look like a factory component once it is installed.

19 The wheel tub rests against the metal strap you previously installed. In order to properly align the wheel well and the floor, mark the metal strap with a Sharpie for cutting to the correct shape.

Mark Inside of Panel

20 Mark the panel in the inside of the car with a black felt-tip pen.

80 CAMARO & FIREBIRD PERFORMANCE PROJECTS: 1970–1981

CHASSIS UPGRADES

Mark Metal Strap

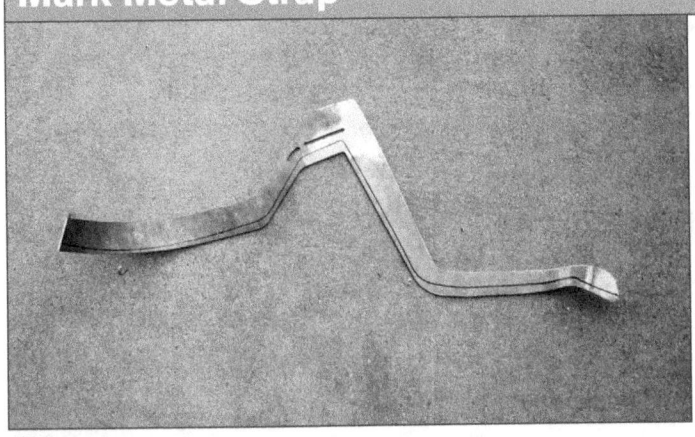

21 Mark the metal strap for cutting from the outside.

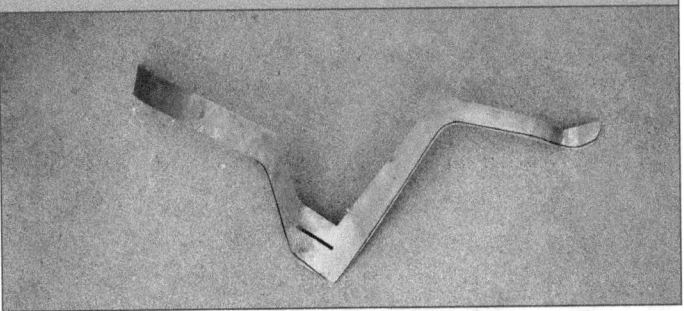

22 Here is the metal strap marked for cutting from the inside. This same marking for cutting has to be done on both sides of the car so both wheel tubs can be connected.

Cut Metal Strap

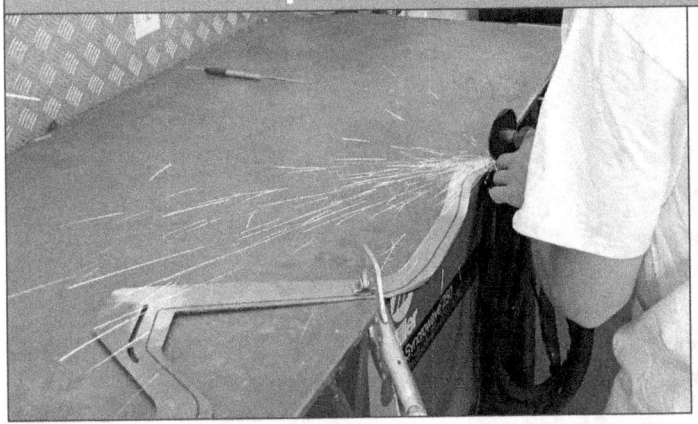

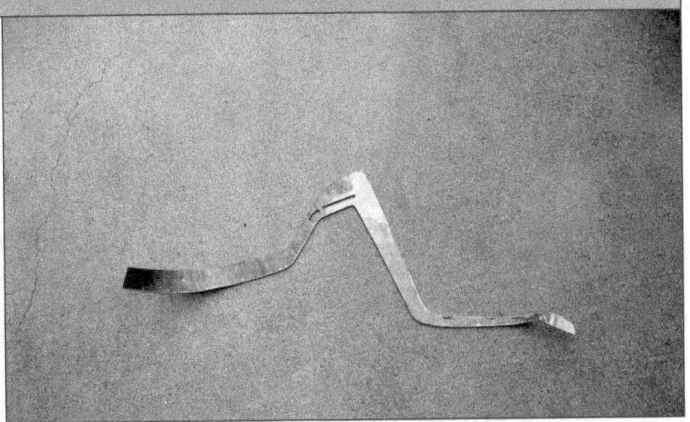

23 Using a 3-inch cut-off wheel, cut the strap following your line (left). The marks are made by using the new wheel tub so you get the pattern required. Here is the strap after the cuts (right). The trimming was extensive but it is now a perfect fit for welding.

Weld Together Floor Section

24 Weld together the floor section and the outside panel for strength prior to installing the wheel tub. Use a MIG wire-feed welder in small sections at a time to avoid warping.

CHAPTER 9

Grind Welds Smooth

25 After the floor section is welded, grind the area smooth with a 3-inch angle grinder. When this is finished it should be difficult to see where the welding was done.

Install Metal Strap and Wheel Tub

26 Install the metal strap along with the wheel tub. Align both and then tack weld the strap to the floor. (The strap is a filler section that securely connects the wheel well to the floor.)

Tack Weld Strap in Place

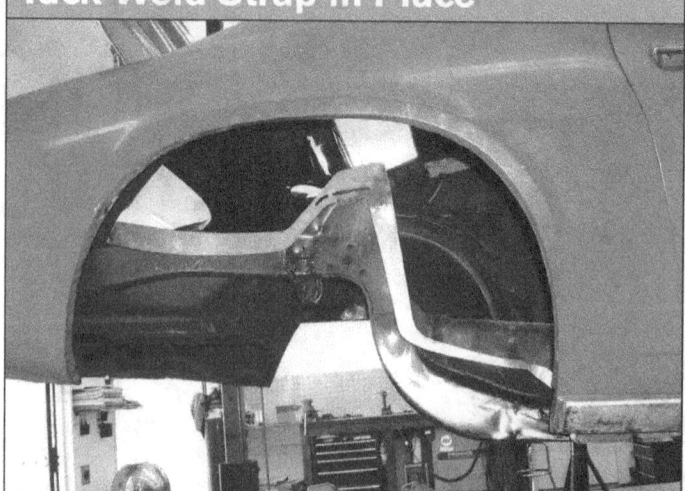

27 Here is the strap after it was tacked in place. This strap is used for mounting the wheel tub.

Weld Strap to Floorpan

28 After the strap is tacked in place, weld it to the floorpan using a wire-feed MIG welder, a little at a time. Move the welder from side to side to keep the heat spread out until the entire strap is welded solid.

Drill Placement Holes

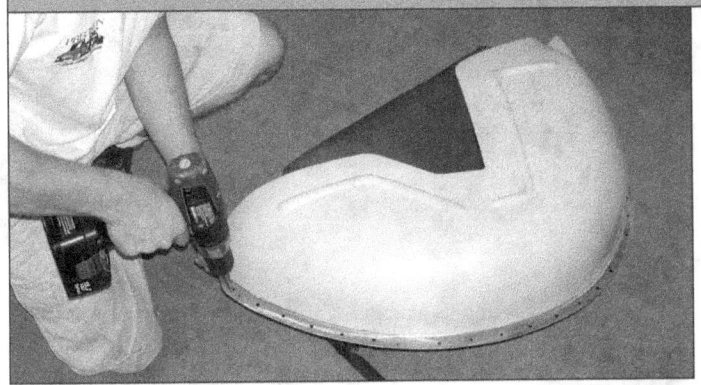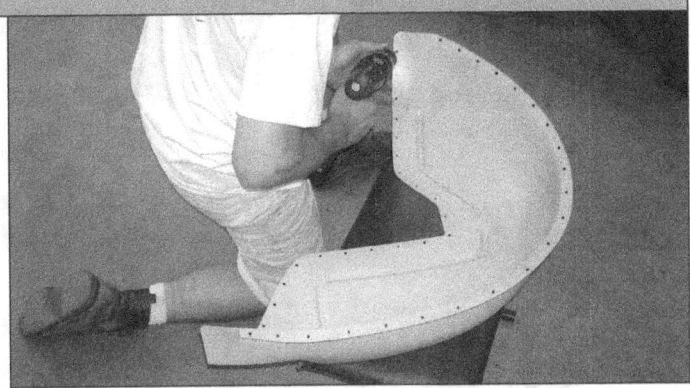

29 Drill holes every 3 inches in the perimeter of the wheel tub in preparation for tack welding the unit in place (left). This connection is done with rosette welds, which are welds through the holes. The result resembles spot welds but are much stronger. The wheel tub will also be welded to the floor at the bottom so drill more holes there (right). This section will be mounted to the strap steel that was just welded to the floor.

Install Wheel Tub

30 To properly fit the wheel tub to the inner wheel well, make sure the wheel tub evenly follows the frame rail. Once you attain the correct position, use sheet-metal clamps to keep it in position on each end. It's much easier to have a helper hold the tub while you clamp it into the correct position. Next, drill through the holes in the wheel tube flange and into the frame rails. Using a MIG welder, place rosette welds through these holes so you get excellent weld penetration and panel strength.

Perimeter Weld Wheel Tub

31 After the outside lower edge of the tub is secure, drill through the wheel tub flange holes and into the chassis. Then place tack welds through all the holes in the tub, which secures it to the body. Also, weld the tub to the Camaro's inner body structure.

Grind and Shape Welds

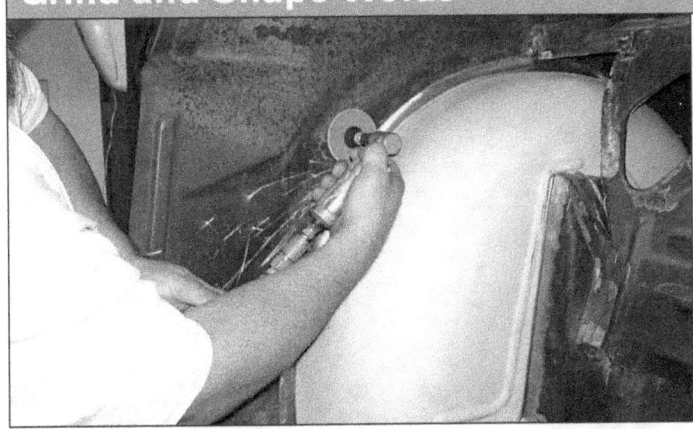

32 After all of the welds are completed, grind them smooth using a 3-inch angle grinder. When the grinding is finished with an 80-grit pad it is difficult to even see the welds.

Check Fitment of Wheel Tubs

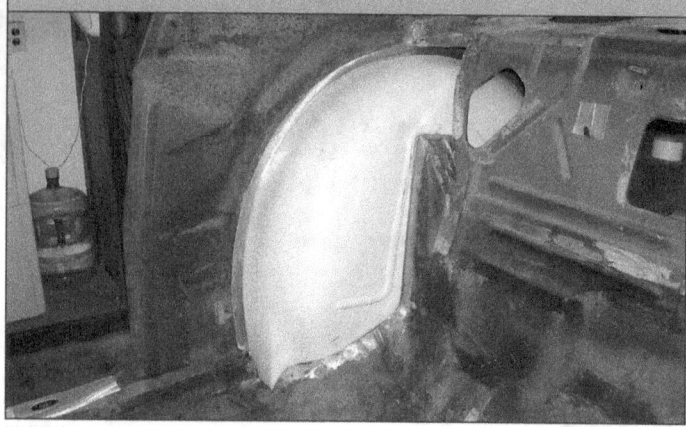
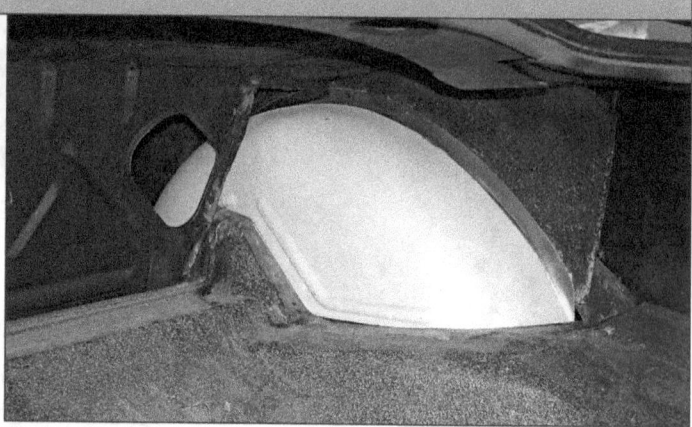

33 Here is the finished wheel tub securely installed and finished off with the grinder. This wider wheel tub looks like a factory installation and that's what is nice about the Detroit Speed kit. Now this Camaro can be outfitted with huge rear tires that look mean and allow the ultimate in handling.

Install Filler Panels

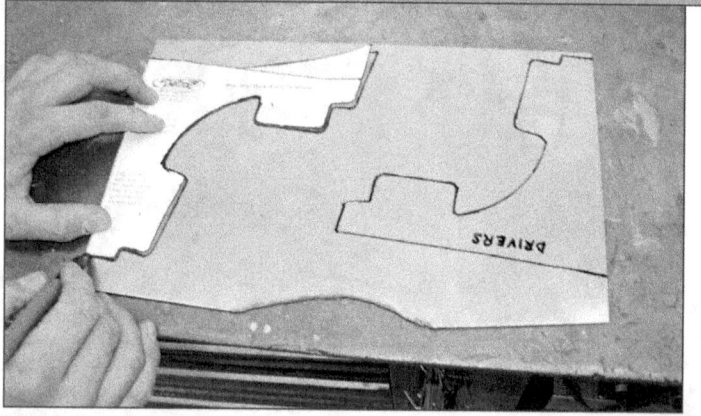
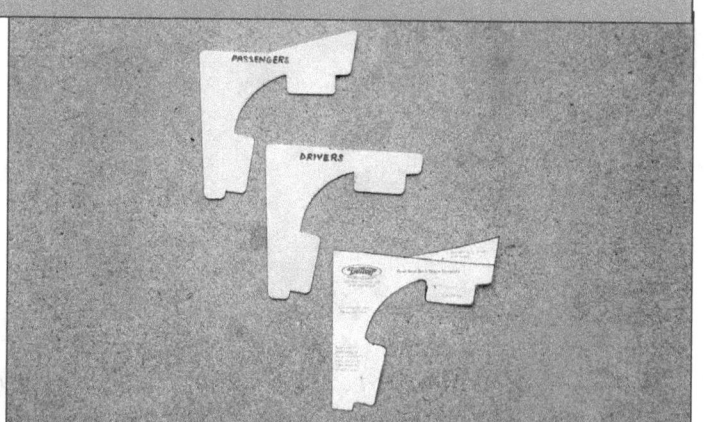

34 In order to complete the installation, one more small filler panel must be made out of sheet steel following one of the templates as a guide. This filler panel is used on the inside of the car on each side of the rear deck section.

Cut Sheet Metal

35 Cut part of the sheet steel with a small shears, as seen here. The shears makes clean cuts in a straight line and it also makes corner cuts.

Cut Panels with Bandsaw

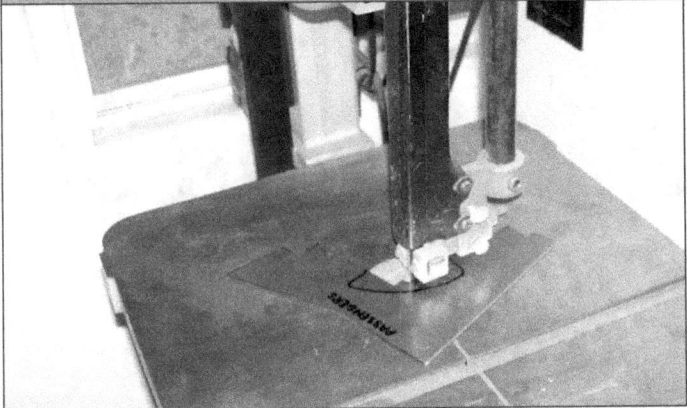

36 Once the seat-back brace has been cut on the band saw, measure the rosette weld holes and drill eleven 1/2-inch holes into the seat-back brace. The bracket supports the top of the wheel tub and fastens to the seat back support.

Bend Metal Tabs

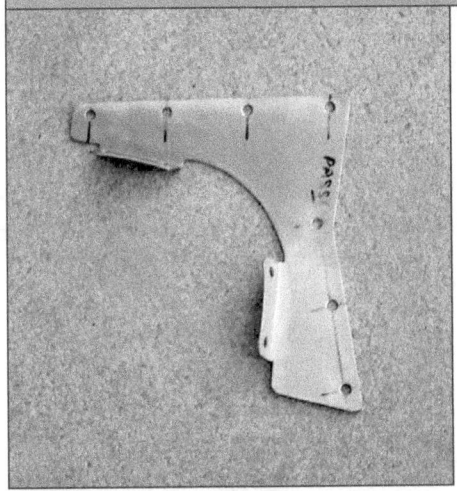

37 Place each metal tab on the seat-back brace into a vise. Align the fold line with the jaws of the vise and then bend the tabs to a 90-degree angle.

Install Filler Panel

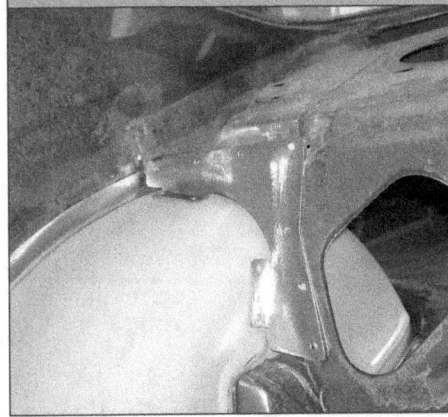

38 Properly position the seat-back brace on the top of the wheel tub and support sheet metal. Using the brace as a template, drill the 1/2-inch holes through the top of the sheet-metal tub and the seat-back support. Then place rosette welds into the wheel tub and seat-back support.

Here is the finished wheel tub and it looks like a factory installation. After you've installed the DSE mini tubs, you can install 335-series tires. With tires of this size, the footprint and, therefore, the traction are enormous, and as a result, the performance of your F-Body car improves by leaps and bounds. Once all the tack welds have been placed in the wheel tub, use an angle grinder with a 80-grit disc to grind them flush with the tub. The finished wheel tub should look like a factory-installed part. Apply the proper paint to prevent rust from forming. Some narrowing of the seat frame is necessary for it to work properly (see Chapter 11, page 118).

CHAPTER 10

FRONT SUSPENSION

Since the second-generation F-Body Firebirds and Camaros rolled off the assembly line in 1970, suspension technology has improved by leaps and bounds. A variety of aftermarket suspension parts and kits can be bolted to the factory subframe to improve handling and road holding. Or, you can replace the entire stock subframe with a complete high-performance aftermarket subframe replete with tubular A-arms, coil-over shocks, large-diameter sway bars, huge boxed frame members, rack-and-pinion steering, and more. Your budget and suspension performance goals determine the ideal parts for your particular car.

If you are not planning on driving the car in autocross racing or other rugged track activities but prefer to build a fine-handling, street-driving car, you can easily upgrade your original suspension to far exceed the factory setup. If you want the ultimate in performance and handling primarily for street as well as track use, and money isn't an object, installing a complete aftermarket subframe is the way to go.

A suspension kit can significantly improve traction, steering precision, and road holding on the street and on the track. I have seen aftermarket subframes transform handling and provide performance that rivals modern cars. Many aftermarket subframes feature lightweight, chrome-moly, rectangular frame tubes; adjustable coil-over shocks; lightweight tubular A-arms; large aftermarket high-performance aluminum calipers, drilled and slotted disc brakes; rack-and-pinion steering (both manual and power); heavy-duty sway bars tailored to the specific subframe design, and many other upgraded parts.

Nearly all subframes are compatible with the stock sheet metal and bodies; however, to get the maximum amount of handling from the cars the wheel tubs (front and rear) may have to be wider for sufficient tire clearance. In addition, most aftermarket subframes carry revised suspension geometry that vastly exceeds stock standards, and as a result, substantially improves performance.

For second-generation cars, 40 years of aggressive driving and stress loading of suspension components can leave the stock subframes fatigued or just plain worn out. Of course, the subframe could be fine, providing that the car was driven conservatively. It is your call when you start to build the car. An aftermarket subframe not only transforms handling and performance, it provides an extra measure of safety, comfort, and driver confidence.

Also, a stock subframe limits the size of wheels and tires you can use, and therefore, it limits the front wheel/tire footprint. As we all know, the more rubber you can put on the road (within certain limits), the more performance you can extract from the car. In some cases, the stock subframe only accepts up to 17-inch wheels, depending on the width of the wheel and on the tire size chosen. In some cases a larger 18- to 20-inch wheel can be used in conjunction with a wider rear wheel well and a wider aftermarket front inner wheel well that are available in carbon fiber. Beyond that, aftermarket subframes are designed to accept modern engine/transmission combinations.

So if you're planning to swap a GM LS engine for a high-performance manual or automatic transmission, most aftermarket subframes accept

FRONT SUSPENSION

Mark Stielow's Camaros

Detroit Speed has proven the performance of its products in competition and in customer satisfaction. In particular, the company has teamed up with Mark Stielow, a GM engineer, to create many all-conquering first-generation Camaros. The Camaros that Stielow has built with support from Detroit Speed have been recognized as ground breaking. These include (but are not limited to) the *Mule*, the *Jackass*, and most recently the *Red Devil*. The *Red Devil* is a 1969 Camaro, but it carries the ultimate hardware that Stielow and Detroit Speed can develop, and it also carries premium off-the-shelf Corvette ZR-1 parts.

Under the hood is a 2010 LS9, but it's no ordinary LS9. It carries a bevy of high-performance parts, including custom cam, Oliver rods, piston oil squirters, and Diamond pistons. But they didn't stop there; the turbo setup has been revised and the engine kicks out an estimated 756 hp, which is far more than the stock 640 hp for the LS9.

While the engine is a giant killer, the suspension system and its performance has elevated the car to the top of the industry. It uses a Detroit Speed subframe (a similar unit is available for second-generation F-Body cars). To complement the front suspension, Stielow installed a Detroit QuadraLink rear suspension; and to make the massive 19-inch tires fit, he added rear mini tubs.

So how does it work together? The *Red Devil* accelerates from 0 to 60 mph in the low-3-second range and covers the quarter-mile in the high-10s. Best of all, this isn't a race car that's impossible to drive on the street. It has a firm yet humane ride, and the engine has ideal street manners, so the car can easily accelerate from a dead stop. Suspension performance and steering precision are astounding. The road-holding capability is immense and cornering speed exceeds that of many other modern sports cars.

Mark Steilow's 1967 Camaro, called Mayhem, *uses Detroit Speed and Engineering's suspension equipment. Like his previous Camaro build,* Mayhem *carries DSE's hydroformed front suspension and Quadralink rear suspension. Steilow drove his new creation to victory in the 2012 Optima Ultimate Street Car Invitational at Spring Mountain Motorsports Ranch in Pahrump, Nevada.*

the powertrain combination. A stock subframe requires different motor mounts and adapter plates for a GM LS engine swap with transmission.

Front Suspension Sources

The second-generation F-body cars had a good front suspension and steering system for the technology of the 1970s. Today, the suspension of the cars can be improved with state-of-the-art parts, such as tubular upper and lower A-arms, coil-over shocks, and rack-and-pinion steering.

Detroit Speed, Inc.

For more than a decade, Detroit Speed has been a leader in high-performance handling products for first- and second-generation Camaros. Former GM engineers Kyle and Stacy Tucker have contributed to or built some of the fastest, best handling 1967–1981 Camaros on the planet; these super Camaros, as they should be called, rival the performance of European super cars. Over the years, Detroit Speed has carved out its niche in the market and is widely recognized as an innovator in the Pro Touring market. While Detroit Speed offers its industry-leading suspension and handling products, it also offers a full line of engine, brake, driveline, body, steering, and other components.

Hotchkis Sport Suspension

Hotchkis Sport Suspension products for the second-generation F-Body deliver exceptional performance at affordable prices. The sport suspension parts have been used in many of the fastest Pro Touring cars and top-handling street machines. In particular, Mary Pozzi has used

Hotchkis suspension components in her 1973 Camaro that has been driven to numerous Pro Touring event wins. It is the suspension that road racing, drag racing, and autocross racing teams rely on.

In recent tests a Hotchkis-equipped early Camaro running an LS2 engine outperformed a brand-new Camaro. The Hotchkis Sport Suspension engineering team has developed vastly improved suspension systems that dramatically increase the pleasure of a street or track driving experience. Driving enthusiasts understand the benefits of a properly engineered aftermarket suspension that includes increased stability and improved handling and maneuverability. In keeping with the company's theme, making a great car even better, the suspension packages provide a comfortable ride, as well.

All Hotchkis Sport Suspension components are tested on the company's 600-foot slalom, 200-foot skid pad, and 14-turn autocross course. Results from the 1/4-mile acceleration and 60-to-0-mph braking tests are compiled. The complete data for stock and Hotchkis Sport Suspension equipped vehicles is gathered and evaluated. Performance gains are documented, and any component not meeting the company's rigid engineering standard of fit and performance is critiqued, redesigned, and retested.

Hotchkis Sport Suspension parts carry attractive and rugged finishes, including gloss powdercoating and anodizing. Hotchkis' newest innovation is the company's TVS (Total Vehicle System) kits that contain engineered and tuned components that work together to improve the performance vehicle's handling. All of the kits have passed the company's rigorous in-house testing procedures. The TVS concept was designed for the driving enthusiast who demands the ultimate in vehicle handling and performance without sacrificing a comfortable ride. The completely tuned suspension package eliminates the poor ride quality and disappointing handling that often result from the use of components produced by different manufacturers.

When General Motors redesigned the platform for the second-generation F-Body in 1970, in preparation for the major restyling of both the Camaro and Firebird, the company actually delivered a much more capable car. While it wasn't a radical rethinking, the suspension geometry was significantly improved over the original 1967–1969 design, creating a more surefooted chassis. Of course that doesn't mean that there isn't still plenty of room for refinement and tuning.

Thanks to roughly 1.9 million cars being built over the following 11 years, second-gen F-Bodies have remained plentiful and affordable, which is great news for budget-minded enthusiasts looking to build a muscle car that handles without a large dollar outlay. Even better news is that General Motors' forethought allowed Hotchkis Sport Suspension to design easy and affordable bolt-on products that cure most of the F-Body's ills and bring it from 1970s handling prowess into the new millennium.

Thanks to a gratuitous helping of oil leaks, the front suspension was in the worst state, so that's where I decided to start. To get a crisp response from this car, I'm going to recycle all the stock stuff and start from scratch with a full complement of Hotchkis products, including upgraded sway bar and end links, Sport springs, tie rod sleeves, and the most important parts of all geometry: corrected upper and lower tubular control arms.

Though everything works in concert to dramatically improve the overall handling, high-speed stability, and tire adhesion, it's the reengineering and analyzing by Finite Element Analysis (FEA) software for maximum strength that went into the control arms that really makes the performance difference on Hotchkis-equipped cars. Using computer-aided design (CAD) software, Hotchkis engineers worked within the limits of the stock subframe and created control arms that offer increased caster for high-speed stability, increased camber gain for improved cornering, and even offset cross-shafts on the upper arms for static negative camber, which helps improve alignment.

Despite all that change, the whole package is little more than an afternoon bolt-on, easily accomplished by one person in a home garage with basic tools. When you're looking to make significant upgrades on a budget, that's a perfect scenario.

RideTech

Formerly Air Ride Technologies, this company is the leader in air-ride suspension systems for street rods, customs, classics, and muscle cars. Today the company's suspension components feature top-of-the-line ShockWaves air shocks and a new line of coil-over shocks. The company also offers a complete line of StrongArms upper and lower tubular A-arms and 2-inch dropped spindles with improved geometry. RideTech makes suspension components for second-generation F-Bodies, and the parts are track tested on the company's 1971 Camaro.

FRONT SUSPENSION

Project 1: Front Subframe Installation

Here you see how Precision Street Rods & Machines installs a Detroit Speed front subframe without removing the front sheet metal. It was certainly an easy and quick method that maintained the sheet-metal alignment the car originally had.

For most enthusiast installers, however, you should carefully remove the front body panels for easier access to the frame connecting points. Body panels are fragile, and paint is incredibly expensive. The paint on these panels can be easily scratched or chipped, so it's not worth the risk unless you have extensive experience installing aftermarket subframes.

The Detroit Speed front subframe was delivered assembled, detailed, and ready to install. The subframe had a factory appearance and featured tubular A-arms, rack-and-pinion steering, and modern spindles that were equipped with Baer Racing 13-inch brakes. The subframe came powdercoated and detailed and was ordered with all the brackets necessary to install an LS engine.

Brake Component Installation

Install Rotors and Calipers

1 *This Detroit Speed kit comes equipped with Baer racing brakes. Two bolts connect the caliper to the bracket that is actually part of the spindle assembly. Install the bolts into the caliper bracket and finger tighten.*

Install Bolts

2 *Using a torque wrench, tighten the bolts following the torque specifications in the instructions. Apply thread locker to the bolts and then tighten them in three steps starting with 50 ft-lbs, followed by 90 ft-lbs, and finally the full 125 ft-lbs.*

CHAPTER 10

Install Banjo Bolts

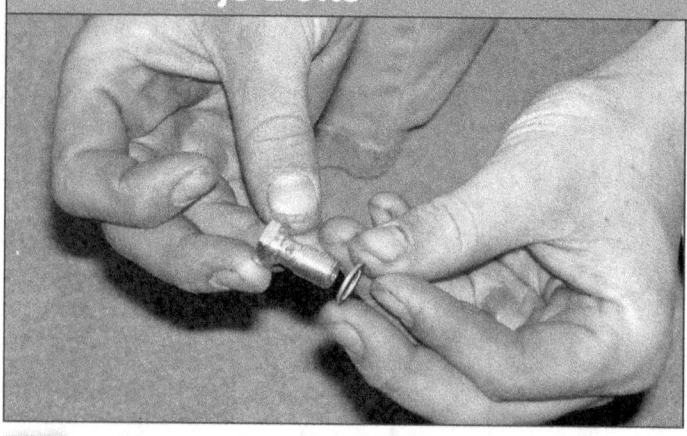

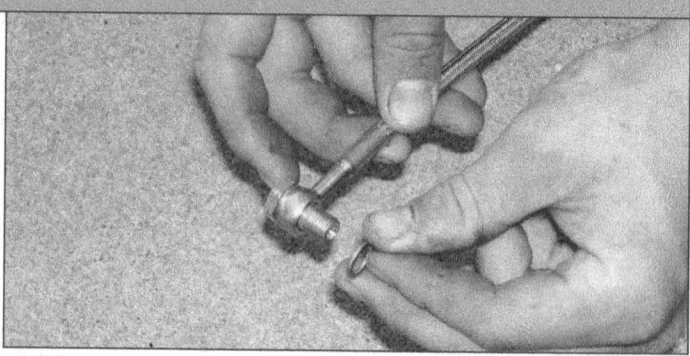

3 To attach the brake lines to the calipers, install the brass washers on the banjo bolt, one at the head of the bolt and one on the other side of the fitting. A banjo fitting is designed so that the hose can be adjusted to come out in a certain desired location. The hose pivots on the bolt.

4 Place the banjo bolt through the braided-steel brake hose as seen here. Place washers on each side of the fitting to seal the hose. These fittings have to be extremely tight to keep the fluid from leaking. Install another brass washer prior to connecting it to the caliper. Tighten the bolt with a box-end wrench, making sure you do not strip the bolt.

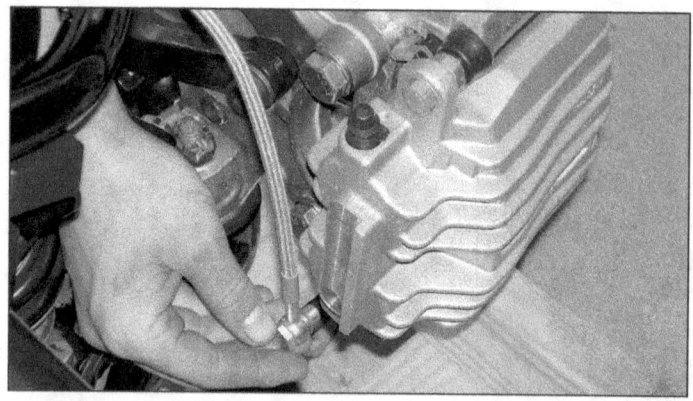

5 Attach the banjo bolt and hose to the caliper. Be sure all brake bolts and hose connections are tight to avoid leaks. Tighten the bolt with a box-end wrench or line wrench.

Here is the Baer Racing brake installed on the Detroit Speed subframe. The system looks nice, and from personal experience it performs great. Baer brakes are some of the best aftermarket brakes offered today. This car is equipped with 13-inch brakes, so larger-than-stock wheels have to be used.

FRONT SUSPENSION

Stock Subframe Removal

Disconnect Steering Column

1 Disconnect the bolt securing the steering rod to the steering column using an open-end wrench. Also remove the bolt in the rag joint on the other end in order to disconnect the steering shaft. The bolt has to be totally removed from the rag joint to disconnect it from the steering column. This is done because the entire original subframe has to be removed for the new one to be installed. To save time and to keep the sheet metal aligned, remove the subframe without removing the fenders and grille.

This car did not have an engine or transmission, so if you are doing the same thing, remember to remove the engine and transmission first.

Remove Spoiler for Installation of Subframe

2 The front spoiler must be removed for additional clearance before the subframe is removed. Disconnect the bolts using a socket wrench and a 1/2-inch socket.

Remove Bumper for Installation of Subframe

3 The bumper bolts must also be disconnected from the subframe with socket and open-end wrenches. The subframe is going to be installed without removing the sheet metal, so every bolt that is connected to the subframe must be disconnected.

Support Body with Jacks

4 In order to remove the subframe, the body must be supported. Here the body is resting on two large bottle jacks. When the jacks are installed they must be under the body pan, not the subframe. Use small blocks of wood on the floorpan to avoid denting it. Make sure the bottle jacks are raised evenly. Make sure the body is raised high enough so the front subframe can be removed and can clear the front of the car.

CAMARO & FIREBIRD PERFORMANCE PROJECTS: 1970–1981

Remove Front Wheels from Car

5 Using an impact gun, remove the lug nuts and take the front wheels and tires off (left). The original wheels are not going to be used because the front brakes on the Detroit Speed subframe are too large. Here is the front subframe minus the wheels and tires (right). Now the subframe can be removed from the car without removing the sheet metal. The unit is still hooked to the body with four original bolts.

Support Front Subframe

6 Before the subframe can be removed it has to be supported, so install a scissors jack to hold it up while the four bolts are removed. There are two forward bolts that hook to an area on the firewall and two more at the rear of the subframe that hook to the body pan. These are large bolts that can be disconnected with a socket wrench and a 15/16-inch socket. If you want to do it quickly use an impact gun.

Remove Radiator Core Support

7 The radiator core support is also attached to the front subframe so the two large bolts must be disconnected prior to removing it. All of the subframe bolts and core support are equipped with rubber cushions so they also have to be removed.

Remove Subframe

8 Disconnect the two subframe bolts that connect to the firewall portion of the car. Do this with a socket wrench and a 15/16-inch socket. Fortunately this car was in good condition so the bolts weren't rusty. It is still a good idea to coat them with penetrating oil, such as Justice Brothers JB-80 or an equivalent.

FRONT SUSPENSION

Remove Subframe (continued)

9 Moving to the other end of the subframe, loosen the two large bolts with a socket wrench and a 15/16-inch socket. When the bolts are loose the subframe is still supported by the scissors jack. Now remove all of the bolts securing the subframe. But before you do that, make sure the jacks are supporting the subframe and the stock assembly is balanced on the scissors jack. You don't want the subframe to slip off the scissors jack.

10 Lower the scissors jack; the subframe is still sitting on the car lift. While this may be common sense, do not stand or lay under the subframe as it is lowered. Place wood blocks (2x4s) on the lift rails and align them with the brake rotors. Lower the subframe onto the wood blocks and remove the scissors jack.

11 Looking at the suspension from the front, you can see that the spoiler had to be removed to provide the clearance required.

12 Position a floor jack under the front subframe and lower the lift so the front subframe lines up with the floor jack. Raise the floor jack so the brake rotors are elevated above the wood blocks. Balance the unit on the floor jack and pull the subframe out from under the car. Use an impact gun to reinstall the front wheels and tires, which makes it easier to move the unit.

CHAPTER 10

Aftermarket Subframe Installation

Inspect and Inventory Parts Kit

1 Detroit Speed has mounts for everything from small-block Chevy engines to the new LS engines. This particular car will be equipped with a powerful LS7 Corvette engine. Shown are the included required mounts for the LS engine.

Tap Top Frame Mounts and Inspect Subframe

2 Visually inspect all components and parts on the subframe to make sure there's no damage or problems. Before the mounts are bolted in, check to see if there is some powdercoating on the threads. Use a tap handle and a 3/8-16 tap to remove the excess. This makes the bolts easier to install.

Tap Side Subframe Mounts

3 Also tap the holes on the side of the subframe to clean out those threads.

Attach Motor Mounts to Subframe

4 Attach the motor mounts to the subframe. These are designed to support an LS Chevy engine. Coat the bolts with thread locker to make sure they don't loosen. Hand tighten the high-strength, 9/16-inch head bolts into the frame at first. Then after the bolts are started, tighten using a socket wrench and a 9/16-inch socket until the bolts are extremely tight.

FRONT SUSPENSION

Inspect Completed Subframe

5 Here is the subframe finished and ready to be installed into the car. This subframe was delivered assembled, powdercoated, and detailed to a show-ready finish. Note the rack-and-pinion unit and the modern spindles that resemble the ones used on the new Camaro.

Raise Subframe into Position

6 Raise the subframe high enough for the car lift. You can do this by holding the front of the new subframe with a "cherry picker" while manually lifting the rear. Place wood strips on the car lift to protect the rotors as the subframe is rolled under the car.

Align Subframe with Mounting Points

7 Adjust the position of the subframe until the mounting points on the subframe look as if they align with the mounting points on the body.

Lift Subframe into Place

8 After you lift the subframe into place, use a large screwdriver to make sure all of the holes in the subframe match up with holes in the body pan.

Inspect Mounting Kit

9 The Detroit Speed subframe was delivered with a mounting kit complete with bolts and mounting pads. The pads supplied are designed for use with this subframe.

Measure Alignment

10 To be sure the subframe is located properly, measure the subframe ends to fixed portions of the body. This is done in a cross pattern to make sure the alignment is the same on both sides.

Square Up the Subframe

11 It is important that the subframe be square. To do that measure the crossmember from one side to a fixed location on the body.

12 Measure the other side to make sure it is the same. It turned out that this subframe was slightly off by less than 1/4 inch, so it was moved accordingly, about 1/8 inch, to make it square.

13 Make one more measurement before installing the frame rails. It's not uncommon to find a second-generation F-Body car with frame rails that are up to 1/2 inch out of alignment. When these cars were manufactured, the chassis' production tolerances were not very precise and quality control was not very stringent.

If you encounter a subframe that is 1/4 or 1/2 inch out of alignment, you can take your car to a chassis shop, so the frame rails and the chassis can be properly aligned. Or you can realign the chassis rails yourself. But I do not recommend that you adjust the frame rails at home unless you have exprience doing it.

FRONT SUSPENSION

Adjust Frame Rails

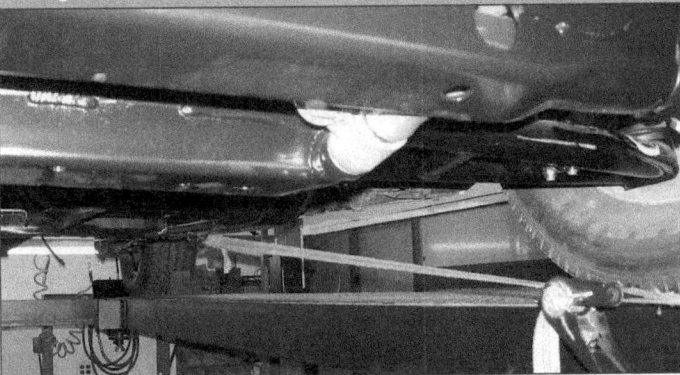

14 Using one come-along on the front left side of the body and one on the back right side, twist the subframe slightly until it appears straight under the body. Take another set of measurements to make sure it is straight. You don't want to make a mistake and have to rebend the rails again.

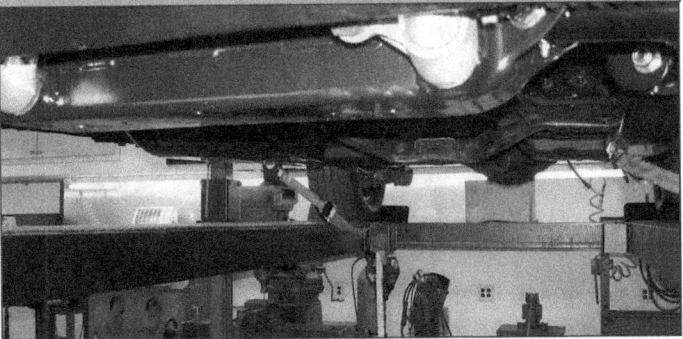

15 Here is the other come-along used to straighten the subframe. The come-alongs are used because it was harder to align the subframe when all of the sheet metal was left in place. By tightening the come-alongs side to side they twisted the subframe until it was square in the frame. When it was finished it was within 1/16 inch square and that's better than it was from the factory.

Bolt Subframe to Frame Rails

16 After your subframe is sitting straight under the body, secure the rear subframe-to-body bolts with a socket wrench and a 15/16-inch socket. Keep the come-alongs in place.

17 Tighten the front subframe bolts, with the come-alongs still in place to make sure the correct measurements are achieved. Secure the bolts using the same socket wrench and 15/16-inch socket.

18 Move to the front of the car and secure the radiator core support to the front of the new subframe. Use a socket wrench and a 15/16-inch socket. This hydro-formed Detroit Speed subframe is one of the best in the industry, and the geometry of the suspension provides a huge leap in handling and road holding. It's made to exacting standards, so when I installed it, all the components lined up with the OEM parts. This front subframe utilizes Corvette steering knuckles and bearing packs.

Attach Bumper Bolts

19 Install the bumper bolts that were removed from the original frame using a socket wrench and 3/4-inch socket. After bumper alignment is checked for straightness, secure the bolts as tight as possible.

Connect Steering Column

20 Connect the U-joint to the steering column as seen here. This is not a straight connection as the original subframe had, so U-joints must be used to make the connection to the rack-and-pinion unit. Connect the appropriate U-joint to the steering column and the other to the rack-and-pinion unit. Install the rod next by loosening the steering column and moving it back. After the rod is in place and the steering column is returned to the proper position, tighten all of the lock screws. It is also important that the two U-joints are in phase, which means that they are lined up so they don't bind.

21 Here is the finished steering connection. You can see why the U-joints are necessary. The original steering box was mounted on the frame in direct line with the steering column and the rack-and-pinion unit connection is offset. The U-joints make this connection possible. Note that even with this offset positioning, there is plenty of room for any engine, from the standard 350 V-8 all the way up to a 572-ci big-block Chevy engine. The LS engines are also a perfect fit.

FRONT SUSPENSION

Connect Power Steering Lines

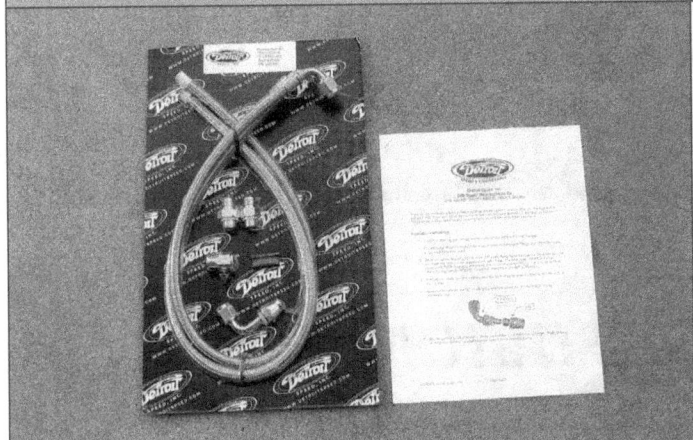

22 The Detroit Speed front subframe comes with power-steering lines. Screw the lines in place and tighten with a line wrench. (This car doesn't currently have an engine so the lines were only connected to the rack-and-pinion unit.)

Note Ground Clearance

23 From the front of the car, you can see that this subframe is straight in the chassis and offers more ground clearance than the original unit. The lower ride height allows the car to have a lower center of gravity for improved handling.

The car was outfitted with a pair of wheels big enough to clear the Baer brakes (left). The original wheels wouldn't fit because they were a smaller diameter. The subframe looks terrific, and it improves the car's ride and handling ability (right).

CAMARO & FIREBIRD PERFORMANCE PROJECTS: 1970–1981

CHAPTER 11

REAR SUSPENSION

The second-generation Camaros and Firebirds were delivered with a parallel leaf spring design that featured a Chevy 10-bolt differential. Many Z28 and Trans Am axle housings were equipped with limited-slip 10-bolt differentials, and they were able to hold up well behind Chevy's LT-1 350 engine and Pontiac's big-block 400 and 403 engines.

The rear suspension had a sway bar and heavy-duty springs to keep the car planted around corners. The differential could be equipped with gear sets ranging from high freeway gears to optional (by request only) low gears for excellent acceleration. The original differentials and suspension worked well in the 1970s and provided excellent handling characteristics for the time. With changes such as springs that lower the car just a little and the use of urethane bushings in the springs and the sway bar, the rear suspension could easily be improved.

This suspension works well on the street and offers a comfortable ride quality, but if you are installing a much stronger running engine, building a Pro Touring type of car, planning to autocross race; or putting the car on the track you probably want a stronger rear suspension that allows adjustability for the specific track. Today numerous companies make new rear assemblies for the second-generation Camaros and Firebirds that upgrade the cars to stronger Ford 9-inch differentials and change from parallel leaf springs to coil-over shocks held in place with four adjustable bars.

The coil-over shocks are adjustable for ride height and shock damping and the four-bar systems are also adjustable to get the desired suspension geometry. Most of the kits available are not just a simple bolt-in arrangement so some fabrication and welding talents are required to complete the installations. Many of the companies I have previously mentioned offer suspension upgrades. All of the upgrades use Ford 9-inch differentials. Be sure to find the one that suits the type of driving you intend to do and the difficulty of installation you feel comfortable doing.

Eaton Detroit Springs

Installing some high-performance springs is an easy way to upgrade your second-generation F-Body. Eaton Detroit Springs can tailor its springs to your particular requirements. To lower ride height and improve handling characteristics, Eaton can provide 1- or 2-inch-lower springs that don't adversely impact the ride quality. The lower ride height improves the overall handling of the car and still works with the factory sway bars or with upgraded aftermarket sway bar kits.

Eaton offers many performance-oriented leaf or coil springs and the upgrade is easy and cost effective. The springs are made in the United States and are manufactured for your particular car, so when they are installed, the car sits just the way you want it to sit.

Project 1: Rear Spring Installation

Springs aren't a glamorous addition to a muscle car but they can make a big difference in the way a car handles and looks. Second-generation Camaros and especially Trans Am Firebirds came from the factory with a low stance to start with so I decided to lower the car 1 inch front and rear. The easiest way to do that was to order 1-inch-lower front and rear springs. The Eaton 1-inch-lower front springs (PN MC 1304-1) and rear springs (PN ML 231) provide significantly improved suspension performance.

Along with the springs I ordered a rear spring installation kit (PN IK GC5003). In the process of installing the rear springs I decided to detail the parts for show and go. Truth be known, during the 1970s the axle housing and rear springs were not painted by the factory in an effort to save money, so if you purchased a new Camaro or Trans Am in the 1970s, and looked underneath, you could see the parts with a layer of surface rust when the car was brand new. In many cases the dealerships sprayed the parts black to give the car a more finished appearance, but the inexpensive paint used didn't last long.

I wanted the car to look nice, so I opted to paint the axle housing semi-gloss black (PPG DP90LF) and the differential cover shiny black for a little contrast. On the springs I used The Eastwood Company Spray Gray, which is a natural metal color. This installation was also completed with polyurethane sway bar parts from Energy Suspension, the same company that makes the Eaton spring installation kit.

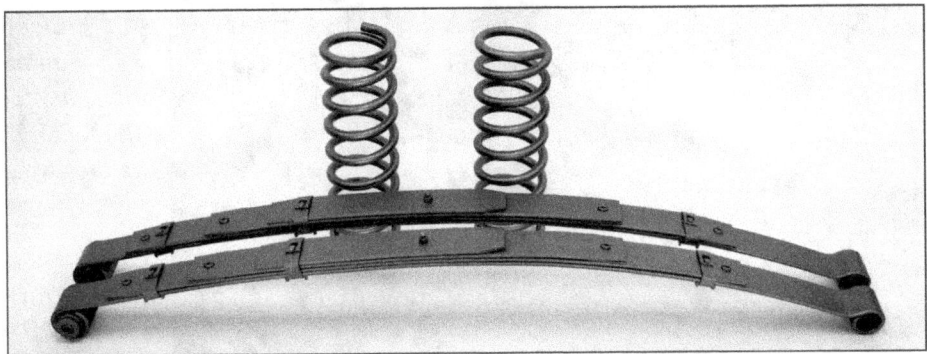

Eaton Detroit Springs can tailor the springs for a particular car, and in this case the springs were made to lower a 1978 Trans Am 1 inch. I installed the front (PN MC 1304-1) and rear (PN ML 231) springs. An Eaton rear spring installation kit was also ordered to complete the installation. Eaton paints the springs black, but I decided to paint them similar to the factory finish, so I used Eastwood's Spray Gray to give them a natural metal appearance.

Remove Rear Springs, Sway Bar and Axle Housing

1 *Remove the rear springs, sway bar, and axle housing as a unit to speed up the process. Remove the axle housing so the individual parts can be disconnected. Here you can see that the complete unit was never painted and is now covered with a thick layer of rust and dirt. General Motors was more interested in making and saving money in the 1970s, so it didn't see a need to paint parts that are never seen, such as axle housings, subframes, and other undercarriage parts.*

CHAPTER 11

Strip Paint from Suspension Parts

2 Clean your rear suspension parts and the differential to bare metal. Here the axle housing is hung on an engine lift so that it can be painted. The factory didn't paint the parts, but I will paint them as they would have looked in the 1960s.

Spray Primer on Axle Housing

3 To refinish the axle housing, you can prime it with PPG DP90LF semi-gloss black. This primer looks like the paint used on suspension parts in the 1960s, so it gives the axle housing a factory appearance, or at least what it would have looked like if GM had done it. This paint works great because it is waterproof and difficult to scratch.

Paint Axle Housing Semi-Gloss Black

4 This axle housing was painted semi-gloss black and the rear cover was painted shiny black for a little contrast. It is not natural metal as it was originally, but I think it looks much nicer. This is a rather rare unit because it was the performance axle with 3.42:1 gears and a limited-slip unit.

Connect Springs to Spring Pockets

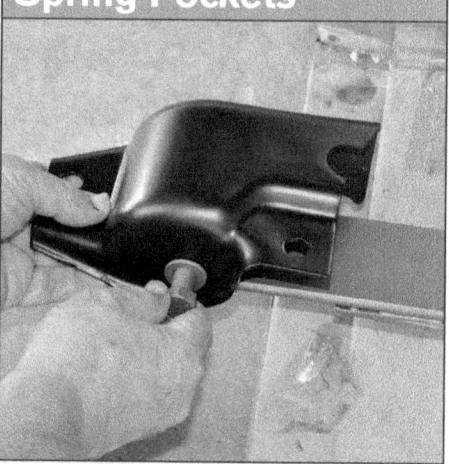

5 Before the springs are actually installed, connect them to the spring pockets. Use one large bolt to fasten the springs. To make everything look nice paint the bolts a natural metal color. Tighten the bolts to the cup with a lock nut. You can paint the pockets semi-gloss black.

REAR SUSPENSION

Install Front Spring Cups

6 Bolt the front of each rear spring into a spring cup with a large bolt and a lock nut that won't back off. Bolt the cup into the car with three bolts per side. The body is equipped with moveable nut plates. Screw three bolts into the nut plates. Tighten the bolts with a socket wrench with a 9/16-inch socket.

Remove Rubber Bushings

7 Remove the old rubber bushings from the aft pivot points where the rear springs are connected. Split the bushings in half so they can be installed one half at a time in the spring and into the bushing cup in the car. Lubricate the bushings inside and out so they slip into the receptacle easily. It is more difficult to get the old bushings out of the springs and car than it is to install the new ones.

Bolt Spring to Body

8 Lift the rear spring pocket into place and install the bolts to secure it to the body. Connect the bolts with a socket wrench outfitted with a 9/16-inch socket. This job is much easier if you have a friend help you hold up the spring while you install the bolts. I recommend tightly securing the spring pocket to the body, but leaving the spring on the loose side until it is fully connected.

Connect Rear Shackles to Upper Pivot Point

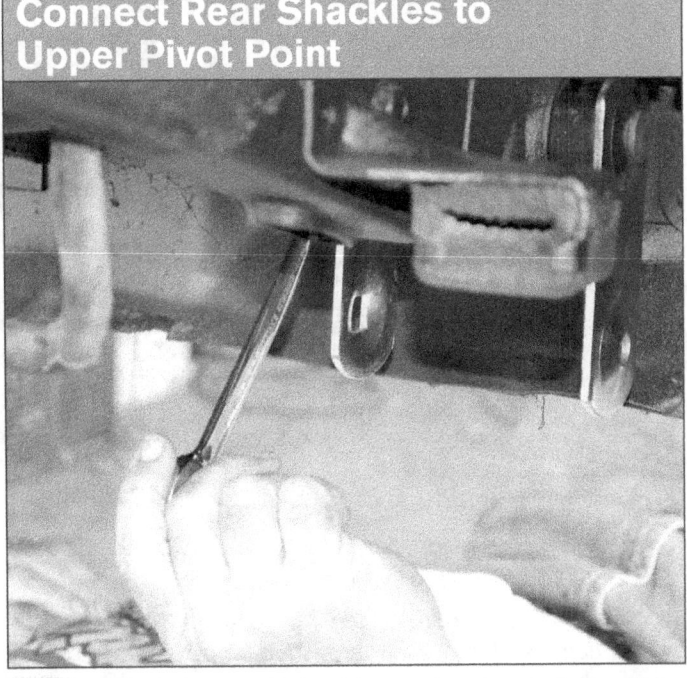

9 Connect the rear shackles to the upper pivot point using the provided polyurethane bushings. Tighten the bolts but keep them loose enough to move around until the axle housing is installed.

CHAPTER 11

Connect Springs at Front

10 Bolt the springs to the front chassis brackets. Let the springs just hang down in the rear until the axle housing is moved in place.

Install Differential

11 Place the painted axle housing on a padded floor jack and carefully wheel it under the car. Center the axle housing over the springs in preparation for connecting the springs to the shackles. The axle housing has to be jacked up high enough so that the shackles can be installed.

12 Although the rear springs are isolated from the axle housing with rubber pads from the factory, I recommend using stiffer and longer lasting polyurethane isolation pads. (The inner portion of the spring pads use special bolts that also attach the sway bar to the axle housing.) These stiff pads are designed to help center the axle housing on the springs and to help the car handle better.

13 Connect the rear springs to the shackles. Hold the axle housing in place with one U-bolt per side. With the shackles installed the axle housing can rest on the springs.

REAR SUSPENSION

Install Bushings

14 *I recommend Energy Suspension bushings in the rear sway bar. To install, lubricate the upper connector and use a vise to press it in. Use new urethane bushings on all sway bar connectors to allow the car to handle better.*

Install Sway Bar Ends

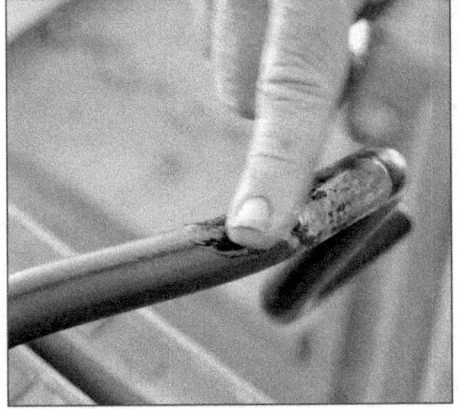
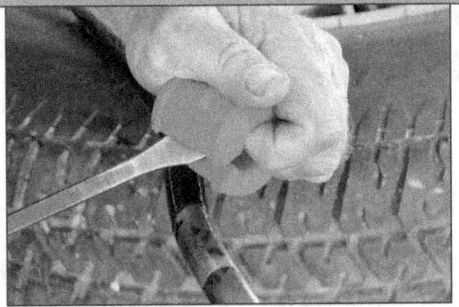
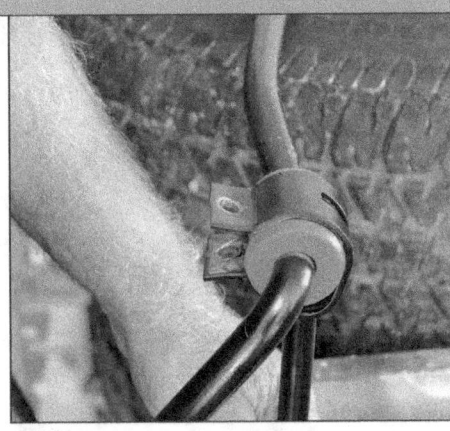

15 *Lubricate the lower connection on the sway bar to help it slide into the mount.*

16 *Using a large screwdriver to split the bushing and slide it over the sway bar in the lubricated area. Once one end is split enough to fit over the sway bar, the rest slides right on.*

17 *Place the lower link over the bushing, install the bolt, and squeeze the link together.*

Place Parts on Sway Bar

18 *Place the end bushing and bracket on the sway bar. This end connects to the spring perch and the bolts secure the sway bar bracket and the axle housing. The upper link connects to the body bracket.*

CAMARO & FIREBIRD PERFORMANCE PROJECTS: 1970–1981

Detroit Speed

Detroit Speed produces some of the finest engineered and quality manufactured products for second-generation Camaros and Firebirds, as well as other GM years and models. The company owners are former GM engineers and their components work as designed to improve a car's ride and handling.

The second-generation Camaros and Firebirds were built with dual rear leaf spring suspension with factory-installed sway bars, and for the mid 1970s the suspension worked well. Today Detroit Speed has designed the QuadraLink suspension system that is state-of-the-art and allows a second-generation Camaro or Firebird to handle extremely well on the street and on the track, exceeding what could be achieved with the original system. This system features a short- and long-arm four-link setup that is used in conjunction with adjustable coil-over shocks and a Panhard bar to center the axle housing.

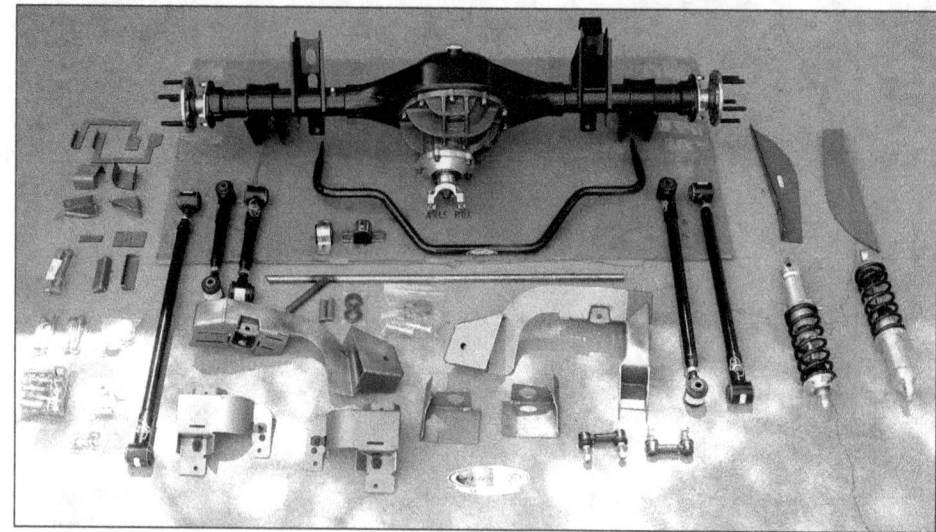

The Detroit Speed Quadralink installation kit comes with the frame brackets installed on the Ford 9-inch axle housing, complete four bars and Panhard bar, high-quality coil-over shocks, hardware, and a complete installation instruction sheet that includes templates for locating the parts and the modifications required.

The complete kit comes with all of the brackets and comprehensive installation instructions, including templates for locating the brackets. The axle housing used for this kit has a strong Ford 9-inch differential, and it comes equipped with the brackets installed. This axle housing mounting system allows for a wide variety of adjustments to the four links and height adjustment for the car's ride height so you can dial-in the suspension to handle just the way you like it.

Project 2: Rear Suspension System Installation

This isn't an easy installation so you might want to have a professional shop do it for you. If you live close to Detroit Speed you can also see if they could do the installation for you. Precision Street Rods & Machines installed this suspension in a 1970 Z28 Camaro.

A complete Detroit Speed subframe assembly was installed on this 1970 Z28. The front sits nice and low but the rear is still in the high stock location. The rear leaf springs were suited for the stock front suspension and ride height, but this stock rear suspension certainly isn't cutting edge and not nearly as good as the multi-link aftermarket rear suspension systems on the market. There is obviously room for improvement for a car that will be used on the track as well as the street.

REAR SUSPENSION

The Chevy axle housing rides on stock parallel leaf springs. The original sway bar was missing on this Z28, but it did have one in the past. Installing a Detroit Speed QuadraLink rear suspension, or another four- or five-link aftermarket rear suspension, is no small endeavor. It requires extensive fabrication, welding, and fitting of components, which takes considerable time. If you've never done this type of work, consider having a professional chassis shop install the kit for you.

If you do tackle it, you need plenty of room to work to complete a professional-grade installation of this suspension system. And although you can cut the frame and body, as well as weld the suspension components while on your back, it is much more difficult to complete the installation. Therefore, I recommend you have a hydraulic service lift, so you can stand under the car to more easily cut and weld. It's also safer.

Stock Rear Suspension Removal

Remove Gas Tank

1 To perform the extensive frame and wheel-well modifications required to install a QuadraLink rear suspension (and use large 20-inch wheels with 40-series footprint) you must remove the gas tank. This allows more room for performing modifications and since welding will be done it is also a safety factor.

Make sure the gas tank is empty; after all, gas weighs about 6 pounds per gallon.

2 Position a floor jack under the fuel tank, but be careful because you don't want to dent it or, worse yet, push it in. Use a ratchet and deep-well socket to remove the bolts securing the tank straps near the axle housing. These straps cradle the gas tank and secure it to the car. Slowly lower the jack and the gas tank. Move the gas tank to a safe storage space where it won't get damaged or be exposed to an ignition source.

Remove Emergency Brake Cable

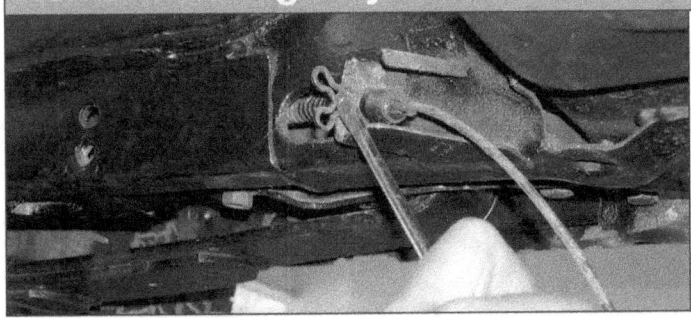

3 Use a screwdriver to pry off the emergency brake cable clips. Slip the cables out of the brackets. Move the cables out of the way so they don't interfere with installing the suspension.

Remove Spring Bolts and Nut

4 Be sure the rear of the car is safely supported with the correct jack stands installed at the frame rails. Ensure that the weight of the chassis is evenly distributed so the chassis does not become twisted, which would mean the suspension is then installed slightly askew and doesn't operate at its full potential.

To remove the old suspension, use an impact wrench to remove the spring bolts from the shackles and the bottom nut of the shock. Often these bolts are severely rusted and may need to soak in WD-40 or another lubricant. If air tools are unavailable, use an open-end wrench and a socket wrench. If the shackle and other parts are stubborn to remove, you can use a hammer to tap the shackle.

Remove Bracket Bolts

5 The front eye loop on the rear spring rides in a spring cup bracket that bolts to the chassis. Remove the three spring cup bracket bolts from the chassis on both sides of the car with a socket wrench and a 9/16-inch socket. This effectively disconnects the spring from the body.

Weld Spring Cup Brackets

6 Detroit Speed brackets are designed to bolt into the same holes, but you can also weld the brackets in place for a much stronger connection.

Remove Rear Suspension

7 Lower the lift and remove the axle housing and springs from the car as a complete unit. Using a floor jack when there is clearance the entire unit can be rolled out from under the car.

Connect Rear Frame Rails

8 In order to keep the chassis from moving during the installation process, connect the rear frame rails to the rack by welding two angle-iron braces in place. This is a stronger connection than the small jacks. (You will remove the angle iron from the car after the new suspension is installed.)

REAR SUSPENSION

Remove Wheel Well

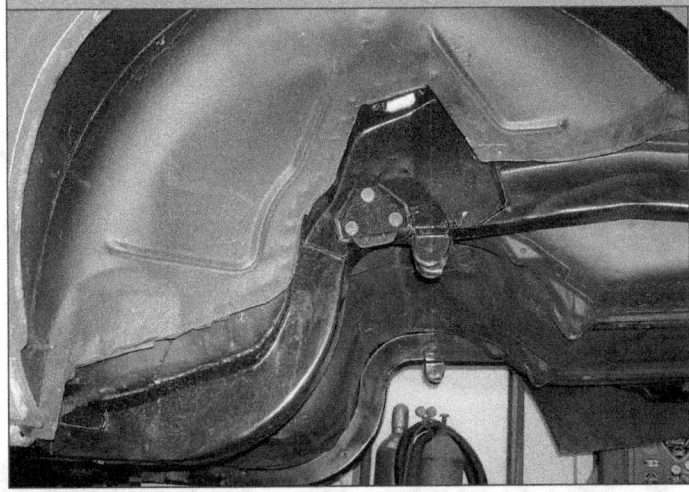

9 Here is the inner wheel well and chassis before any work was done. A wider wheel well is necessary to house larger tires so the factory wheel tub has to be removed. The installation of larger wheel wells or tubs is detailed in Chapter 9.

10 Carefully outline where the inner wheel well meets the trunk and the floor of the car. Mark this from inside the passenger compartment and the trunk. Use a 3-inch cut-off wheel to carefully cut around the wheel well. See Chapter 9 for the removal process. The tub was released in a way that works with the new Detroit Speed wide wheel tubs.

Remove Brackets

11 Use a 3-inch cut-off wheel to remove a small bracket from the rear frame section. Take your time and make a clean cut. Once it has been removed, grind the remainder of the bracket away so the frame rail has a clean appearance.

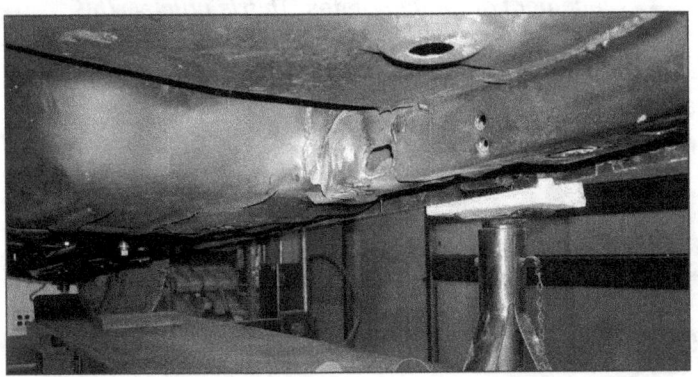

12 Use a 3-inch cut-off wheel to remove the other small bracket located on the inside of the frame. Sand the area to bare metal and it is ready for the next step.

13 Remove the rear frame section after the bracket. After the bracket is removed, sand the entire area, including the rear frame rails, to bare metal in preparation for the modifications. Bare metal promotes better welding.

CHAPTER 11

Rear Chassis Modification

Place Template onto Frame

1 The installation instructions include templates that make it easier to figure out where modifications have to be made. The templates indicate where the frame rails have to be modified and where brackets have to go. Tape the rear frame rail template into place. Mark the frame rail where it needs to be narrowed. Much of the frame strength is temporarily removed at this stage, so make sure you have jack stands at the corners to evenly distribute the weight of the chassis and to maintain the body integrity. Also, support the body in the middle to make sure there is no chance of bending or flexing.

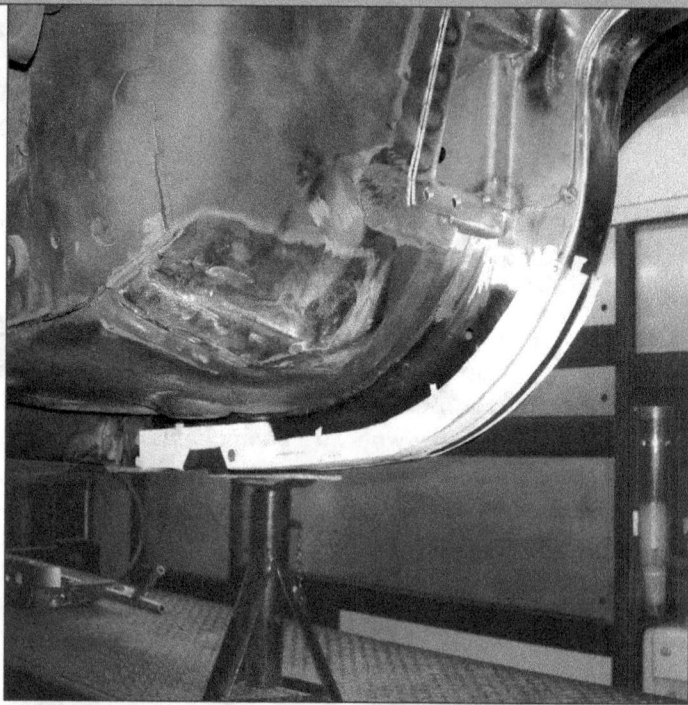

2 A portion of the frame rail needs to be cut away so the lower control arm has an adequate amount of clearance and can move through its entire arc of travel. At the front of the template is a notch that needs to be cut in the frame rail for the suspension mount. The same template must be used on the other side of the rear frame. Make marks for the notches prior to cutting out the sections on each side of the car.

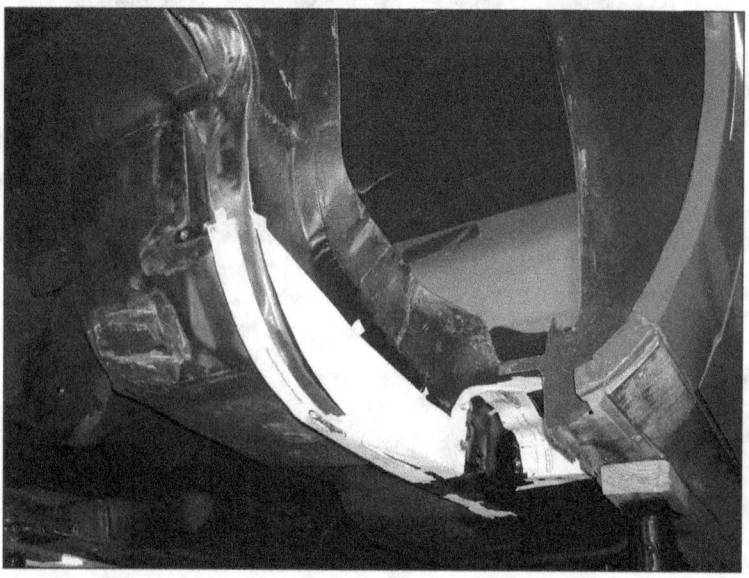

3 Make sure the template has been placed in the correct position, so the proper cuts can be made. Be sure each side has been accurately and precisely marked and cut, otherwise the suspension won't properly align. Take your time and verify the placement of the templates. This is crucial. This template is used to make adjustments for the installation of the front four-link bracket. The template shows the areas of the car where metal has to be removed.

REAR SUSPENSION

Mark Off Rear Floor Section

4 Using another template, mark the rear floor section and cut accordingly. Make a small notch using a 3-inch cut-off wheel. After the metal is removed, sand the area smooth and to bare metal using a 3-inch angle sander.

Notch Out Wheel Well

5 In step 2, I showed you where a notch has to be made. It was marked when the template was in place and now the area is being cut out using a 3-inch cut-off wheel. After the area is cut out, sand it smooth to bare metal to promote welding.

Cut Out Section of Rear Frame

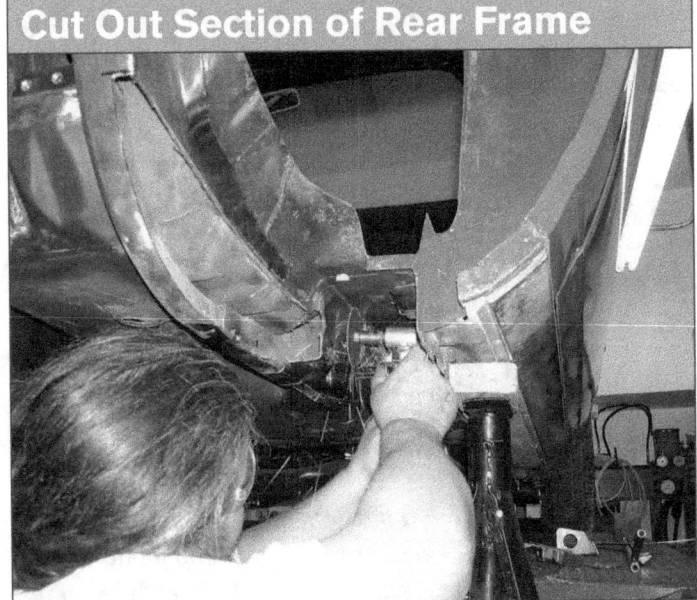

6 Use the 3-inch cut-off wheel to cut the rear frame rails to the specified shape. Once this step has been completed, use the cut-off wheel to notch the frame rail for the spring mount. (Here, the frame rail was narrowed all the way through the profile around the wheel well.) Once all the cuts have been made, use a 3-inch cut-off wheel and then sand it to bare metal. Smooth all edges with a small 3-inch angle sander.

Modify Bracket

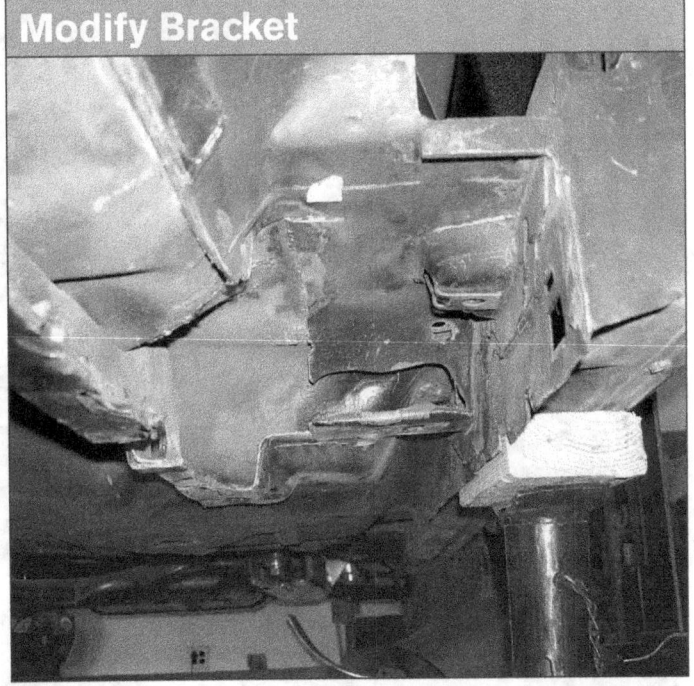

7 When working on 30-plus-year-old cars, you're going to run into unforeseen obstacles. In this particular case, this area of the car was damaged in the past, so Precision Street Rods modified the bracket in the kit to make sure the installation was stronger. Weld the brackets into the chassis for improved strength.

CAMARO & FIREBIRD PERFORMANCE PROJECTS: 1970–1981

Modify Rear Bracket

 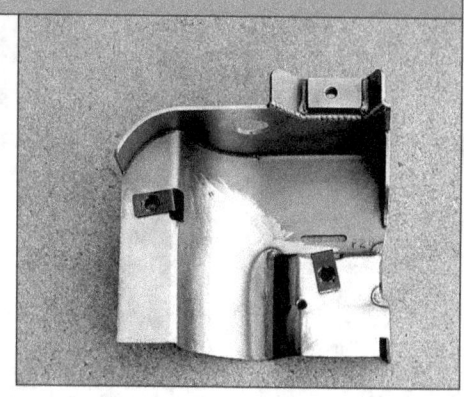

Cut and Reinforce Frame

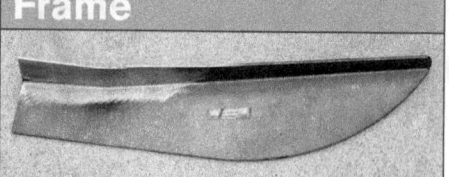

8 Here is the rear bracket that is furnished in the Detroit Speed kit (left). This bracket is designed to bolt to the spring pocket holes. This bracket comes welded and ready to bolt in. Note the three connection points. This is the modified spring pocket bracket (right). It has been welded and ground so it was completed. The welding and sanding was done so well that the unit looks like it was built that way.

9 At this stage, the frame has been narrowed slightly so it can accept the four-link suspension and provide clearance. Detroit Speed furnishes patches for each modified frame rail to cap both of them off. Cut back a section of the frame about 1 inch and then weld another section of metal back in to add strength. This section has to be made for the up-and-down movement of the four-bar.

Cut Frame Rail

10 Here is the frame after a section was cut out for four-link clearance. Note the frame rail and trunk have been cut. Use a 3-inch cut-off wheel for a precise cut, and don't risk using a plasma cutter even though it's easier to use. Sand the area prior to welding in a new piece.

Suspension Kit Installation

Position Frame Rail Patch

1 Place the frame rail patch against the frame and use Vise-Grips body clamps to clamp it into the desired position. Use the 3-inch cut-off wheel to clean up and modify any areas. Extensive cutting may be needed to narrow the frame rail. It is often required to clean up the cuts on the frame rail so the patch effectively caps the frame rail. Small adjustments may be needed to get it to sit exactly where it should be. Make the adjustments using a 3-inch angle sander to smooth off the frame or modify the panel. Notice that the four-link bracket is also in place, and it connects to the patched area.

Make Room for Frame Patch

2 Some interior modifications must be done to get the frame patch in place. Installing a wheel tub kit requires some fabrication, and therefore you typically have some finish cutting, trimming, and fitting in order for all the components to properly line up. This particular notch was made earlier; the floor also has to be sliced for it to seat properly.

Weld Four-Link Bracket in Place

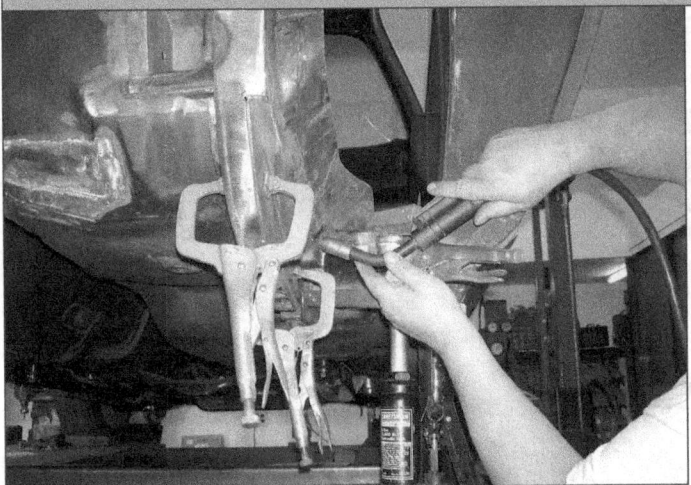

3 After the frame patch and four-link bracket are in place, use the MIG welder to tack weld the patch to the frame. Place tack welds every 4 inches. Verify the position of the patch weld. Now lay down a full bead of weld and connect the tack welds together. Alternate welding at each end of the patch panel and quench the welds with air or water if necessary. This spreads the heat around so you don't warp the patch. While this procedure can be done with a TIG welder if you have one, most use a MIG welder at a low-amp setting. Use this process until the entire area is welded together.

Weld Floor Section from Above

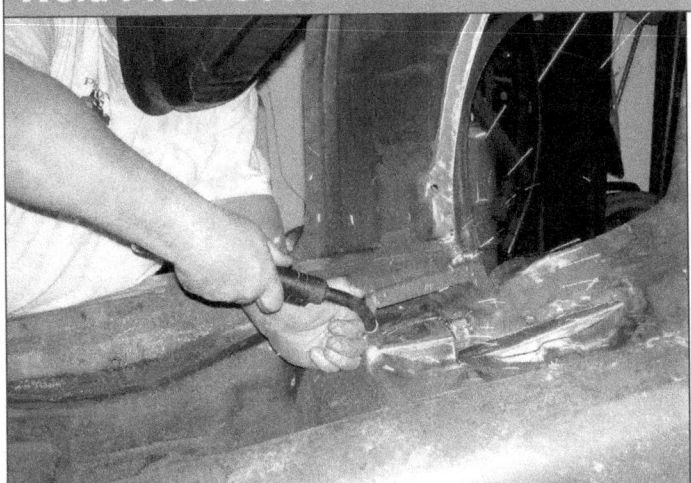

4 The metal sections protruding through the floor must be perimeter welded in for superior strength. Notice the nice welding job.

5 Here is the floor section after the welding was finished. Sand the welds for a nice smooth finish (even though they are never seen after the seat is in place).

Sand Welds

6 Once you have tack welded the frame patch into position, stitch weld between the tack welds. Alternate from one side of the patch to the other in order to spread the heat around and not warp the patch. If necessary, quench the welds with air or water so the frame rail does not get too hot. Once all the welding has been completed, use an angle grinder with an 80-grit disc to grind smooth the surface of the patch so it looks finished.

Clean Up Patch Panel

7 Use an 80-grit grinding wheel to clean up the patch panel. Once the suspension system has been installed, prime and paint this area so that it appears factory new. Here is the other side of the car with the patch in place. This provides another look at how the frame was notched to clear the long four-link bar.

Weld In Four-Link Bracket

8 Like other brackets and patches, make sure the four-link bracket is properly positioned. Tack weld the four-link bracket into the chassis about every 4 inches. Then lay down a full perimeter weld by welding one side and then the other. As always, manage the application of heat to avoid warping the thin sheet metal.

Measure Area for Templates

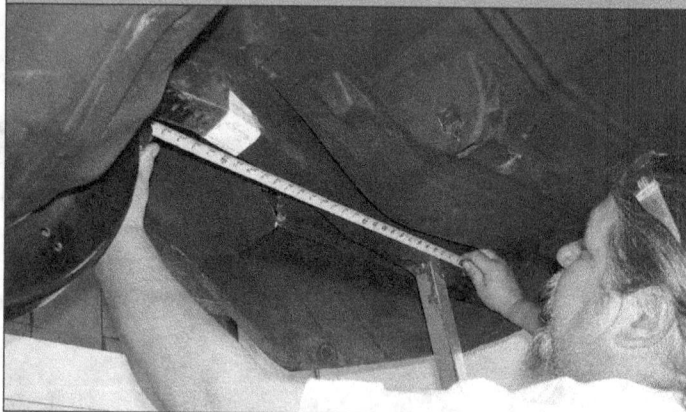

9 Use templates to mount the upper four-link attachment brackets. The templates make the installation a little easier because less measuring has to be done. Take correct measurements so the templates are located properly and are attached to the inner frame structure. Use these measurements to verify that the template is in the correct location.

REAR SUSPENSION

Mark Location of Template on Frame

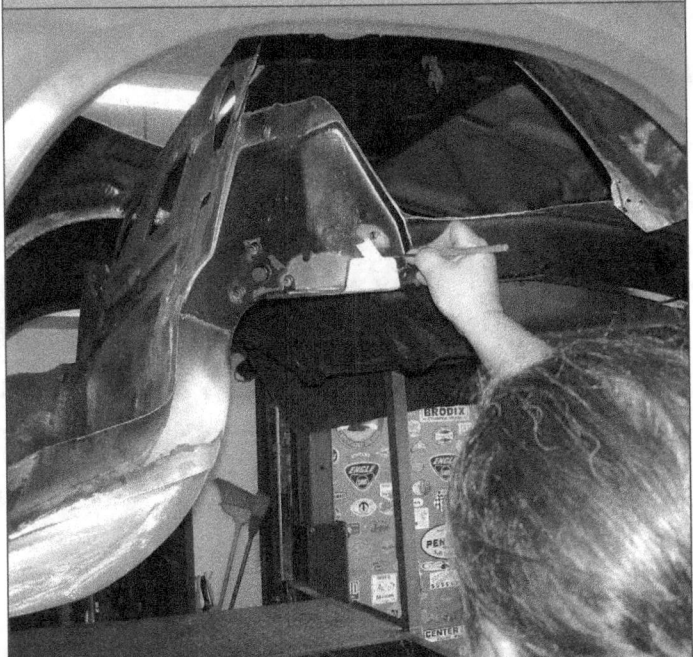

10 When the measurement is completed and you are confident that the template is in the correct location, mark the perimeter of the template on the frame.

Mark Location of Upper Link Bracket

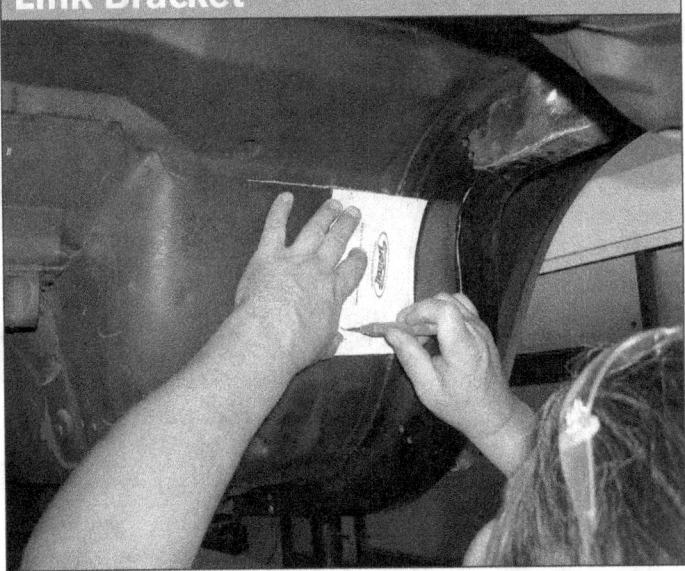

11 The upper link mount pocket is a critical anchoring point on the vehicle. Ensure that the cut-out line is properly marked, so the suspension link is mounted in the ideal position. Using another template, mark the inner floorpan for the installation of the upper link pocket.

Cut Out Link Pocket and Frame Mount

12 Use a silver pen or another suitable marking device to mark the upper pan and the area to be cut out. Use a 3-inch cut-off wheel on a pneumatic rotary tool to carefully cut out the metal for the upper link pocket. Using the same tool, also cut out the frame notch accordingly.

Install Bracket

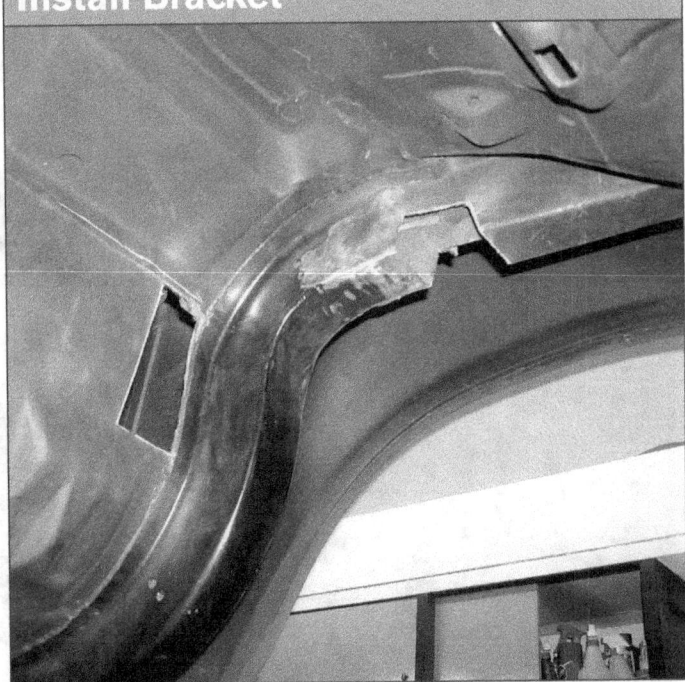

13 Here are the upper floorpan and the frame section after the cuts have been made. The bracket supplied in the kit connects to these points. This is a one-piece bracket that slides right into place for welding.

Weld On Frame Bracket

14 Use a set of locking pliers for bodywork to clamp the mount bracket into position of the notched frame. Make sure the mount bracket sits squarely and at the correct depth in the notched pocket. Use a grinding tool if necessary to clean up the area and fit the bracket. Once clamped in place, use a MIG welder to tack weld the bracket to the frame rail, then to other brackets lay down a perimeter weld. After the welding is completed, grind it smooth for a factory-like appearance and to enable better welding for the main bracket.

Trial Fit Upper Link Mount Pocket

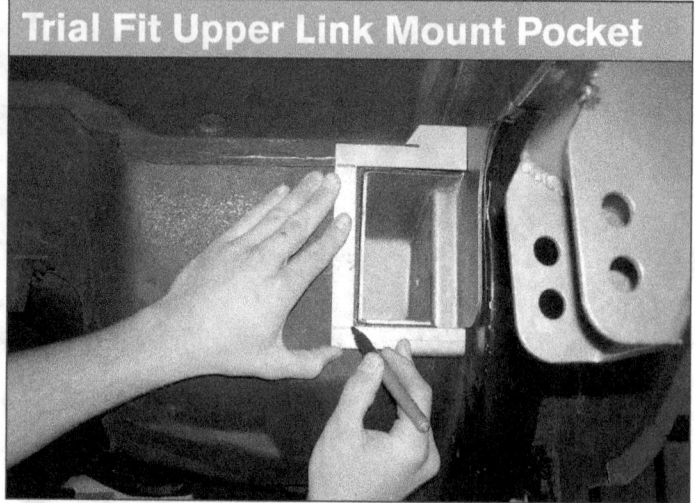

15 Trial fit the upper link mount pocket. Make sure that it properly aligns with the rest of the suspension mounting points. Once placement and alignment is verified, tack weld the mount pocket to the frame. Detroit Speed makes a framework for the upper four-link bracket. Here the frame is held in place to see how much of the bracket protrudes so that the area can be trimmed off prior to welding the framework to the bracket. Trim the area that protrudes with a 3-inch angle grinder.

Weld Framework of Bracket

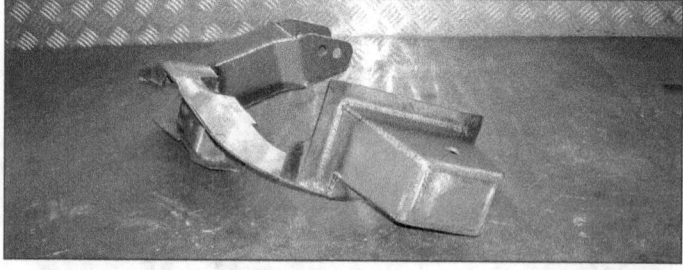

16 Weld the framework of the bracket for additional strength and support. Remove the bracket from the car and weld the front and back of the framework. This double-sided welding provides more penetration and allows for some smoothing on the side that can be seen.

Insert Bracket into Floor and Weld In

17 Place the bracket into the cut-out area and perform one last final check. Make sure it is sitting flush against the floorpan. Once in position, place tack welds at the corners to hold it into position. Then drill through the mount pocket flange and the floor using a 1/2-inch drill bit. Drill holes every 2 to 3 inches, so spot welds can be placed through the bracket and floor. Then spot weld the pocket and be sure to manage heat application. Tack weld the bracket to the frame rail so it securely attaches to the chassis in the desired position. Weld the bracket on both sides for maximum strength. Tack welded it first, then finish weld.

REAR SUSPENSION

Spot Weld Pocket Bracket

18 From inside the passenger compartment, you can see the spot welds were placed every few inches and the brackets have been tack welded into position.

Install Panhard Bar Bracket

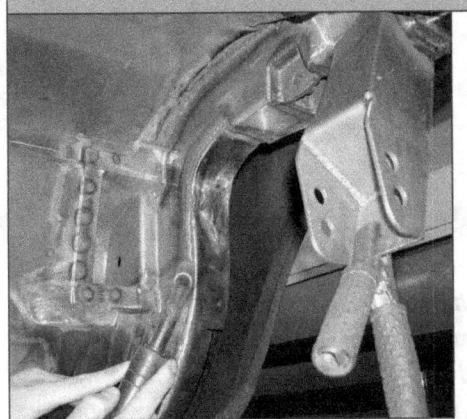

19 The entire bracket includes an upper four-bar mount and a bracket mount for the Panhard bar. Place a perimeter weld between the tack welds on the bracket. Carefully weld the multi-use bracket into place. (Notice that the bracket has two holes so the rear axle can be adjusted according to where the upper four-bar is located.)

20 Mark the pan for the location of the Panhard bracket brace. This is a tubular unit that runs from one side of the car to the other.

21 Detroit Speed provides a Panhard bracket brace that also strengthens the rear frame section (above). This bar runs from one side of the rear frame to the other and adds strength to the connection.

Carefully position the bar on the brackets and make sure that the bottom and top attachment points are correctly positioned. Once in proper alignment, tack weld on each side to secure it into position (right). Using a MIG welder, weld the brace to the Panhard brackets on each side of the car. Make sure the gas tank mounts are not damaged or altered.

Install Panhard Bar Bracket (Continued)

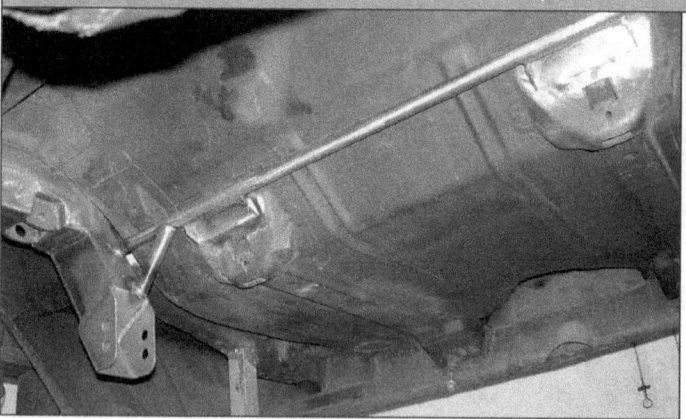

22 Here is the bar welded in place. The bar is attached to the bracket to give it strength from both sides of the car and the body pan. The Panhard bar runs from the axle housing to the bracket and it is used to keep the axle housing centered. (Note that the gas tank strap mounting locations have not been altered so the stock gas tank can be reinstalled.)

Paint Undercarriage

23 Make sure all welds have been cleaned up and the surfaces of all the brackets have been wiped down. Use acetone to clean the surfaces. Apply a layer of primer and the desired tint of paint. In this case, the undercarriage was painted flat black.

Install Wide Wheel Well Tubs

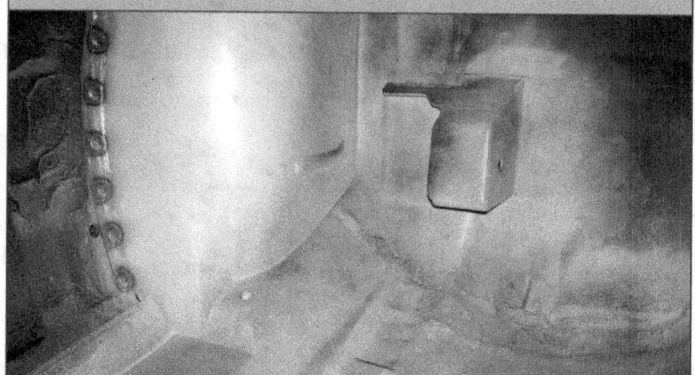

24 Install aftermarket wheel tubs to accommodate the larger wheels and tires to run with this high-performance rear suspension. Follow the procedure for installing the wheel tubs found in Chapter 9. After the tubs are in place on the floor section, coat them with gray primer.

Modify Rear Seat Frame

25 These deep wheel tubs take up more interior space and specifically reduce the amount of rear seat space between the wheel tubs. You need to reduce rear seat width by trimming the seat frame to fit between the wheel tubs. Most wheel tub installations for most second-generation F-Body cars typically require trimming 2 inches off the seat frame.

Place the seat frame between the two wheel tubs and mark the points of contact on the frame with a Sharpie. These are the areas that require cutting and trimming. Use an angle grinder with an abrasive 3-inch disc to cut, relocate, and reattach the center support rod and also the stamped center section at the bottom of the seat frame.

REAR SUSPENSION

Install Axle Housing

26 Many Camaro and Firebird owners opt to install a Curry 9-inch rear end or similar unit. Have an assistant lift the axle housing into place in the rear end. Slip the bolts through the mount brackets on the chassis and mount brackets on the axle housing. Trial fit the axle housing and suspension to make sure everything is aligned and before torqueing the bolts to final specifications.

Once the housing is installed, start attaching the upper and lower link rods. Install the rod in the bracket for the upper link rod and then slip the bolt through and hand tighten.

Get inside the passenger compartment and have a friend guide the rod into the mount pocket, line up the bolt holes, and slip the bolts through. Align the lower link rods on the axle housing brackets and then in mount pockets. Slip the bolts through and hand tighten the nuts.

Now take side-to-side measurements and forward-to-aft measurements. Verify these measurements with the instructions. Make sure the axle housing and suspension are square on the body before proceeding.

Install Shocks, Sway Bars, Brake Lines

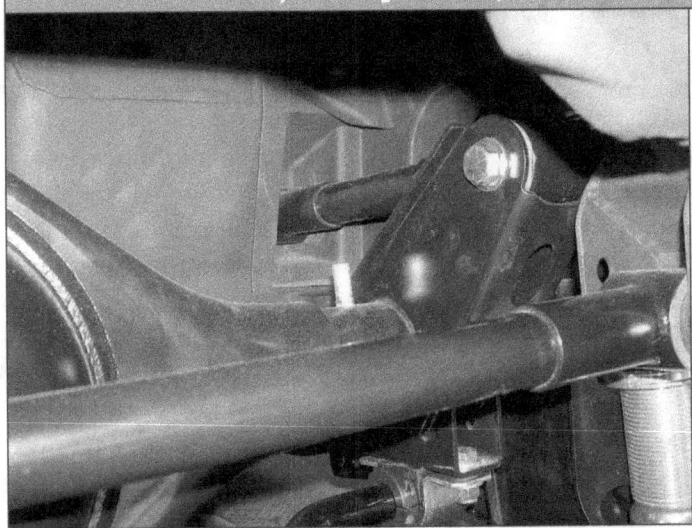

27 Align the shock eye loop with the upper shock mount on the chassis. Thread the bolt through and hand tighten the nut. Align the bottom eye of the shock with the axle housing. Again insert the bolt through the bracket and shock eye loop, and hand tighten. (At this stage, the upper four-link rods are also attached to the axle housing.) The upper rods are very short but work well and are fully adjustable.

Mount the sway bar to the assembly. Align the sway bar on the lower shock mount brackets and insert the bolts. Install the brackets over the bushings. Torque all bolts and fasteners to specification.

Reattach the emergency brake cable, attach the brake lines, and bleed the system.

After installing the wheels, step back to see the complete installation that includes the four-link design, the large strong Panhard bar, and the top-quality coil-over shocks that display plenty of adjustability. The axle housing is a Ford 9-inch limited-slip unit. Gear selections can be made for street driving and road racing, or even low gears for drag racing.

CHAPTER 12

PERFORMANCE BRAKES

Muscle cars in the 1960s were equipped with drum brakes that worked fine for normal transportation, as long as the streets were dry and conditions were favorable. When the manufacturers in Detroit started installing high-performance, large-displacement engines in small sedans, the brakes certainly needed improvement. So in 1967 many manufacturers began offering manual and power disc brake options.

The 1967 disc brakes stopped the cars fine when they were working properly, but this first design proved to be very troublesome. All of the car manufacturers were buying disc brakes from the same source, so all of the companies were having similar problems. In 1968 another design was used with a single piston, and many manufacturers adopted the basic design with their own changes and mechanical improvements.

Camaros and Firebirds were optionally equipped with single-piston disc brakes and they were a big improvement over the drum brakes. They were so trouble free that they continued to be used for a long time. This basic brake design was used from 1968 through 1981 with a drum rear brake as standard equipment.

In 1979 General Motors started offering a rear disc brake option as part of the Trans Am WS6 suspension upgrade, so some of the last Firebirds could be ordered with improved four-wheel disc brakes. In 1979, Camaros and Firebirds were also equipped with new, improved front spindles, which was the only big front brake change made between 1970 and 1981.

If you are driving your Camaro or Firebird for normal transportation the standard disc brakes probably work fine. But if you like canyon driving, or if you are going to use your car for track or autocross racing, you may want to make an improvement. The original brakes heat up on the track or on the street under hard use such as high-speed curvy canyon driving, and the brakes start to fade quickly.

Brake Sources

Today there are several aftermarket companies making high-performance brakes that are designed for hard use and racing-style applications, including Stainless Steel Brakes Corporation, Baer, and Wilwood Engineering. Also, they all make sure their brakes are attractive for show use.

Stainless Steel Brakes Corporation

As a family-owned business, Stainless Steel Brakes Corporation (SSBC) first pioneered the stainless-steel-sleeved caliper for classic Corvettes and Mustangs in 1975. The company has expanded its facilities and continues to set the industry standard for high-quality brake systems and components. It offers a complete line of disc brake conversions and performance brake upgrades for classic muscle cars, late-model performance vehicles, street rods and customs, trucks, SUVs, and sport compacts.

At SSBC, braking is all it does. The company continues to improve its capabilities. Some recent steps include successfully passing an ISO 9001, utilizing state-of-the-art CAD, using FEA software, and installing a coordinate measuring machine (CMM) to measure product tolerances.

In addition, the company has invested in a cutting-edge CNC bridge-and-rail system that utilizes plasma/oxy-fuel sources to mass-produce various brake components to precise standards. These improvements give the company design, testing, quality, and manufacturing capabilities that very few aftermarket companies can match.

SSBC's signature line of aluminum calipers was first introduced in the late 1990s. These lightweight calipers greatly reduce unsprung weight, which improves handling and ride quality. Most are available polished, and all can be powder-coated a variety of colors for added visual appeal. They are available in both front and rear kits and come in single-, two-, four-, six-, and eight-piston configurations.

Baer Brake Systems

In the late 1980s Hal Baer was involved with the road-racing scene as a driver and later as a team manager. In 1993 Baer Brake Systems was started with Hal's brake knowledge, Robert Sommers' financial backing and the late Todd Gartshore's marketing skills. As the team started making brake systems for several popular cars the business grew. Today Baer makes a wide variety of brake systems for everything from early street rods to brand-new Camaros and everything in between. Baer specializes in upgraded brakes for many GM, Ford, and Chrysler vehicles, and that includes second-generation Camaros and Firebirds. Baer also works closely with companies that build chassis upgrades, and many of the elite companies use Baer brakes as their standard choice.

Baer has developed a large variety of caliper and rotor choices in several different price ranges. All of the brakes the company produces are installed, tested, and improved upon before they are released to the public. Enthusiasts who purchase the brakes are always pleased with their fantastic stopping ability.

Baer brakes have been very successful on the track and on the street and have earned a reputation for being the best aftermarket brakes available. The company makes brake improvement kits in several price ranges, but they all work much better than the original brakes they replace.

Baer is one of the most popular aftermarket brake companies because it produces high-quality disc brakes for an affordable price. Many enthusiasts think it produces the best aftermarket brakes, and some of the aftermarket suspension manufacturers agree. Detroit Speed uses Baer brakes on many of their suspension systems.

In Chapter 11, a Baer rear brake is installed on a 1970 Z28 Camaro, which is equipped with a Detroit Speed rear suspension system. This kit works on almost any Ford 9-inch axle housing, but check with Baer to determine the best kit for your particular application. Baer specializes in large, powerful brake systems for a variety of muscle cars, including Pro Touring cars and street machines, even those still equipped with their original rear axle housing. These brake kits with 13- and 14-inch rotors require 17-inch-and-larger wheels. You can check with Baer to source kits that may work with smaller wheel sizes.

Wilwood Engineering

Wilwood started building racing brake systems for NASCAR race cars and branched out to cover a wide variety of other racing endeavors. Wilwood saw the need for street rod brakes and is currently the leader in the field. Wilwood also saw the need for improved brakes for 1960s muscle cars so it started offering brake improvement kits. The company offers improved brakes for Corvettes and has also expanded to offer improved brakes for second-generation Camaros and Firebirds. Wilwood has brake kits ranging from a basic caliper replacement kit all the way up to large-rotor-diameter kits that are a favorite of Pro Touring and road race enthusiasts.

All of the second-generation Camaro and Firebird kits are available in the standard black finish, or the kits can be upgraded to include red calipers, which look nice when large-diameter wheels with big windows are used.

Project 1: Front Brake and Shock Installation

When I was building this 1978 Trans Am, I installed an SSBC front brake improvement kit that is a complete, easy-to-install, bolt-on installation. The kit features drilled-and-slotted rotors and aluminum two-piston calipers that can be used with original Firebird spindles and brackets. This kit is lightweight and gives the car improved stopping ability and better handling.

CHAPTER 12

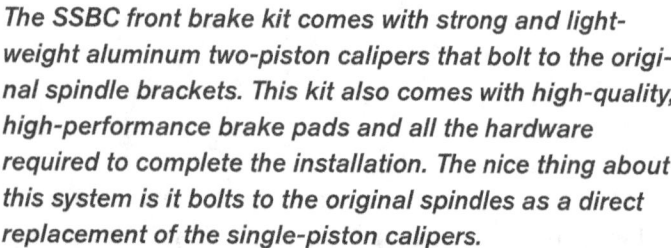

The SSBC front brake kit comes with strong and lightweight aluminum two-piston calipers that bolt to the original spindle brackets. This kit also comes with high-quality, high-performance brake pads and all the hardware required to complete the installation. The nice thing about this system is it bolts to the original spindles as a direct replacement of the single-piston calipers.

This car was upgraded with top-quality SSBC drilled-and-slotted rotors that are designed for use with the original-style bearings. The bearings and dust caps are ordered separately and are available from SSBC or you can purchase them from your local auto parts store. They are the same ones used for the original rotors.

Here are the old front brakes. This entire front suspension required restoration before new brakes could be installed.

This car was equipped with the original single-piston GM calipers and the original brake hoses. The parts were delivered to the sandblaster to strip everything to bare metal, and then they were all painted the appropriate colors to keep them from rusting. Many parts were painted cast-iron gray to match the factory color. Other parts were painted semi-gloss black for a clean look.

Select Bearings and Seals

1 Use new bearings and new grease seals with the rotors. The nice feature of this kit is if you need to repair the car for any reason the parts are readily available. No special parts are required.

Pack Bearings with Grease

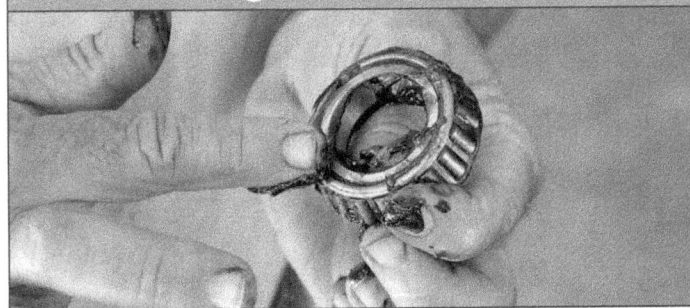

2 It is important to pack the bearings with high-quality grease, such as Sta-Lube Hi-Temp Disc Brake Bearing Grease. Many different wheel bearing greases are available, but make sure you buy the correct one for your car. Pack the large inner bearing with grease prior to installation. Do this by hand, as seen here, or purchase a special grease-packing tool from your local parts store or restoration supplier.

Install Races and Bearing

3 Install the races on the disc brake rotors and install the bearing after you pack it with grease. The NAPA bearings work perfectly with the SSBC-supplied races.

Install Grease Seal

4 After the large inner bearing is resting in the race, install the grease seal on the rotor. Place the seal in the opening, put a round shaft of aluminum over the bearing, and tap it in with a hammer. There are special tools for seal installation that are available from your parts supplier or restoration shop.

Clean Spindle

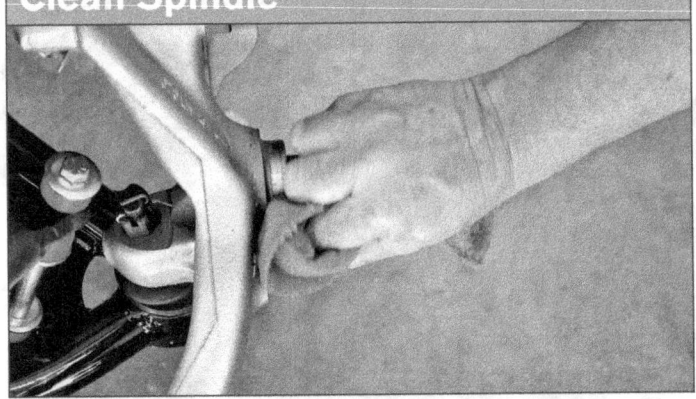

5 Before the rotor is installed, clean the spindle with a rag soaked with lacquer thinner to remove any debris or paint overspray. A small layer of paint could inhibit the installation of the tight-fitting bearings. Metal debris could damage the bearings.

Install Rotor

6 Place the rotor on the spindle and install the large castle nut as seen here. The nut must be snug, but not over-tight, because that can cause premature bearing failure. After the nut is snug, use a cotter key to keep it from backing off.

Install First Brake Pad

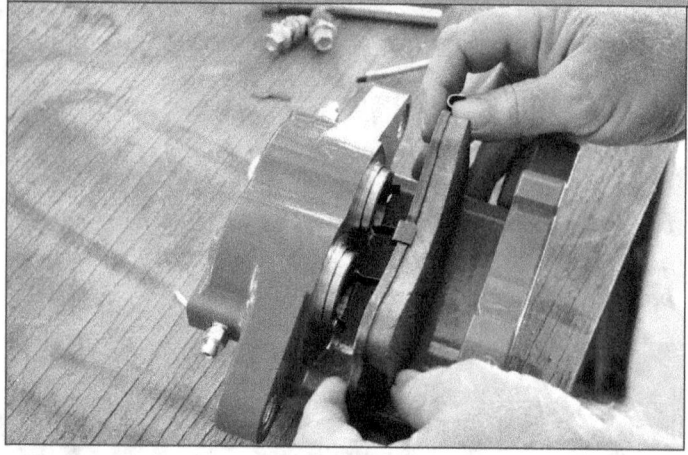

7 Outfit the piston-side brake pad with a pad clip. These high-performance pads were supplied by Stainless Steel Brakes Corporation, but if new pads are needed you can buy them from the original supplier or purchase similar pads from your local auto parts store because they are the same design as the ones used in single-caliper GM units.

Adjust Spring Tabs

Install Second Brake Pad

8 The rear brake pad is held in place with two spring tabs that connect to the caliper. Some adjustment may need to be made to the tabs for the pad to sit properly. You can bend them just a little to get them to work better.

9 Install the other brake pad in the caliper prior to installing it to the spindle bracket.

Install Caliper

10 Carefully place the caliper over the rotor and line it up with the holes in the bracket. Install and tighten the bolts using an Allen socket and wrench (left).

Here is the caliper after it was installed over the rotor (right). I outfitted the car with a bright red, powdercoated, two-piston caliper. This caliper looks nice against the black and cast-iron gray parts. Here you notice that the car features upper and lower A-arms that also allow the car to handle better.

PERFORMANCE BRAKES

Inspect Brake Hose

11 The brake hose has a banjo-style fitting that is used with two brass washers for sealing. Here is the hose and the bolt prior to installation. The brass crush washers are used for sealing.

Connect Hose to Caliper

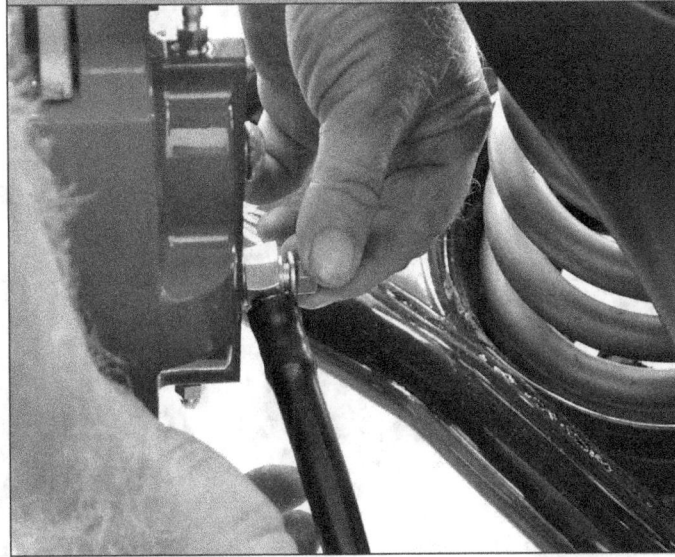

12 Connect the hose to the caliper and install it finger tight. Position the hose to make it a direct fit to the chassis-mounted steel brake lines.

Connect Hose to Frame

13 Connect the other end of the hose to the bracket on the frame with a spring clip. Tighten the nut in the caliper. Tighten all brake lines to avoid leaks.

Here is the finished drilled-and-slotted rotor and bright red, two-piston caliper. This brake system not only works superior to the old system it also looks terrific.

Install Shocks

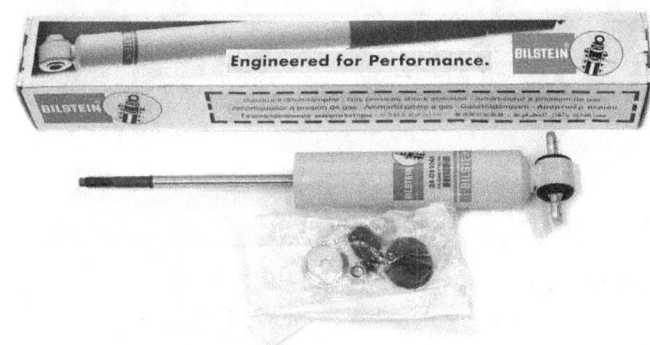

14 Along with the highly improved front brakes, I installed the new Bilstein shock absorbers. The shocks are top quality and used with the Heidts A-arms. They really improve the handling ability of this suspension system.

CAMARO & FIREBIRD PERFORMANCE PROJECTS: 1970–1981

Install Shocks (Continued)

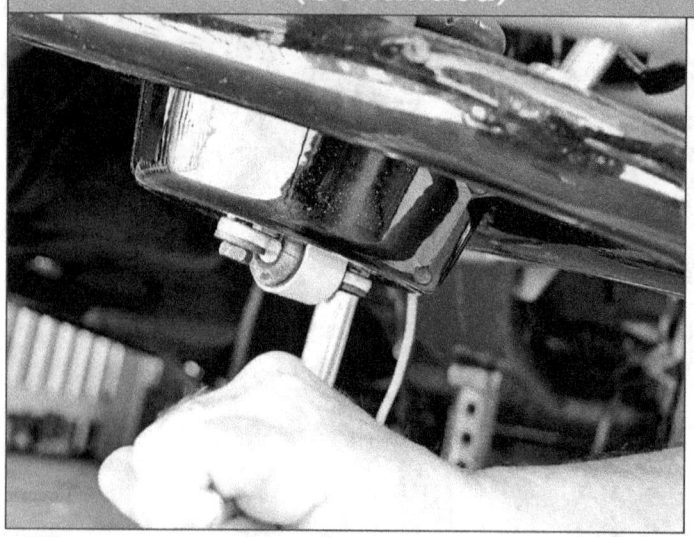

15 Place the shock up through the hole in the lower A-arm assembly and line up the upper portion with the shock hole in the frame. Before the shock is installed, be sure it is outfitted with the large washer and rubber cushions.

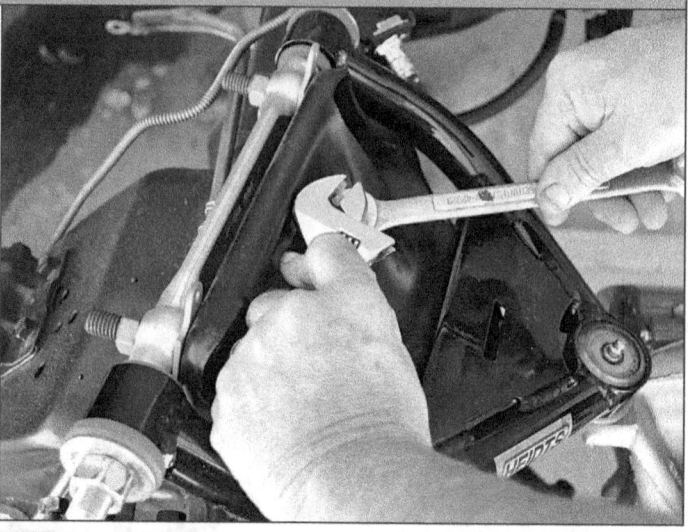

16 Install the other cushion on the shock, along with the smaller washer and then the locknut. Tighten with an open-end wrench and a small Crescent wrench to secure the shock shaft. Another small nut came with the shock, and it is used as a jamb nut.

Here is the complete front suspension with the Heidts tubular A-arms, Energy Suspension bushings and dust caps, Stainless Steel Brakes Corporation disc brake system, and Bilstein shock absorbers. With all of these suspension improvements this car will be fun to drive.

Project 2: Drum to Disc Brake Conversion

Here, the rear drum brakes are upgraded with SSBC's rear brake improvement kit that features drilled-and-slotted rotors, hydro-mechanical calipers that improve clamping force, and a built-in parking brake mechanism. This kit is lightweight and gives the car improved stopping ability and better handling.

PERFORMANCE BRAKES

The car is going to be outfitted with an A125-30R rear disc brake kit that includes drilled-and-slotted rotors, hydro-mechanical red calipers, caliper brackets, and all hardware required to make the conversion. This conversion features large calipers, so 16-inch-or-larger brakes are required; however, the calipers work with some 15-inch wheels with minor modifications.

Before the SSBC rear brake and Bilstein shock installation was completed, the axle housing, rear springs, and undercarriage were restored. The parts were removed and taken to the sandblaster where they were returned to bare metal. New Eaton springs were installed and the axle housing was painted semi-gloss black. All the small parts were restored for a nice finish and attractive appearance. This 1978 Trans Am was originally equipped with rear drum brakes.

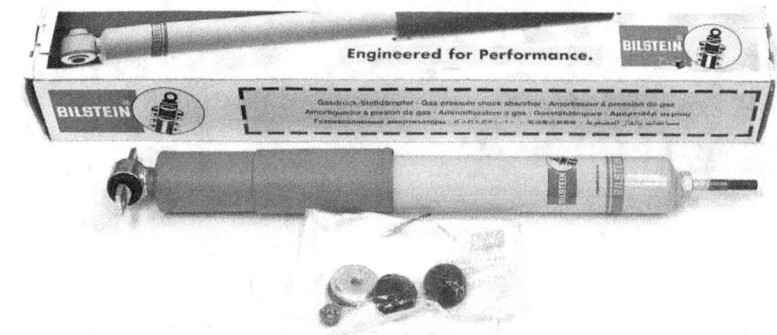

While performing the brake installation I also chose to install the Bilstein shocks to make sure I had the caliper-to-shock clearance required. This car was outfitted with staggered shocks so the calipers also had to be staggered, which looks different but works fine.

Remove Brake Drums

1 To start the installation, remove the brake drums. First turn the lower spanner to back off the linings because they might be too tight to release the drums. If the car has been sitting for some time, the linings may not back off, so spray them with penetrating oil to free them up. Let the oil soak in and eventually the drums release.

If it's been years since the drums have been removed, they will likely be stubborn and difficult to free from the hub. Use a hammer to send a sharp blow through the drum brake cover, but be sure to stay away from the wheel studs because you don't want to damage the threads. Some drum brake housings have two bolt holes; a wrench and 8x1.25 bolts can be used to drive bolts down onto the wheel hub to force the cover off the hub. In this case, the brake drum was in good condition, not old and rusted, so it came off smoothly. Although the original drum brakes worked well, disc brakes will make a big difference in this car's stopping ability.

CHAPTER 12

Remove Axle C-Clips

2 In order to install the disc brake brackets, the axles have to be removed. Place a drop pan under the axle housing. Remove the drain plug and allow the fluid to drain into the pan. Use a socket and ratchet to remove the 10 or 12 bolts on the differential cover. Remove the large pinion shaft pin to gain access to the C-clips that hold the axles in place. Turn the axle shafts until the carrier is in the correct position, the shaft pointing down.

Use a 1/4-inch socket to remove the pinion shaft lock bolt; the pin simply falls out. Do not move the axles at this point because the spider gears can fall out and need to be re-installed. Use a block of wood to push in both axle hubs as far as possible so the C-clips become accessible. Pull the C-clips out with a needle-nose pliers. After the C-clips are removed the axles slide right out. If they don't, use a slide-hammer-style axle puller.

Remove Axle Shafts

3 After disconnecting the C-clips, remove the axles from the axle housing. Be sure to mark which axle goes with a particular housing so you don't mix them up when they are re-installed. There may be a small length difference between them.

Remove Backing Plate

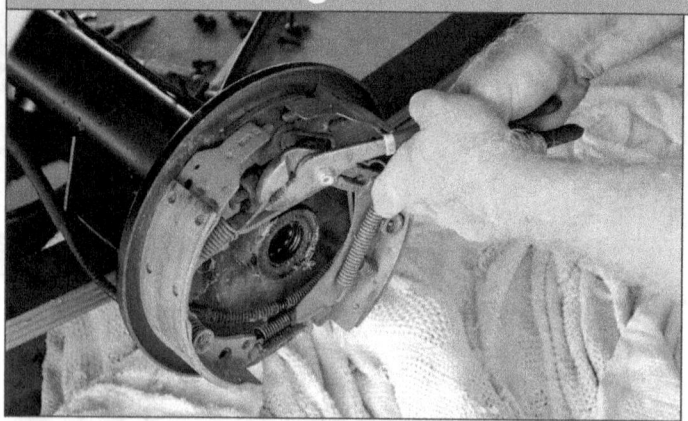 

4 In order to access the backing plate bolts, use a spring hook tool or locking pliers to stretch the brake springs and disconnect them to remove the brake shoes. Using a brake spring hook tool or Vise-Grips, remove the large springs from the assembly. Be careful, because the springs are tight. Use the spring hook tool to disconnect the two retainer springs. Remove the shoe assembly from the backing plate. Use a socket wrench with 9/16-inch socket to remove the four backing plate bolts. Lift the backing plate off the axle housing.

Remove Old Seals

5 Clean the axle housing end using a wire wheel and solvent.

6 Drill two holes so that a slide hammer can be used to pull the seals out of the axle. They may be tight, so spray the circumference of the bearing with penetrating oil to loosen the bearing.

7 Insert a screw into the seal and attach it to the slide hammer. Slide the handle back and forth and tug the seal out of the axle housing. Remove the bearing by sliding the weight back. Alternate the slide hammer from one side to the other so the seal comes out straight.

Install Bearings and Seal

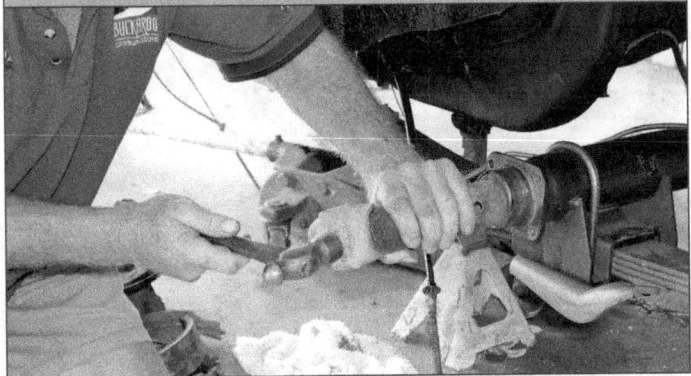

8 After inspection, this bearing was not excessively worn and was in good condition. So it was packed with grease, and then the new seal was installed. However, I recommend playing it safe and always replacing the bearings.

Place the seal on the lip of the axle housing. Use a socket or a used bearing that has a slightly larger diameter. Tap the seal with a hammer to make sure the seal is seated evenly around the bearing into the axle, and make sure it isn't skewed while tapping it into place.

Install Shock

9 Line up the shock absorber eye loop with the upper mount and feed the mount bolt through the bracket and eye loop. Then direct the bottom mount stud through the spring plate and secure it with a nut.

Install Caliper Mounting Bracket

10 The brake caliper needs to face forward. Use a box-end wrench to hold the nuts on the back of the bracket and use a torque wrench to torque the bolts to 65 ft-lbs. Once installed, it became obvious that the spring would interfere with the caliper mounting bolt. Since this kit didn't come with detailed instructions part of the installation had to be trial and error.

11 Adjust the axle housing bracket and angle it up slightly for the other mounting holes. By re-adjusting the bracket the spring does not come in contact with the bracket. Using the torque specifications in the instructions, tighten the bolts accordingly. Reinstall the axle by reversing the procedure used to remove it (Steps 2 and 3 on page 128).

Install Disc Brake Rotor

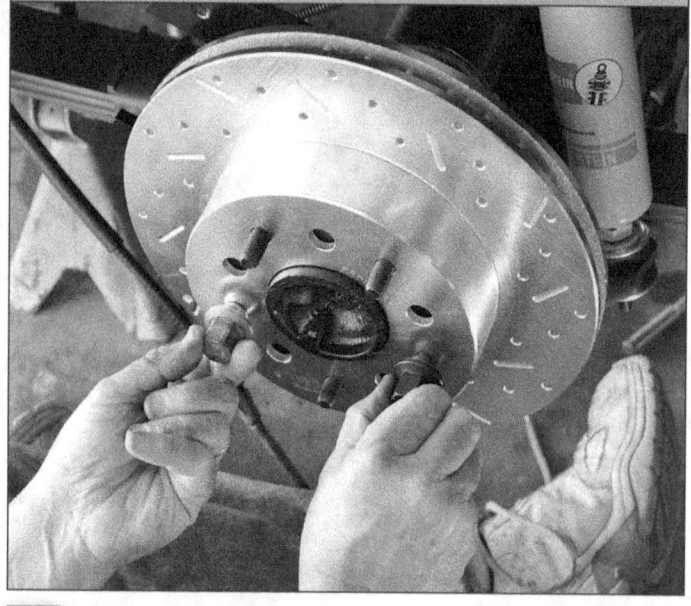

12 Fit the wheel studs in the rotor. Then install and secure the bracket. Torque the two lug nuts to secure the drilled-and-slotted disc brake rotor into the proper position.

Install Disc Brake Caliper

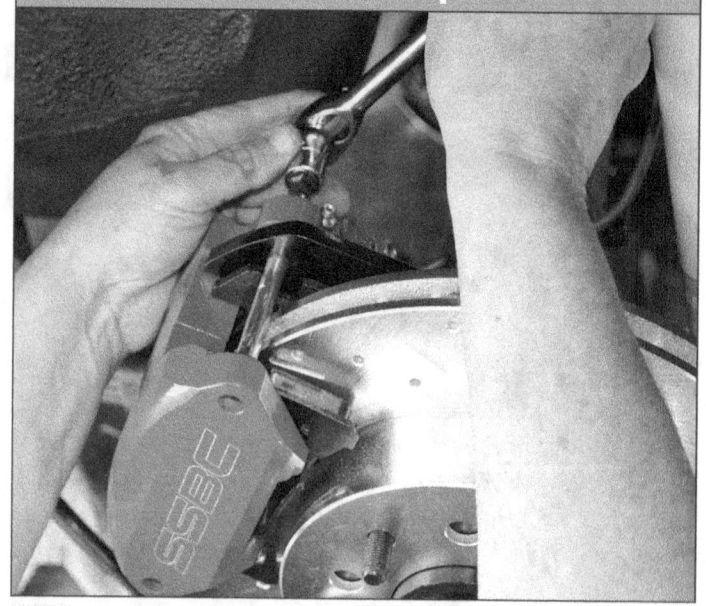

13 Place the caliper over the rotor, line up the mounting holes with the bracket, and tighten the bolts using a socket wrench with an Allen-head socket. Make sure the caliper is centered over the rotor.

PERFORMANCE BRAKES

The dual-piston SSBC caliper and drilled-and-slotted rotor deliver a huge improvement in braking performance and safety. This brake uses hydraulic pressure for braking and mechanical activation for the parking brake (aftermarket brake cables need to be installed to activate the parking brake).

Install Brake Lines

14 The braided stainless-steel brake lines attach to the hard lines installed on the axle housing. Once the OEM rubber brake lines have been removed, the system is open and air enters the system. Therefore, the new brake lines must be properly bled to correctly and safely operate.

Mock up the brake line path to the caliper and make sure that the brake line is long enough for the entire range of travel. In addition, make sure the brake hose does not come in contact with any suspension part; any contact could cause damage and eventual brake loss.

Fasten the brake hose to the caliper and connect the other end to the original brake line as seen here. If the brake lines need to be shortened, use a brake line cutter and crimper. Install the copper washers between the caliper and the banjo bolt. The banjo bolt slips through the brake line end. Use the brake line wrenches to properly fasten the banjo bolts and to prevent over torqueing.

Correctly Orient Brake Calipers

15 Since this car is equipped with staggered shocks, the passenger-side caliper is positioned behind the shock absorber. Position the driver-side caliper on the front side. This is a little weird but you can only see one rear caliper at a time.

Here is the finished SSBC brake installation, the Bilstein shock absorber, and the restored undercarriage, all ready for action. The rear calipers are large so they require a 16-inch-or-larger wheel.

CHAPTER 13

COOLING SYSTEM

A high-horsepower engine needs a high-performance cooling system to match it. A stock radiator with a cooper core was commonly fitted to most muscle cars of the 1960s and 1970s. While these radiators performed capably for muscle cars at stock horsepower levels, they were heavy and inefficient compared to the high-grade aluminum radiators of today that often provide far superior cooling.

Many stock engines produce between 300 and 400 hp, but many high-performance street engines these days produce 500 to 700 hp. This is a significant increase in horsepower, which means a dramatic increase in heat production. If you've invested thousands of dollars in a high-performance engine buildup or have swapped in a cam, heads, and intake, you need to protect your investment. And to do that you need a cooling system: radiator, fan, shroud, water pump, and other accessories.

The radiator's cooling capacity, the water pump's flow rate, and the electric fan's airflow capacity are the three most important components of the cooling system. First, the larger the volume of water flowing through the system, the more cooling capability the system has. Second, the surface area of the radiator needs to be larger or of better material (e.g., aluminum) to have a better cooling rate. Third, a more efficient fan, such as a dual electric version, to stream air across the radiator's fins is another crucial element for cooling.

How many times have you seen a Pro Touring car or street machine cruise into a car show with steam coming from the engine compartment and a big green puddle underneath when it stops? I've seen many, and sometimes several in one show from a variety of cars. To avoid that situation, an engine must remain in the desired temperature range under all conditions. For example, the cooling system should be able to keep the engine at the correct operating

This 1970 Camaro was built as an ultimate show machine, so the small-block Chevy engine has been detailed to perfection. The car features an aluminum radiator, a high-end flex fan, and a custom radiator hose.

COOLING SYSTEM

temperature in the winter months when the temperature can drop below zero in many parts of the country. The car should also be able to maintain an operating temperature in bumper-to-bumper traffic or on the highway when you are cruising at 70 mph or more.

In the end, remember that investing in good-quality parts is the key to having an efficient cooling system.

Radiator

Heat transfer is created when air flows through the radiator. When the air flows through, it has to escape from the engine compartment. If the air can't escape, an air bubble forms inside the engine compartment and keeps air from flowing through the radiator, and no airflow means no cooling. This became a common problem with the smoothie street rods that eliminated louvers in the hood. The Ford factory installed the louvers in the hood to let the hot air escape. It was critical for Ford trucks, which worked harder than a car, to have more and larger louvers in the hood. If you are building a Pro Touring car and you are modifying the engine compartment it's important to keep airflow in mind.

When you look under the hood of your new car, you may be surprised at the size of your radiator. In many cases it's much smaller than you would have imagined. Cost is one big factor. Weight is another factor that is considered because less weight translates to better fuel economy. That is why many radiators being used in new cars feature an aluminum core with plastic tanks.

If you are building a high-performance street car, Pro Touring car, street machine, or street/strip car, you have many cooling options. You can use an aftermarket aluminum radiator, electric water pumps, electric fans, and more. If you are restoring a muscle car to original condition or concours standards, you need a stock or stock-appearing radiator, and that limits your cooling options and capacity. You could be faced with installing an OEM-type copper and brass radiator, but that's not a bad thing because some of the high-density cores are very efficient.

Size is Important

In general, if you have a radiator that is designed for your engine size and a strong fan that can draw plenty of air through it, you should be fine. "Should" is the key word because keeping you car cool can be more difficult than it seems. You need to be sure the cooling system is in optimal operating condition. Unidentified problems can hinder a cooling system. Blocked water passages, low-performance water pumps, thermostats that don't work properly, fans that don't work properly, and many other possible problems can reduce the system's cooling ability.

If your car runs at the correct temperature on the highway at typical road speeds, the radiator size

Radiator Design Evolution

In 1970, General Motors released a cross-flow, saddle-mount radiator on the second-generation Firebird and Camaro. This was a big step up from the down-flow radiators used on some of the earlier Chevelles and LeMans sedans. These cross-flow radiators were used from 1970 to 1981 on F-Bodies and almost every other car of the era with copper-brass construction. These radiators dissipated heat well and could be manufactured and repaired easily, but this material was also somewhat heavy. Manufacturers discovered that adding more tubing provided greater surface area and, thus, increased cooling capacity in a high-density core.

Aluminum radiators gained prominence and displaced the copper/brass radiators in the industry for two basic reasons. First, they were light, and all of the auto manufacturers were trying to find ways of making the cars lighter. The aluminum-and-plastic radiators were about 1/3 the weight of copper/brass radiators. Second, the lower cost of aluminum/plastic radiators made economic sense.

These days, most cars on the road are equipped with aluminum radiators. Big-block and small-block cars were fitted with a 26 3/8-inch core. Aluminum radiators are available in two-, three-, and four-core models for the second-generation Camaro and Firebird.

For the ultimate in cooling and the highest horsepower engines you should use a four-core aluminum radiator. AFCO makes a four-core, direct-fit radiator that measures 31 1/4 by 17 3/4 inches and does not require any fabrication work to make it fit. It accepts the factory fan but in most cases owners opt for the aftermarket electric fan. It is brazed and TIG welded, as well.

is adequate for the engine size. If that same car gets hot when it is in bumper-to-bumper traffic, the fan is not drawing enough air through the radiator at low speeds or at idle. If the car runs hot on the highway but runs cool at low speed, the water pump may be running too fast, so the coolant is running through the radiator too quickly to allow enough time for the transfer process to work properly.

If the engine runs hot all of the time, the radiator may not be adequate or there is a blockage in the engine. In the case of some engines, such as a Pontiac, the aluminum pump housing and metal plate may have deteriorated and coolant isn't being circulated correctly. A failing thermostat could also cause an engine to run hot all of the time.

Engine Overheating

Engine tuning is another factor. If an engine is running lean, it runs hotter than one with the correct air/fuel ratio. This may not sound like a problem, but think of a cutting torch. After you have your oxygen and acetylene adjusted correctly, all it takes is additional oxygen to get the flame hot enough to cut metal. This same principal happens inside the cylinders, but fortunately it's not hot enough to melt metal.

The most common problem seen in Pro Touring cars and street machines is overheating at slow speeds and in bumper-to-bumper traffic.

The more exotic the engine is, the more problems you may have in keeping it at the correct operating temperature. Most newer cars have high-tech aluminum radiators and electric fans to keep them cool so you should engineer your specialty car with a similar system. The fans used by manufacturers today are generally top quality with the correct number of blades, a large motor, and a temperature-sensing unit in the radiator, which turns the fan on when it is necessary and off when the car is running at or below the normal operating temperature.

Modern cars are computer controlled and they have to run hotter for cleaner emissions, so that makes it even more difficult to keep the engine running at the correct temperature. This doesn't seem to be too difficult, but you may purchase an aftermarket fan that doesn't work as well as the factory unit or a radiator that doesn't have the same cooling capacity. If you plan to install a new Corvette LS engine in your specialty car, for example, make sure you study the source car to make sure you have the same or better parts in your car.

A second-generation F-Body car producing more than 450 hp should be equipped with a larger, 26-inch radiator. Otherwise, you could be faced with a hot-running engine and potential engine damage. Typically, you should have 1 square inch of cooling surface area for each horsepower produced. Therefore, a 450-hp engine should have a radiator with 450 square inches of radiator surface. Even with the 26-inch width, a height of 17 inches limits the total surface area to just 442 square inches. For most high-performance vehicles, this should provide enough cooling capacity, except for the hottest days under a heavy load.

When a Pro Touring car or street machine is having a cooling problem the first thing the driver blames is the radiator. If you are trying to use a stock radiator to cool a larger displacement engine it certainly could be the culprit. I've seen people try to cool a high-horsepower Chevy 350- or 383-ci V-8 with a radiator designed for a stock 307-ci Chevy engine only to have cooling problems. If you have a radiator with a core designed to handle the engine size and horsepower output, it's probably not the radiator.

If you are into traditional cars and you plan to install a small-block Chevy engine, there are additional things to think about. For example, if you are using a new crate engine you should have no internal problems, so cooling should be straightforward. If you are going to rebuild a wrecking yard engine, or you buy one from a rebuilding source, make sure you use top-quality shops that thoroughly clean the engine block. In many cases it is a good idea to take the engine block to a professional stripping shop that has a de-rusting tank so that all of the internal passages are free from rust blockage.

Airflow

Another thing to think about is the type of fan belts you are using. If you are using standard belts the installation of the water pump and accessories is straightforward. If you are equipping your engine with a serpentine belt system there are a few things to keep in mind. First, a serpentine-equipped engine generally powers the water pump and fan in a counterclockwise rotation instead of clockwise as with standard belts. This means that the water pump should be designed to work in a counterclockwise direction.

The impeller inside the water pump is a superior design. If the serpentine engine is outfitted with a fan it also must be designed to draw air through the radiator, so you have to buy one with a reverse pitch. If you install the wrong water pump or the

COOLING SYSTEM

wrong fan you will have a car that runs hot or overheats even in typical weather conditions.

Remember that when a radiator is working properly the air has to flow unrestricted through the radiator so that the heat transfer can be completed properly. That shouldn't be a problem in a stock second-generation Camaro or Firebird, but it could be if the engine compartment was modified in a way that restricts the air.

I have seen cars that were modified in a way that keeps the air from flowing rapidly through the radiator and an air bubble gets trapped in the engine compartment. You can't see it but if an air bubble is in your engine compartment no more air can enter the compartment, and that eliminates the possibility of air flowing through the radiator, so the heat transfer does not work properly.

If you modified your engine compartment and the car is overheating you can test the theory by removing the hood and driving the car to see if the cooling starts working properly. If it does, some changes have to be made to eliminate the problem. This is more likely to happen with a mechanical fan.

Transmission Cooler and Overflow Tank

Many radiators are available with a built-in transmission cooler, which may be fine for some cars with large cross-flow radiators. Most muscle cars used this system and were able to cool efficiently.

If you are building a Pro Touring car with a smaller radiator I recommend ordering a radiator that doesn't have a built-in transmission cooler so it doesn't have to work harder than necessary to keep the engine temperature down. I recommend using a remote transmission cooler. I generally use a B&M transmission cooler because the units are small and easy to install and the polished units are an attractive addition.

I also recommend installing an overflow tank so that your coolant doesn't escape. If the car runs warm, the overflow catches the coolant, and when it cools off, it returns to the radiator.

Radiator Sources

Several top manufacturers make high-performance radiators for high-performance muscle cars, such as Walker Radiator Works, U.S. Radiator, Brassworks, Mattson's, and many more.

If you are working on a street machine, a muscle car, or a Pro Touring car there are many top-quality companies making radiators, and there are local radiator shops that are able to rework your stock radiator to the way it came from the factory or improve it with a more efficient core. Think about it, if you install a big-block Chevy engine in a Camaro that was originally equipped with a 307-ci engine, that radiator needs major improvement.

Core Size

When I order a radiator for a car I generally order one that has a larger core than what is really needed. You will run into problems with over-carburetion and camshafts that are too large, but you will never have problems with a radiator that is larger than required. Car manufacturers use a radiator that is just large enough to do the job to save money, so some radiator engineers may not agree with radiator overkill. But I always increase the core size and have never had a cooling problem, even when the cooling system is a little weak in other areas.

Perhaps I should clarify this just a little, because cooling deals with air transfer. The radiator is filled with a coolant mixture that transfers the heated coolant to the tubes and fins. When the cool air flows through the radiator the outside air cools the fins and the tubes, and on the other side of the radiator you can feel the warm air escaping. The hot coolant should remain in the core long enough for this process to take place.

This is where overkill can become a problem because if you have a really thick core there is a chance that the air can't flow through it efficiently, so the heat transfer does not happen the way it should. The problem is compounded when you combine a thick core with an A/C condenser in front of it. The other problem is if there are too many tubes in a really thick core, the coolant flows through the radiator too quickly and does not cool completely. Most radiator shops are aware of these problems, so most limit the core size to five rows for extreme cases. Most engines only need a high-efficiency four-core style.

CHAPTER 13

U.S. Radiator manufactures a radiator where the coolant flows through the core three times before it exits the radiator. This design keeps the coolant in the radiator longer so the complete heat transfer occurs. This is also a good radiator to use when your engine is equipped with a very efficient water pump because it's almost impossible for the coolant to flow through the radiator too quickly.

Top-quality radiators are expensive but they are worth the price when you can drive anywhere without the worry of overheating. Other radiator manufacturers have their own designs that seem to work well, too, and some believe that aluminum radiators are the answer to the problem. Aluminum radiators work well to cool a car, and they are lightweight, which also helps handling.

If you are working on a Camaro or Firebird you have to clean or upgrade the radiator. This high-efficiency radiator built by Mark 7 Machine & Radiator looks like an original, but it is actually an aluminum radiator that is anodized black to look like the factory radiator.

If you want to maximize your radiator's cooling ability it can be built without an internal transmission cooler. You can instead have a separate transmission cooler located under your car.

This dual-fan unit with a built-in shroud can be adapted to a large crossflow radiator and provides plenty of cooling at low and high speeds.

Water Pump

Another important cooling component is the water pump. It's the heartbeat of the engine that keeps the coolant flowing, and if it isn't working properly an overheating problem can occur. If you are building an engine to install in your second-generation F-Body, make sure you use a high-quality pump that flows a high volume of coolant. If you are using one of the newer engines you have no choice; you have to use the original-equipment pump that was designed for the engine.

Several excellent water pumps are on the market today, including the aluminum FlowKooler by Weiand. It is made of cast aluminum, CNC machined, and features a six-blade impeller. FlowKooler pumps are designed to push twice the coolant at idle and low RPM, and that makes the car run better in bumper-to-bumper traffic conditions. Weiand also makes a variety of top-quality water pumps for Chevrolet, Pontiac, and several other makes.

When car manufacturers were building cars in the early days one way of changing water pump performance was to use different-size pulleys. If a small-diameter water pump pulley is used with a large-diameter crank pulley the water pump turns faster, so changing the upper pulley diameter to a smaller or larger size can increase or decrease the water pump speed and, ultimately, output. The desired performance in a Pro Touring car engine is to have the pump turn fast enough to deliver plenty of coolant to the radiator but not so fast that the coolant runs through the radiator before the heat transfer is complete.

Serpentine belt systems present a problem because the water pump pulley spins counterclockwise, so you have to use a water pump that is designed for a serpentine belt. If you install a serpentine belt on a regular water pump it does not work properly when it turns backward and overheating occurs rapidly. When you purchase a serpentine belt system for your engine, check with the manufacturer for a water pump recommendation. Since serpentine belt systems have become popular with enthusiasts, most of the high-end pump manufacturers offer both clockwise and counterclockwise water pumps.

Electric Water Pump

There are several companies offering electric water pumps for small- and big-block Chevy engines. The pumps work well but they are primarily designed for drag race cars, not for street use. Most of the engine accessory bracket kits are designed to be used with mechanical pumps, so that is also a problem, along with the fact that a standard fan can't be used. They are great for a drag car because they are small and light.

Fans

Fans are one of the most important parts of the cooling system because their job is to keep the heat transfer operating properly when the car is in stop-and-go traffic. I started building street machines before electric fans were available, and the only thing you could use was an original fan or a flex fan. Today electric fans make cooling a little easier.

Mechanical or Electrical

If you have plenty of room and can use a large-diameter mechanical fan it should work well because that's what the car manufacturers used for years. Some cars don't have a lot of space under the hood or the engine sits low in the frame, so it makes more sense to use an electric fan that can be mounted in the middle of the radiator.

Unfortunately, the first aftermarket electric fans were a good idea that didn't work well. They were built with small motors that actually slowed down as they heated up so they weren't able to keep the radiator cool. Today small-motor fans are still being made, so if the price of the fan is really low, the quality is probably also low. Manufacturers realized the problem and now the motors are strong and do not slow down when the radiator heats up.

I have used both 16- and 17-inch fans with large motors on some street machines, and they work great. In fact, one of them is equipped with a 16-inch fan, and when the weather is at 100 degrees, the engine runs at just under 200 degrees all day long when the car is idling in the driveway.

Pusher or Puller

There are two types of fans: pusher and puller. A pusher fan is mounted on the front of the radiator, and it pushes air through the radiator to improve cooling. A puller fan is mounted behind the radiator, and it sucks air through the radiator just like a mechanical fan. A puller fan is actually more effective than a pusher.

When you buy a fan, make sure you talk to the manufacturer to verify that it works properly for the particular puller or pusher setup. Some really top-end fans, such as those by Flex-a-lite, are also equipped with built-in shrouds, and if you have room they really work great. Some Flex-a-lite fans have airflow rates that are double the airflow rate of many other electric fans. It is also a good idea to make sure the wires are connected properly because if you reverse the wires, in many instances it changes the direction of the fan, and that's not a good thing if it is turning in the opposite direction that is needed.

Some cars have room for two fans, a mechanical fan that draws air through the radiator and a pusher electric fan at the front of the radiator. I use a dual-fan system in three cars, and it works great in really hot California weather. Most of the time the mechanical fan is the only one used but there are times when a little more airflow is needed in low-speed applications.

Flex Type

You can find a good flex fan in most speed shops and regular auto part stores. You can also buy them from mail-order suppliers. Most are built with six blades and they generally work fine. Flex-a-lite makes a seven-blade fan that can be found through Walker Radiator Works if you can't find one locally. More blades mean more airflow, so use the largest fan that fits your application.

If you are looking for maximum cooling this aluminum radiator was outfitted with a pair of extremely strong fans. This one is designed for a Camaro/Firebird.

CHAPTER 13

If your Camaro or Firebird is equipped with a shroud it is a good idea to restore the unit and use it with your upgraded or new radiator. This one needed some minor repair work, and then it was painted semi-gloss black.

Remember, if you outfit your engine with a serpentine belt system your water pump pulley is turning counterclockwise, which means your fan is turning the same way. If you install a regular mechanical fan on your car with a serpentine belt it is turning in the wrong direction to be effective, so you have to find a reversed-pitch fan to cure the problem.

Shroud

If you are building a street machine or Pro Touring car most restoration companies sell reproduction shrouds for second-generation Camaros and Firebirds. If you can't find one for your car, or if you want something special, you can always have one fabricated by a good tin bender.

Thermostat

The thermostat is designed to get the engine up to the operating temperature and keep it there. It also slows the coolant circulation so it doesn't flow through the radiator too quickly. Thermostats are sold in a variety of heat ranges such as 160 and 195 degrees. Higher temperature thermostats are used in computer-controlled vehicles because a hot engine runs cleaner. A normal street machine with a carbureted engine generally runs a 160-degree thermostat but when that temperature approaches the 200-degree mark, rodders start to panic. A computer-controlled engine starts running well at the 200-degree mark, so rodders with new engines have to recondition their thinking. If you look at the temperature gauge in a new car the 200-degree mark is in middle of the gauge.

It is also possible to use a lower temperature thermostat in a computer-controlled vehicle to keep the temperature lower. Most of the companies that specialize in newer computer-controlled engines say that the engines work better at the higher temperatures. Alternatively, I have run a 1987 tuned port engine with a 160-degree thermostat with no problem at all. The engine ran at a constant 175 degrees in hot or cool weather, it had plenty of power, and I got 25 mpg.

Restrictor Plate

If you are not worried about your engine running at a constant temperature you can eliminate the thermostat and run a restrictor plate. This is a trial-and-error process to get the right one, but when you do the engine generally runs very cool and stays that way.

I have a restrictor plate in one of my street machines, and the car runs very cool all of the time. The only thing I have noticed is that when the outside temperature is cold, the engine temperature on the highway

Flex-a-lite makes several aftermarket radiators in a variety of sizes, so you are able to find one that fits into your engine compartment. This aluminum radiator is outfitted with a very strong fan with a built-in shroud.

runs at 120 degrees, which is very cool. Even when the weather warms up, the engine still runs at 150 to 160 degrees, and I generally drive the car on the highway with the electric fan turned off.

This system works great for a California car but I don't recommend it for a car in a much cooler climate. In most areas a thermostat warms the engine enough to run efficiently when it is very cold outside.

This restored Trans Am engine compartment is equipped with a Mark 7 aluminum radiator that works perfectly with the factory shroud and the original seven-blade declutching fan. The factory designed this system, so it should work even better with an aluminum radiator.

CHAPTER 14

WEIGHT-SAVING MEASURES

Removing weight from the car improves performance by following the laws of physics. If your engine is delivering a certain amount of horsepower, the car accelerates faster and has a higher top-end speed when weight is removed. In turn, this increases the power-to-weight ratio. This same principle applies to drag racing.

When Gasser drag racing was gaining popularity, many racers ditched their Buicks and Oldsmobiles and installed their engines in the lightest cars they could find, such as the early Willys, Anglias, Austins, and even Henry Js. All of the cars were small and light, and when you installed a strong engine they were fast. Racers wanted them even lighter, so companies started producing fiberglass fenders, hoods, and even doors, which eliminated a lot more weight, and the cars became even faster. Side glass was also replaced by lightweight plexiglass. On many of the early gassers the interior metal was also removed from the doors and rear quarters, and sometimes the floor was removed and replaced with sheet aluminum. The racers knew that every pound counted.

Another popular drag racing endeavor was Super Stock racing, which became very popular in 1961. In 1962, Chryslers, Plymouths, and Dodges were downsized and used unitized bodies, making them very lightweight. When Chrysler combined that strategy with its strong-running 413-ci engines the company became a force in Super Stock racing.

In an effort to be competitive Pontiac and Chevrolet had to make their cars lighter, so the factory started releasing aluminum fenders, bumpers, doors, and other parts on the cars they produced for their factory-backed racers. Pontiac lightened the frames under its cars by drilling holes in the frame, and they became known as Swiss cheese Pontiacs.

As proven in the past, removing heavy parts from a 1970–1981 Camaro or Firebird improves performance. There aren't many ways to remove weight from many of the early Camaros and Firebirds because they weren't necessarily loaded down with options. By the mid 1970s that changed, as the cars featured many options, because that's the way the dealers ordered them in an effort to make more money. And obviously,

In the 1950s, speed parts manufacturers started building intake manifolds and heads out of aluminum because it was lighter and easier to cast. The car manufacturers noticed what the aftermarket was doing, so they started experimenting with aluminum, and many of the early Corvette intakes were cast out of aluminum. Today custom intakes continue to be cast from aluminum, such as this Edelbrock aluminum high-rise intake.

from the increasing sales, the buyers liked them that way. The later cars also had more smog equipment to improve emissions, which also added weight.

Today, car designers and engineers know that reducing weight not only makes the car's power-to-weight ratio better, which improves performance, it also improves emissions because it takes less fuel to move the car down the road. If you are building a street driver, you can reduce the weight of the car and still meet the emissions standards. If you have an earlier car that doesn't have to conform to emissions laws, you have many more options for weight reduction.

Many aftermarket appearance items are also manufactured from aluminum. One example is finned aluminum valve covers, which are light but probably weigh about the same as sheet-steel covers.

Early racers found that losing weight helped the car go faster and handle better, so Edelbrock and other companies started manufacturing aluminum water pumps that weighed less than half of a cast-iron pump.

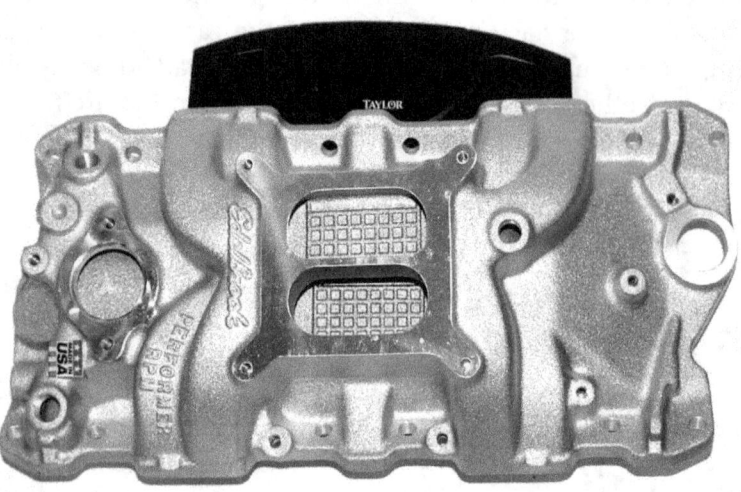

An aluminum intake weighs less than half as much as a comparable cast-iron intake. An aluminum manifold weighs about 17 pounds, and a comparable cast-iron unit weighs almost three times as much.

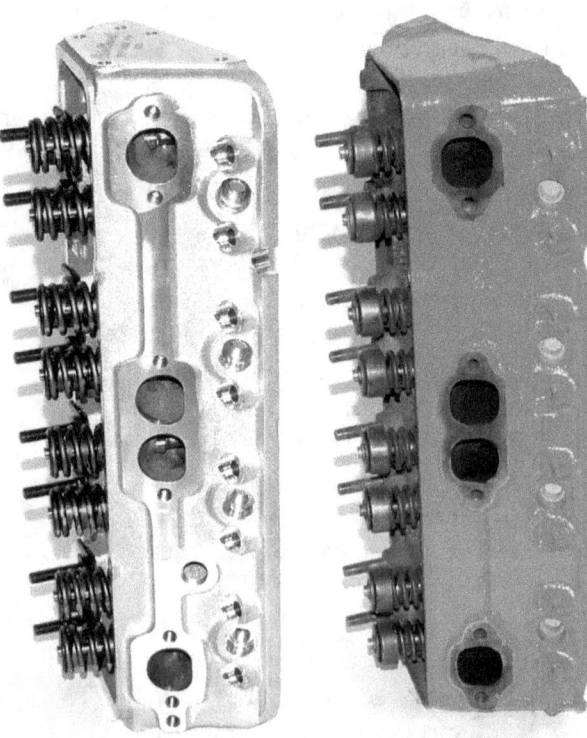

An Edelbrock head (shown) delivers more power than a performance steel Corvette head, plus it is lighter.

WEIGHT-SAVING MEASURES

Edelbrock manufactures AFB carburetors that are light and offer excellent performance. AFB stands for "aluminum four barrel."

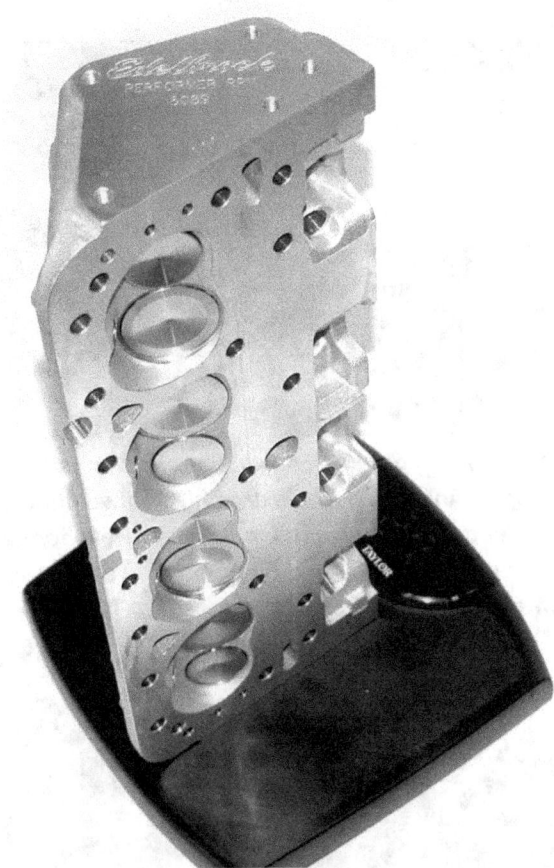

The steel head weighs 47½ pounds. The aluminum head weighs 27 pounds, so the weight savings of the head is 20½ pounds. With each weight-saving measure you will save significant weight, and it all adds up.

Stock hood hinges and springs are heavy, so the weight can be lowered by installing billet-aluminum hood hinges that are suspended by a small gas-charged shock. This is a case where every pound counts.

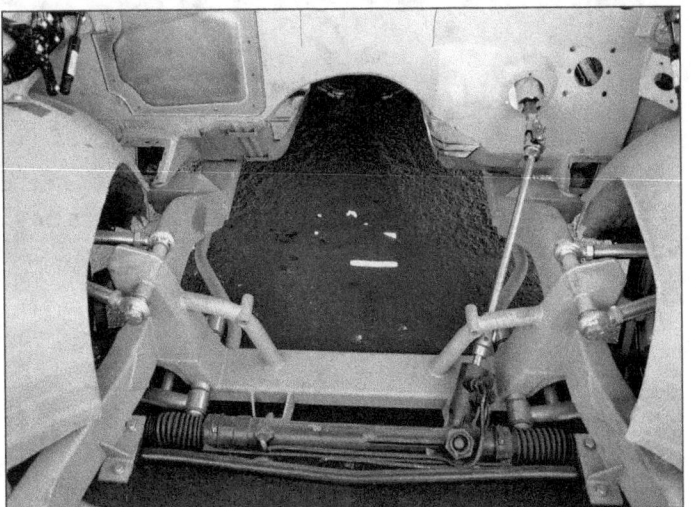

A variety of aftermarket companies manufacture front subframe kits for the 1970–1981 Camaros and Firebirds. This subframe features lightweight rectangular tubing, lightweight tubular A-arms, coil-over shocks, and a lightweight aluminum rack-and-pinion steering unit. All together, this subframe weighs less than half of the original.

CHAPTER 14

Fiberglass is light and carbon fiber is even lighter and stronger. Anvil produces extremely lightweight carbon-fiber fenders, hoods, and inner fender wells for second-generation Camaros and Firebirds. The carbon-fiber parts can eliminate hundreds of pounds.

The lightweight Camaro is powered by an all-aluminum, twin-turbocharged, small-block Chevy engine. This engine produces more than 800 hp, making it an awesome car to drive.

The original steel Camaro wheels are heavy, and can be replaced with super-lightweight, large-diameter wheels and tires as seen here. The wheels look terrific and also lower the weight of the car by a large margin.

Looking through the windows in the wheels, note the aluminum Baer racing brakes. They dramatically increase the stopping power of the car, plus the brakes are much lighter than stock units.

Here is an all-aluminum, small-block, 383-ci engine built to power a 1970 Camaro. This engine features an aluminum block, aluminum heads, an aluminum intake manifold, and a variety of other aluminum parts to effectively lower the weight of the engine.

142   CAMARO & FIREBIRD PERFORMANCE PROJECTS: 1970–1981

CHAPTER 15

WHEELS AND TIRES

Wheels and tires have come full circle since the early days. Some of the earliest cars and trucks were equipped with large woooden wheels and hard, solid-rubber tires. That turned out to be a bad idea because when the rubber tire was worn out the owner of the vehicle had to buy a new wheel and tire combination, which was very costly. In an effort to change that, early tire manufacturers came out with tube-type tires that could easily be replaced. Some of the early tires were white but they got dirty fast, so black tires started to appear, and some early companies started making whitewall tires.

General Motors used 14-inch wheels and tires on many of its standard cars and muscle cars in the 1960s. The performance models, such as the Z28 Camaro and Firebird Trans Am, were equipped with larger 15-inch wheels and the new 60-series

If you are doing a restoration or a resto-mod-styled Camaro or Firebird you may want reproduction tires. Many cars were originally equipped with blackwall tires such as this BFGoodrich bias-ply tire. Radials didn't come out until the mid 1970s.

If you wanted your tires to have a little flash you could order a set of narrow whitewall tires. Many Camaros and Firebirds were equipped with U.S. Royal Safety 200 whitewall tires. The tires are wrapped around custom, chrome-plated, steel wheels that are outfitted with the early-style rally cap.

Narrow-stripe tires in white, red, and gold were available for muscle cars. Shown here is a narrow whitewall, BFGoodrich radial tire wrapped around a custom chrome wheel with a late-style Chevy rally cap.

CAMARO & FIREBIRD PERFORMANCE PROJECTS: 1970–1981

CHAPTER 15

White-letter tires became popular in the early 1970s; one of the favorites was the Firestone Wide Oval tire. Wide Ovals were used by the factory on many Camaros and Firebirds.

If you want redline tires on your car, but want the nice ride quality of radial tires, you can outfit your car with BFGoodrich redline radial tires. These tires are wrapped around chrome wheels with early Chevy rally caps.

tires because they were wider and offered improved handling over the 14-inch, 70-series tires.

Throughout the late 1950s and early 1960s performance enthusiasts were installing custom wheels and tires on their cars. In the early 1960s, companies such as Halibrand, American Racing, Cragar, and Ansen were making custom wheels that became very popular. They offered wheels in 14- and 15-inch sizes and in various wheel widths to accept wide, custom tires.

Car manufacturers were aware of what enthusiasts were doing with wheels and tire combinations, so they started offering their own custom wheels in the form of rally wheels. Pontiac started by offering Rally I wheels in 1965, and they looked nice on the GTO models but many enthusiasts still wanted custom wheels. In 1967, Pontiac came out with Rally II wheels, and they had a more custom appearance and became a favorite of Pontiac buyers. Chevrolet also came out with its own rally wheel style, and it was popular, but enthusiasts still liked the custom wheels better.

As time went on, car manufacturers were designing nicer custom wheels, and they started competing with the designs. Pontiac was very successful with its honeycomb wheels and later snowflake wheels. Chevrolet also came out with several wheel designs with five-spoke rally wheels for the early Z28 Camaros and then other designs for the 1977- and-newer Z28 Camaros.

Handling became a focus of the 1970s Camaros and Firebirds, so both Chevrolet and Pontiac worked on improving the cars with wider wheels and performance tires. In 1973, Pontiac installed radial tires on its cars, and designers tuned the suspension to take advantage of the new tire technology.

When you look at the dash of a mid-1970s Trans Am you see a little badge that says "Radial Tuned Suspension." Enthusiasts wanted improved handling, so the factory responded with wider wheels. Through testing it found that larger diameter wheels with lower profile tires increased the handling ability of the Camaros and Firebirds. All of the second-generation Camaros and Firebirds were equipped with 15x7- or 15x8-inch aluminum wheels as an option. In the early 1980s Chevrolet released the IROC Camaros and Pontiac offered a GTA Trans Am, both equipped with 16-inch wheels running the new Goodyear Gatorback unidirectional tires. The Corvette was also equipped similarly. This was the start of the large-diameter wheel technology seen today.

Sidewall Flex

It is true that a car with large, wide wheels equipped with extremely low profile tires goes around corners better than a car with smaller wheels and higher profile tires because there is no sidewall flex. There are pros and cons to using large-diameter wheels. It all goes back to the early days when Ford started using tires with a larger sidewall.

Basically, cars that are equipped with large wheels and extremely low profile tires ride like those early cars with solid-rubber tires. A tire with some sidewall flex in an up-and-down direction softens the bumps in the road. The thing that happens when a car with low-profile tires hits a deep bump or rut in the road is that the small sidewall allows the rim to hit the rut with no cushion, and the result is a bent or broken wheel. I feel that it is important to have more sidewall for cushion than what some enthusiasts want. The handling difference is generally less than they expect, especially for those who are not professional drivers. In fact, a professional driver can generally compensate for the sidewall difference.

Today you can find a variety of 15-, 16-, 17-, 18-, 19-, 20-, 22-, and 24-inch wheels on the market. Just as many enthusiasts think bigger is better with cams and carburetors, they also think that bigger wheels must also be better, so they jack up their cars to be able to run 24-inch wheels and tires. The result is an unattractive car that really doesn't handle that well. When you jack up the car to install large-diameter wheels you effectively change the car's center of gravity, so the handling is compromised. Most second-generation Camaros and Firebirds look and work fine with 17-inch wheels, and I have seen some with highly modified chassis running 18-inch wheels. In general a second-generation Camaro or Firebird looks great with 17- or 18-inch wheels but starts to look like a Mattel Hot Wheels car with larger wheels. When large wheels are used the car should also have the right stance. Camaros and Firebirds look nice when they are lowered. In general the stance of any performance car, especially one that is designed for ultimate handling, looks better when lowered.

In keeping with street rod and even road racing standards cars can also look great with larger rear tires and smaller front tires. That has even been a consideration by factory engineers because the newer Corvettes use larger rear wheels and tires. Today's Corvettes are equipped with P245/40ZR18 front tires and P285/35ZR19 rear tires.

Wheel Design

Selecting a wheel design for your car is subjective. It has to please you, the owner, but it should also enhance the appearance of your car. The wheel you choose also has to go along with the style of the car you are building.

For instance, if you are going for a stock look you want to use nicely detailed original wheels and tires that were similar to what was used when the car was new. If you are

With the value of second-generation Camaros and Firebirds increasing, many enthusiasts want to restore the special models, such as this 1978 Gold Special Edition Trans Am. In this case it is beneficial to restore the original 15x8-inch snowflake wheels.

Here is a nice 1975 Camaro built as a mild street machine. It features custom billet wheels, and it is powered by a hot 350-ci engine.

building a wild Pro Touring car you probably want 17- or 18-inch wheels running low-profile tires. If you go bigger than that the wheels might look out of proportion for the size of the car. In general five-spoke wheels always look nice on a Camaro or Firebird, and there are literally dozens of those on the market.

If you are going for the stock look but want the car to look more modern, there are a few larger diameter, factory-appearing wheels that have been released by the aftermarket. Today you can get 1970 Z28 Rally wheels and snowflake wheels in 17-inch form. There are also 17-inch Rally II Pontiac wheels being made. These are options if you are building a mild Pro Touring or resto mod car.

This 1970 Z28 features a super-low stance due to a custom front and rear subframe installation. Check out the large-diameter wheels and extra-wide, low-profile tires. This is definitely a very nice Pro Touring car with fantastic handling ability.

Some enthusiasts like resto mod styling, and here's a really nice Firebird 400 running the original honeycomb 15x7-inch wheels and Goodyear Eagle tires. The car is running a hot 455-ci engine.

WHEELS AND TIRES

In 1970, Chevrolet released this unique five-spoke rally wheel, and it was very popular with enthusiasts. This restored wheel is used on a 1970 Z28 that is built in a resto mod style. The BFGoodrich tires are perfect for this car.

This Pro Touring car is running large-diameter wheels and low-profile tires. The black wheels are very popular with ultimate-handling enthusiasts.

Enthusiasts who want a modified car that resembles the original styling can improve a car with large-diameter wheels that look like the original Pontiac Rally II wheels. These were seen on a 1968 Firebird but they also work on a second-generation model.

CHAPTER 16

INTERIOR

If you are restoring or modifying a second-generation Camaro or Firebird the last part of the project is the interior. Depending on how you want to build your car you have many interior choices, from a completely restored appearance to a wild custom interior with racing-style seats. Thanks to the aftermarket suppliers and restoration shops you can achieve your goals. If you want to restore or mildly modify your Camaro or Firebird with a stock interior it can be done, and the restoration interior parts (such as seat covers, carpets, and door panels) are reasonably priced. If you are not worried about the cost of your buildup there are many wild things that can be done with the interior of a Camaro or Firebird—from a wild, custom-fabricated dash to front and rear racing seats with a custom full-length console.

Seats

The seats in some early sports cars built in England and Europe were rounded in the back and resembled buckets with cushions installed. Their unusual shape gave rise to the nickname "bucket seats." Soon after, every single-passenger seat in a car was called a bucket seat, even if it didn't resemble a bucket.

1960s

The 1960s bucket seats were rather flat because the performance models, such as the Camaros and Firebirds, were designed to go fast in a straight line. In fact all of the muscle cars of the time were small, light cars with a big engine and quarter-mile performance; they were the engineers, as well as the enthusiasts, were looking for. There were a small number of engineers working on Trans-Am race cars, where they were looking for a strong-running small engine under 305 ci in a car that handled well.

The Trans-Am cars were raced on road courses that were built with a wide variety of turns and level changes. Powered by a small-block engine the Camaro was well balanced, and with a variety of suspension modifications the early cars were track ready and cornered really well. All of the car companies involved in Trans-Am racing had to also have a street version that was offered for sale to qualify. But in the muscle car years enthusiasts wanted a small car with a big engine, so they didn't sell that many to start with.

The 1967 Z28 Camaro wasn't particularly popular, and only 602 street models were sold. Ford was the king of the road course in the earlier years; however, the 1967 Z28 Camaro race cars were very successful, so Ford was striving to design a car that was competitive. The big problem wasn't the car's suspension; it was the fact that Ford didn't have a small-block engine that was competitive with the Chevy engine.

Toward the end of 1968 the powertrain engineers and the race car engineers came up with the Boss 302 engine, which combined the 302-ci small-block Windsor cylinder block and the new Cleveland heads. Together they produced the horsepower required to be competitive with the Chevy engines. There was also going to be a body improvement in 1969, so when the Ford interior engineers were designing the seats and door panels they came up with

INTERIOR

The 1970 Z28 Camaros came with a choice of two interiors. The standard interior is shown here, and the deluxe version featured bucket seats with larger side bolsters. An all-vinyl upholstery and a matte-black dashboard finish are the key elements of a standard interior. Optional custom features include a higher grade of cloth or vinyl upholstery with a dash and console that have wood accents.

The deluxe Firebird seats feature a high back with larger side bolsters that help keep the driver from moving around when the car is driven hard around corners.

high-back, large, bolstered bucket seats that worked well to keep passengers planted in the seats when the new performance models with improved handling ability were driven.

Chevrolet management saw a major sales improvement for the Z28 over the years when enthusiasts saw its performance prowess. Chevy's interior engineers also saw a need for improved seats because the 1969 Z28 Camaro featured excellent handling, and high-bolstered seats were definitely needed. Chevrolet and Pontiac had to justify the new seat design, so the improvement was incorporated when the new models were being planned and designed.

1970s

In 1970 a high-back seat with improved side bolsters was released by both Chevrolet and Pontiac. The seats not only worked better they also looked nicer. (High-back seats were only offered if the buyer purchased the deluxe interior.) Over the second-generation years from 1970 to 1981, there were many seat changes and improvements that corresponded with the car's improved handling ability, such as the WS6 suspension system used by Pontiac. In the later years the seats were also available with a cloth insert, which helped to keep enthusiasts from sliding around in their seats. Many of the interior designs used in the mid to late 1970s Camaros and Firebirds were as nice as any professional upholsterer could create.

Racing-Style Seats

Many high-end sports cars (such as the Ferrari) that were being built in Europe were outfitted with racing-style seats with very high bolsters and some that could be used with racing harnesses.

Recaro is a favorite seat manufacturer of the big car companies, as well as of the racing enthusiasts. Some of its seats feature fully adjustable side bolsters that can be tailored to the driver's and passenger's physique. Some of its custom seats can be folded forward to allow entry for rear-seat passengers. Some are not designed to

This is a typical high-back bolstered racing-style seat in black vinyl. The side bolsters help prevent the driver from sliding around the seat while behind the steering wheel, and the two holes in the top are designed for use with racing-style seat belts. These seats fold to allow rear passengers to enter the vehicle.

CHAPTER 16

Luxury Features

Another interesting change in the automotive world happened in 1971, due to the EPA laws that discontinued the use of leaded gasoline and mandated better fuel economy. Chevrolet and Pontiac started lowering compression ratios and were aware that engine performance was only getting worse, so they started improving the suspension for better handling as well as adding luxury features to the interior. Instead of going fast in a straight line, their cars became excellent road cars with enough power to be fun to drive.

By the mid 1970s most of the second-generation cars were optionally available with power seats, air conditioning, cruise control, tilt steering columns, power windows, 8-track stereo radios, and power door locks. They had all of the amenities you could find in a Cadillac, including high-bolster seats that were very plush. The Z28 and Trans Am models were also available with nicely designed gauge clusters instead of idiot lights. General Motors found that the more extras it made available, the better the cars sold, plus the options made the company plenty of money. The highest sales year for both the Camaro and the Firebird was 1979, so it showed that the GM management strategy was working. People of all ages were purchasing Camaros and Firebirds. They were no longer a car for young buyers because they were expensive when all of the options were ordered.

The interiors of the mid- to late-1970s cars were very nice, and a custom upholsterer had a difficult time making big improvements. That can't be said for the earlier cars because they were not as sophisticated, and many of the Camaros, especially the Z28 models, were sold without expensive options because the people who purchased them knew the cars were lighter and faster without heavy power options. Today many of the earlier Camaros and Firebirds are being turned into Pro Touring cars, but with all of the new handling improvements, including new front and rear subframes and complete custom frames, enthusiasts quickly find that the seats are not adequate for the cornering ability the cars can attain if driven on slalom courses or on the track. Yes, the new seats available in the 1970 Camaros and Firebirds were built with higher bolsters that were probably fine for the cars with stock heavy-duty suspension, but certainly not good enough for the fantastic cornering ability of the modified cars, especially if the cars are driven on a slalom or road course.

The early Camaros and Firebirds were available with standard and deluxe interiors. The standard interiors were certainly not designed for cornering because the seats are almost flat with no side bolsters at all. If you ordered the deluxe interior you received the high-back seats with reasonable bolsters. GM interior designers were aware of the variable size of customers, so it had to make the seats comfortable for small people as well as large people.

Over the years the seats were continually improved, along with the carpeting and door panels, and by the mid 1970s the interiors were very plush and comfortable. Pontiac had the lead in the interior department because the Firebird was marketed as a step up from a Camaro.

fold, and they are more like race car seats. They also have very high bolsters, and they really keep the driver in place during extreme cornering.

Recaro, as well as other racing seat manufacturers such as Corbeau, sells seats fully upholstered. You can install them as they are delivered with a non-matching surround of door panels and a rear seat, or you can have your trim shop match the door panels and rear seat with a similar design and material so the seats look factory installed. The seats are designed to fit an average-size driver (say, 5-foot 10-inches, 170 pounds), so if you are a larger person you will probably have a difficult time squeezing into the racing seats unless they are custom built to fit you.

Stock Camaro Seat Drawbacks

Many of the early Z28 Camaros were ordered with all of the go-fast options and none of the frills. A 1970 Z28 has a standard bucket seat interior with an optional console. The seats were an improvement over those in the first-generation Camaro but they were still very flat with only small side bolsters. If the car is going to be driven to shows and not for track action the standard seats can be used and improved upon with bigger side bolsters when they are reupholstered.

INTERIOR

Enthusiasts who are building a mid-1970s to 1981 Camaro or Firebird may want to keep it in close-to-original condition, or what I refer to as a resto mod car. This is a car that looks fairly original in appearance but has various performance improvements that may or may not be easily visible. The reason for the mild modifications is that, in many states, the later cars must meet emissions requirements and are tested biannually, so it makes more sense to restore the cars with the addition of legal improvements. That means that many enthusiasts retain and restore the original interiors because by the mid 1970s they were extremely nice.

Fortunately for everyone who is building a later F-Body Camaro or Firebird there are several companies that make restoration parts, including new interior kits, that make the cars look as good as new. Some of the excellent restoration companies include National Parts Depot, Classic Industries, Year One, and Ames Performance.

Project 1: Seat Reupholstery

One of the best companies making interior kits is Legendary Auto Interiors. I have been in the process of restoring a 1978 Pontiac Special Edition Trans Am, so I purchased a set of new seat covers and door panels from Legendary Auto Interiors. This car has been sitting in California's high desert, and the original velour and vinyl interior rotted in the hot sun. I decided to make the interior more durable, so I ordered the deluxe all-vinyl seat covers that were also available in 1978. Along with the seat covers I also ordered new door panels. The seat covers were installed in a matter of a few days, giving this Trans Am interior a new lease on life.

This 1978 Special Edition Pontiac Trans Am had been sitting for more than 20 years in Ridgecrest, California, overlooking the Mojave Desert. Before the car was parked the interior may have already been in worn condition, but sitting in the desert with the sun shining through the T-tops rendered the interior to be in very poor condition. Basically, everything needed replacement. This car featured velour seat covers, but I am going to replace the covers with the vinyl covers that were also available at the time because the material can handle more abuse.

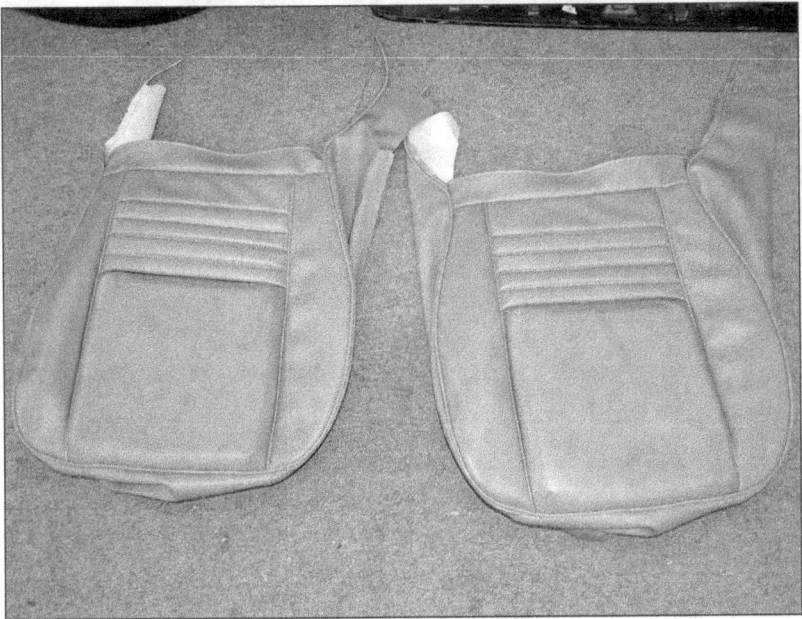

This Special Edition Trans Am was originally ordered with the best of everything, including the camel-colored deluxe interior. Legendary Auto Interiors makes complete interior replacement kits for Firebirds and Camaros of every vintage, including these replacement pieces.

CAMARO & FIREBIRD PERFORMANCE PROJECTS: 1970–1981

Seat Disassembly

Remove Plastic Seat Back

1 Use a No. 2 Philips screwdriver to remove the screws at the bottom of the seat back, and then slide the plastic cover off. Fortunately this unit was in good, reusable condition but did have some wear and fading.

2 There is a plastic chrome edging that can be restored or purchased new. In this case I restored the edging using Dupli-Color Instant Chrome spray paint #CS101. This provides a chrome-like appearance that looks nice with the new seat covers.

Remove Lock Mechanism Bolt

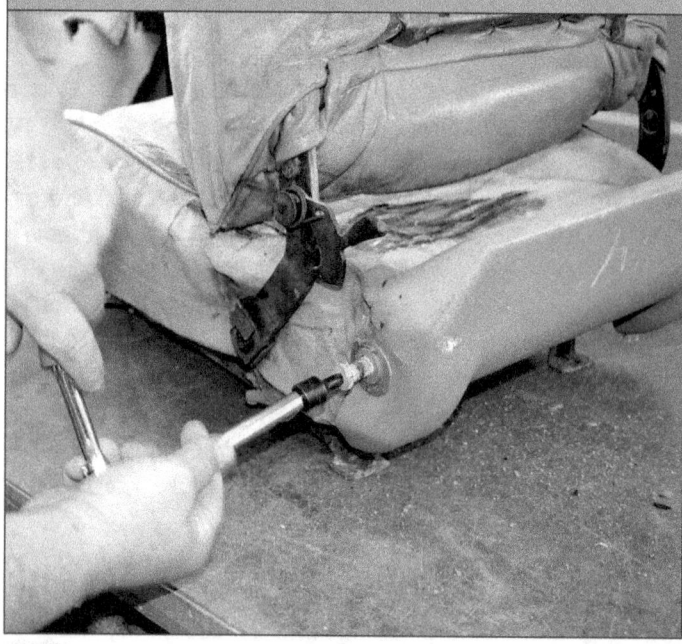

3 Use a socket wrench equipped with an Allen-head socket to remove the bolt/lock catch from the seat in preparation for the removal of the original material.

Remove Plastic Guard

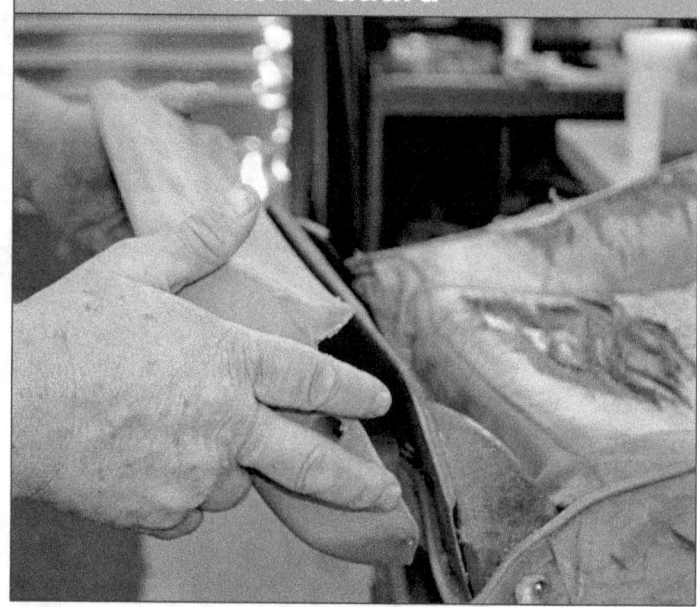

4 Remove the plastic guard cover. This one was faded but in good condition for restoration. Remove all the other pieces such as seat-belt connector, hinge cover, etc.

INTERIOR

Remove Seat Cover

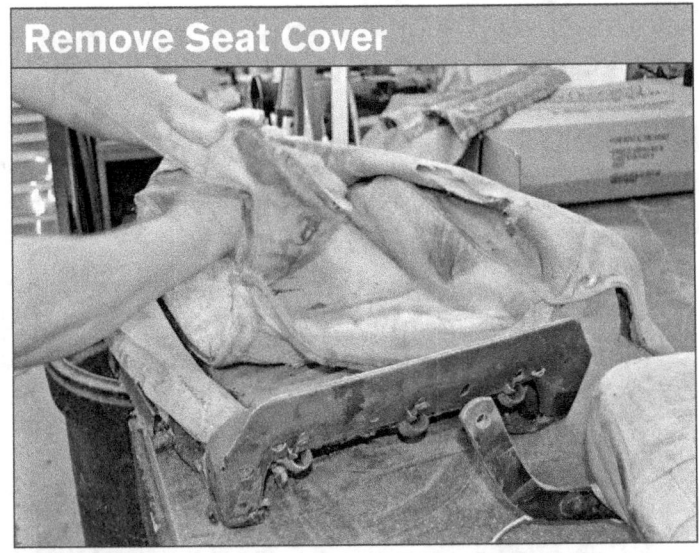

5 Remove the old seat material after cutting the hog rings along the perimeter and at the wires. This has to be done with large, sharp diagonal cutters.

Remove Seat Foam

6 The original foam may be starting to crumble from age and sun exposure, so it needs to be replaced with new foam. If you're tempted to reuse the old foam, remember that it may leave foam crumbs under the seat and on the carpet after the seats are installed.

Seat Assembly

Inspect New Foam

1 American Cushion Industries makes new foam kits for the various Firebird and Camaro seats. These cushions were designed for use with the deluxe Firebird interior seats. Notice the reasonably high side bolsters for the 1978 seats, which were designed to keep the driver in place but not so high that a large person couldn't sit in the seats.

Inspect New Covers

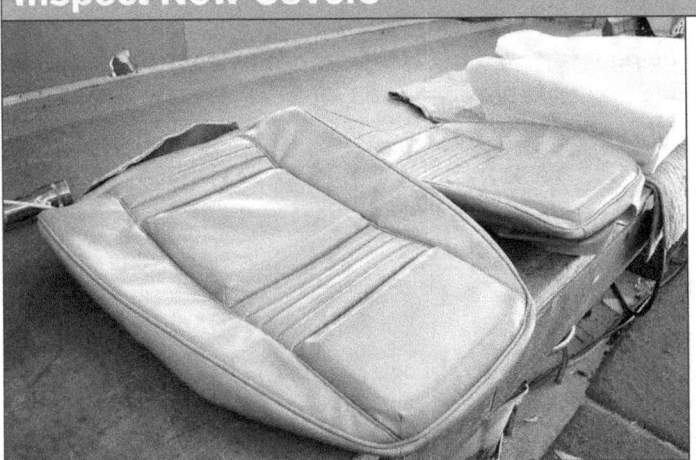

2 The 1978 deluxe seats are stitched with a padded back with a high- and low-rolled-and-pleated design. These seats are very comfortable and provide good side support for normal driving conditions. The 1978 interiors were nicely designed to go along with the luxury performance image of the Trans Am models.

Paint Seat Frames

3 Sandblast the upper and lower seat frames to strip them back to bare metal. After they are cleaned, paint them with semi-gloss black paint. The original seat frames weren't painted at the factory, so now they are better than new.

Reinstall Seat Spring

4 Reinstall the original wire seat spring to support the cushion. Pound the spring clips down to support the wires.

Install Carpet for Seat Springs

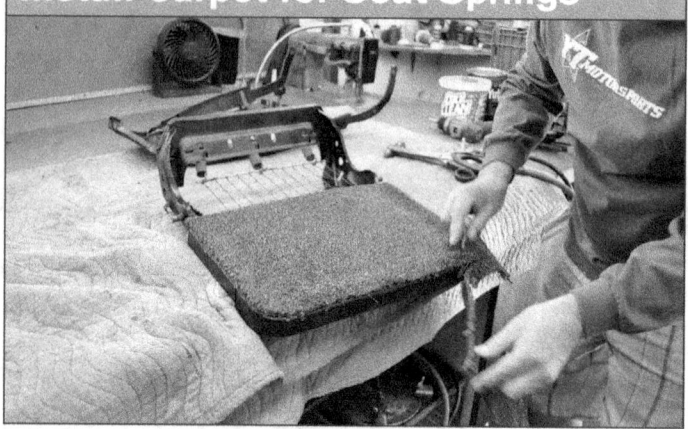

5 Cover the seat spring with the lightweight carpet in the kit. This carpet provides a more secure base for the new cushion and makes the seat feel firm. Cut the carpet to the shape of the seat frame.

Attach Seat-Cushion Foam to Frame

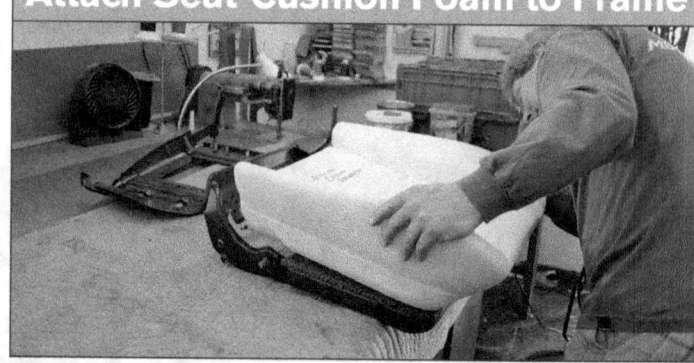

6 Spray the seat-cushion foam and carpet area of the frame with 3M contact cement. (This is commonly called upholstery glue.) You coat both parts that are going to be glued together and allow the glue to dry just a little. When you put the two components together, they immediately stick.

Attach Middle of Seat Cover to Frame

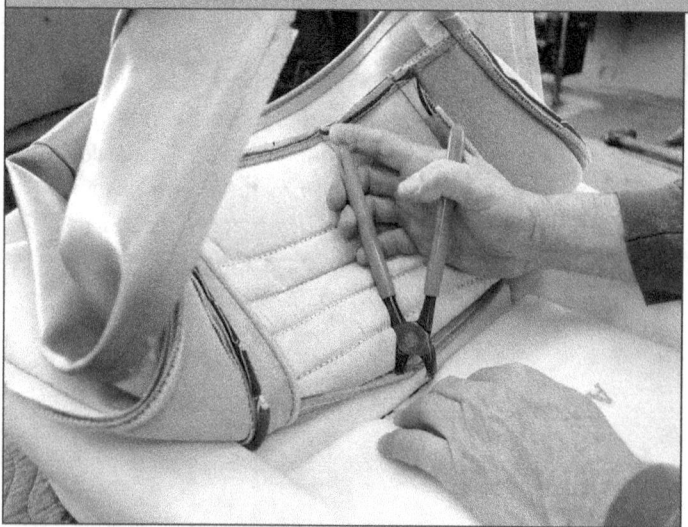

7 Connect the seat cover to the foam-covered frame using hog ring pliers and hog rings. The seats must be perfectly aligned before this can be done because once the hog rings are connected the seat covers are not moveable.

Install Seat Cover over Foam

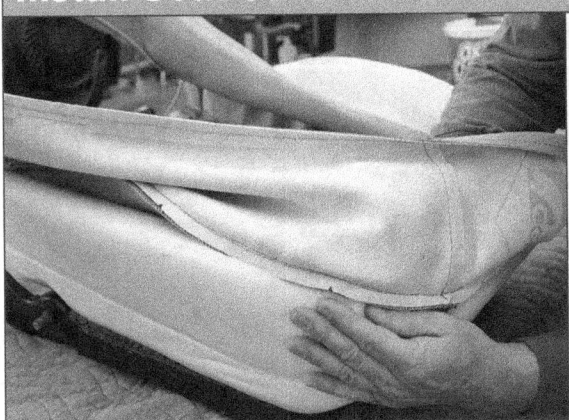

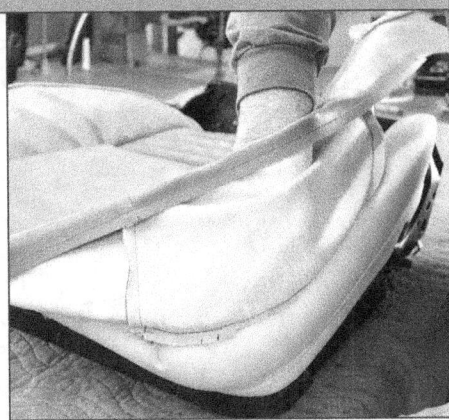

8 Align the seat cover corner with the curve of the foam. Making sure the alignment is correct reduces the chance of getting wrinkles in the material. This may require some arm muscle as you stretch and adjust the vinyl covers. Make sure the covers do not have serious wrinkles and are in the correct position. If you see wrinkles or creases in the vinyl covers, contact the supplier and return the vinyl covers for another set. You don't want to go through the entire installation process and find out that you cannot remove the wrinkles or creases from the vinyl and have to start all over again.

9 Stretch the cover over the foam. You can spray the seat cover and seat foam with silicone spray to make it a little easier.

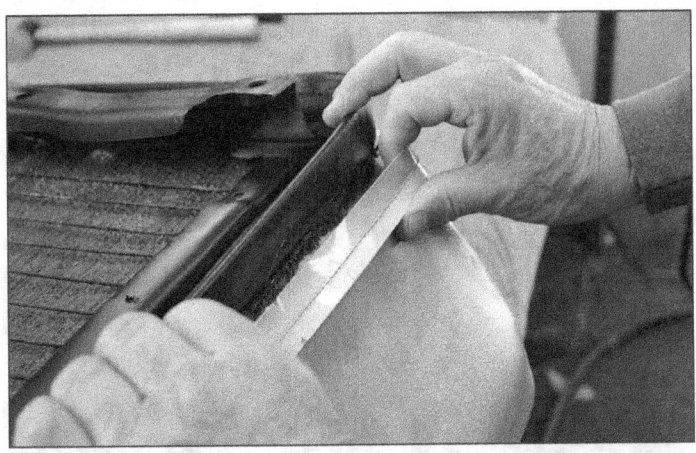

10 The back of the seat cover uses a strip of plastic that hooks into the seat frame as seen here. The seat cover requires stretching for the plastic to sit properly into the channel.

Attach Seat Cover Sides to Frame

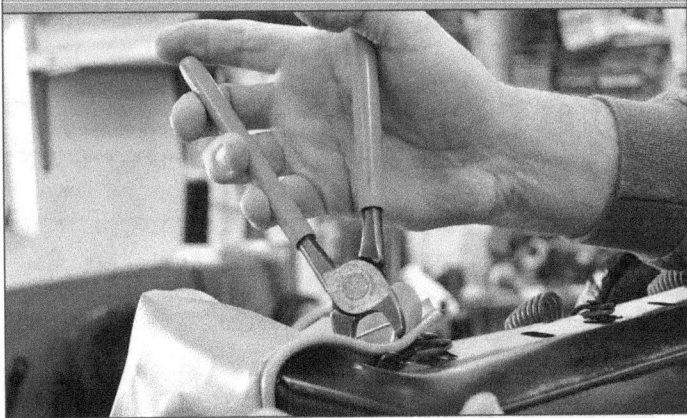

Cut Lock Bolt Hole

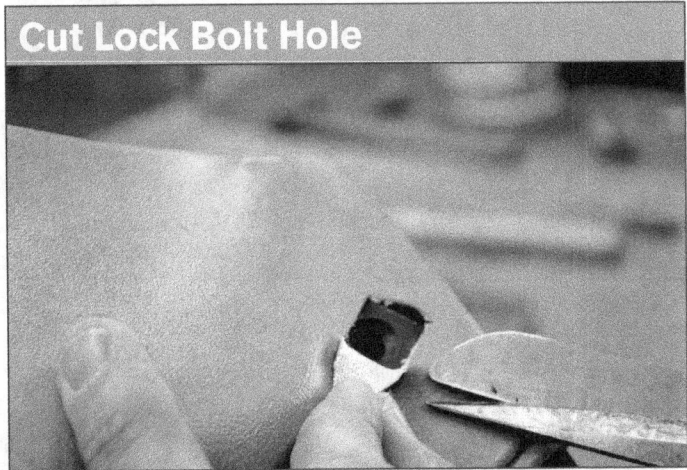

11 The seat frame has hog ring mounting holes, so grasp the hog that's attached to the corner of the vinyl cover and stretch the fabric until you can hook the hog ring into a hole and then crimp the hog ring.

12 Locate the hole for the lock-mechanism bolt. To cut away the vinyl, you can use the pointed end of upholstery scissors to pierce the vinyl and then use the scissors to neatly cut away the fabric around the hole.

Reinstall Plastic Guard

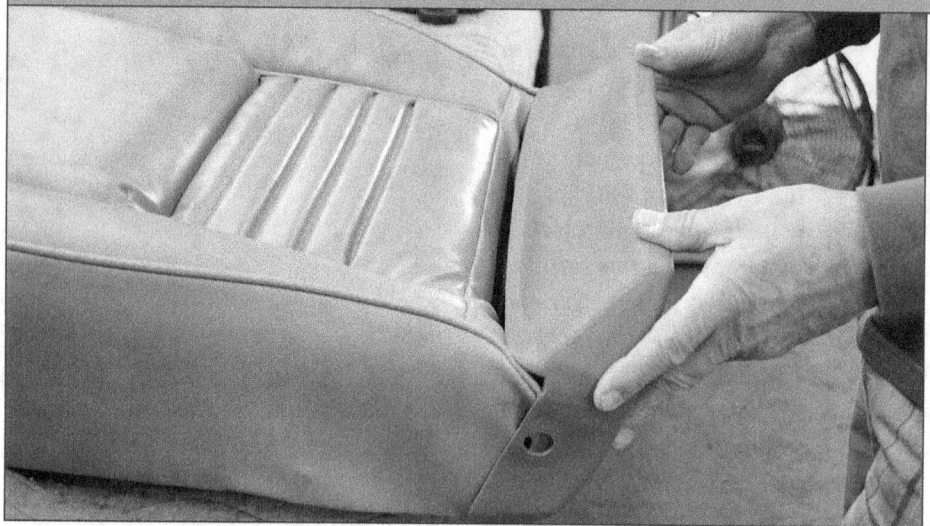

13 Paint the plastic seat-back guard to look new (here, with Original Equipment Reproduction's Camel Tan interior dye #PP820). Then align and install it over the rear of the seat bottom.

Reinstall Lock-Mechanism Bolt

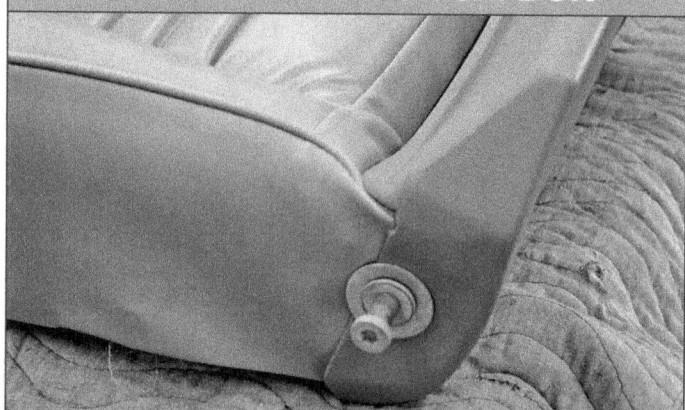

14 Align the plastic seat guard with the latch holes on each side of the seat bottom. Use a Torx driver to tighten the lock-mechanism bolt on the seat bottom.

Install Seat-Back Pin

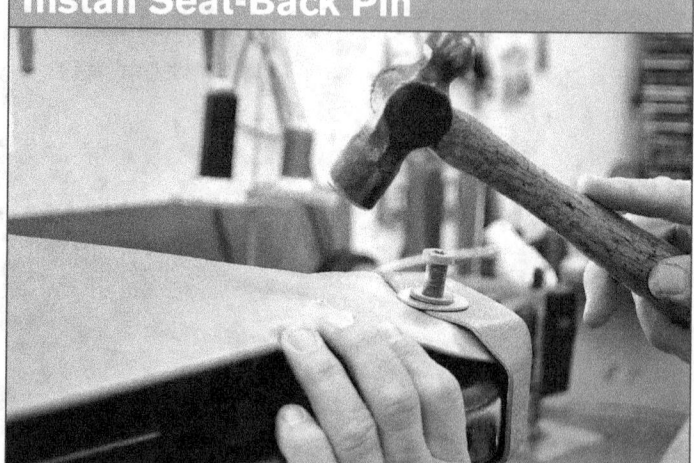

15 Tap on the seat-back pin to cut the material tightly around the pin.

Install Seat Tracks

16 These seat tracks were stripped, painted, and lubricated prior to installation on the seat bottom. This car originally had manual seats but power seats were also available.

INTERIOR

Attach Seat-Back Foam to Frame

17 Here is the seat-back frame for the high-back bucket seat. The frame was sandblasted, and then it was painted semi-gloss black. Fortunately, it was in good condition, so it didn't need to be replaced and it was easy to install the new cover on it.

18 Evenly spray upholstery contact cement (3M or other suitable type) on the foam and seat-back frame. Lay the frame over the formed seat foam and make sure it is properly positioned. Give the seat back enough time to adequately dry and then reattach the seat-back bracket.

Reinstall Seat-Back Bracket

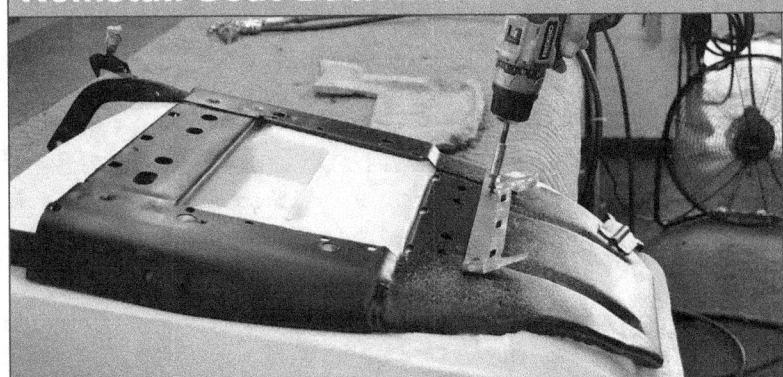

19 To reinstall the bracket, align the bracket with the mounting holes on the seat-back frame. The mounting tabs are oriented toward the top of the seat. Use a screwdriver or a drill with driver bit to reinstall the mounting screws through the bracket and into the frame.

Reuse Seat-Back Foam

20 The small section of original foam used at the back of the high-back seat can be retained and reused if it is still in perfect condition. Glue it to the back of the seat using 3M contact cement. If it's not reuseable, use this piece to cut a new piece from the same type and thickness of foam.

Install Seat-Back Cover

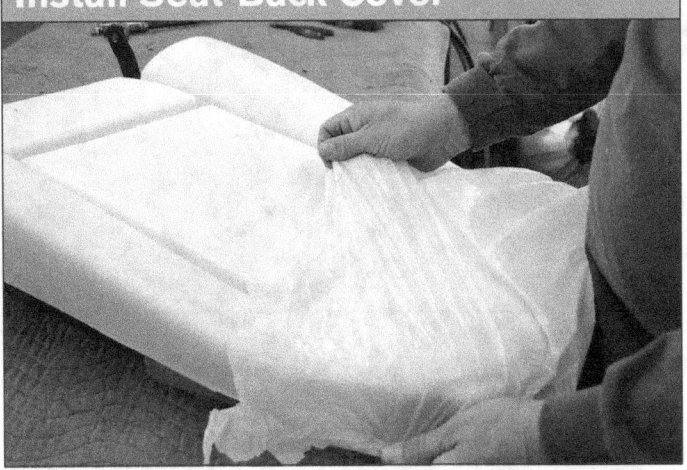

21 A little upholstery trick to get the seat-back upholstery properly stretched over the seat is to use a plastic bag over the top of the foam. This allows the material to slide easier over the foam because the material and foam tend to stick together.

CAMARO & FIREBIRD PERFORMANCE PROJECTS: 1970–1981

Install Seat-Back Cover (Continued)

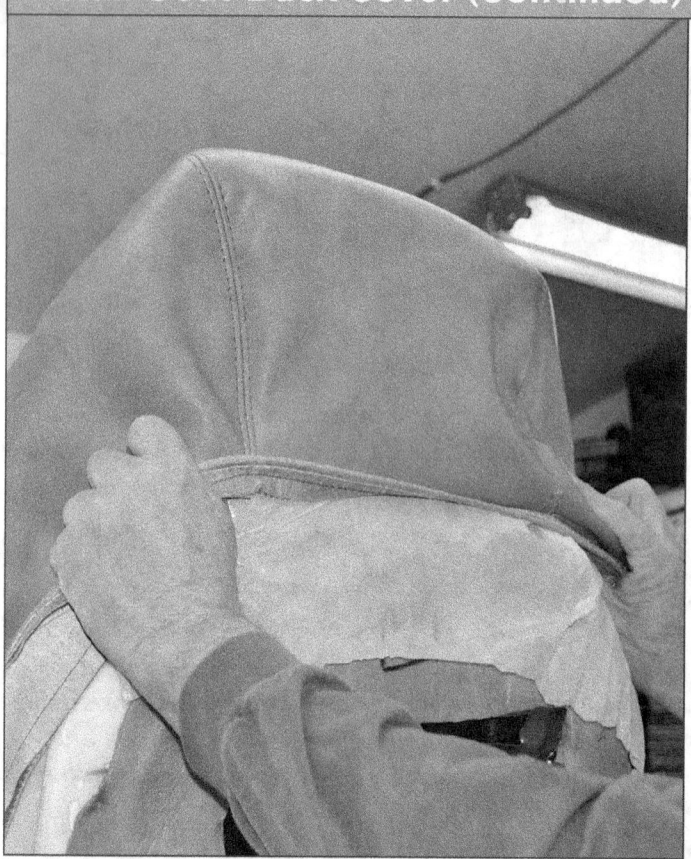

22 If you have wrinkles in the seat bottom or the seat back, you can carefully apply heat from a heat gun to smooth them out. If you need to smooth out wrinkles in the vinyl, slowly apply the heat and not too much. You don't want to misshape the vinyl covers.

23 Here is the seat cover stretched over the seat-back frame. Be sure that the cover stretches all the way to the seat-back bracket.

Attach Seat-Back Cover to Frame

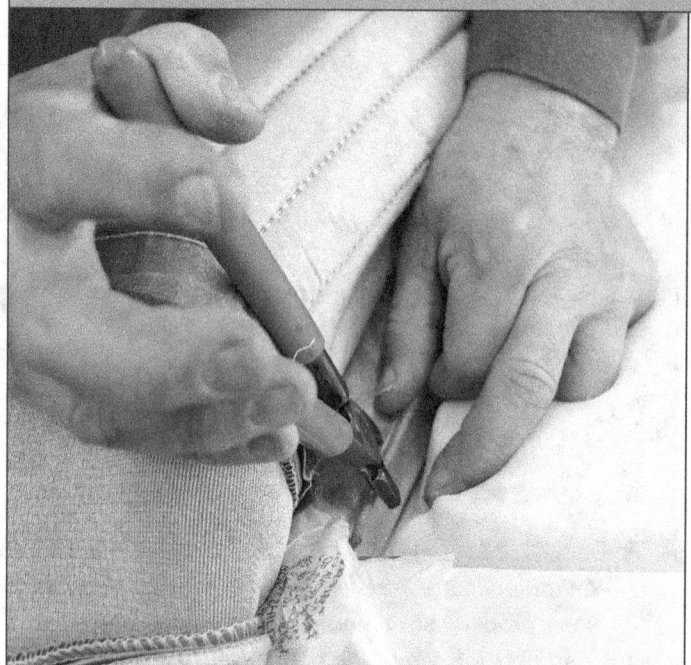

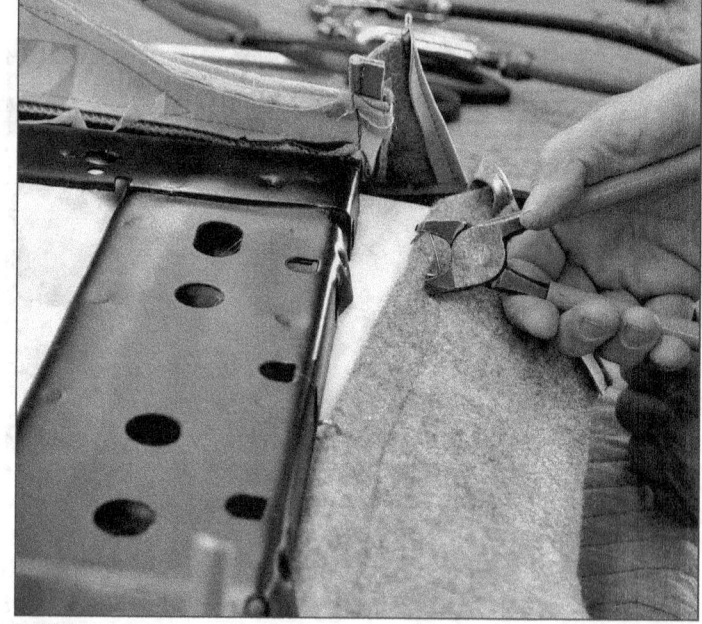

24 Use hog ring pliers to connect the seat wires to the seat cover.

25 Attach the seat cover to the perimeter of the frame using hog rings and hog ring pliers. It is a good idea to use plenty of hog rings to make the connection.

INTERIOR

Reinstall Seat Belt Connector

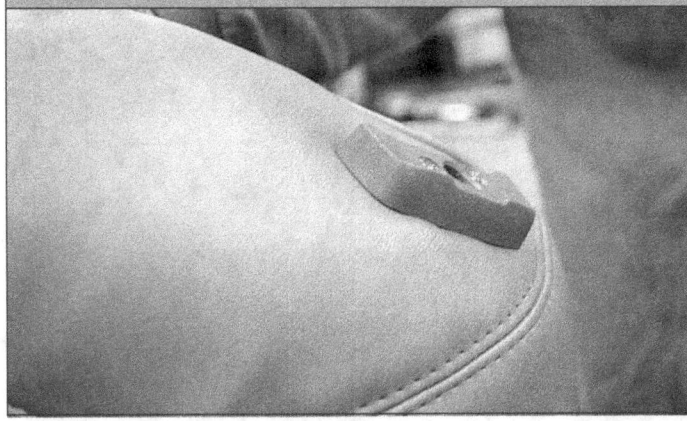

26 Secure the plastic base for the seat belt connector to the seat using the original screws.

Install Seat Back

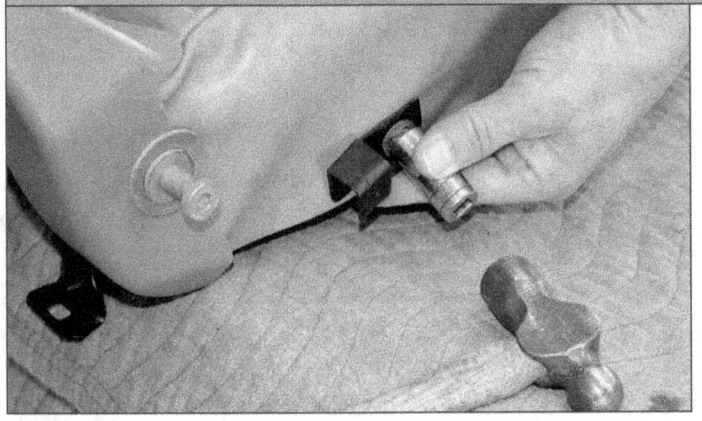

27 Find a socket that's the same diameter as the hinge cover. Using the socket and a hammer, gently tap the plastic cover into position over the hinge, using light taps so you don't shatter the cap.

28 Gently lower the seat back on the studs with the spring clips.

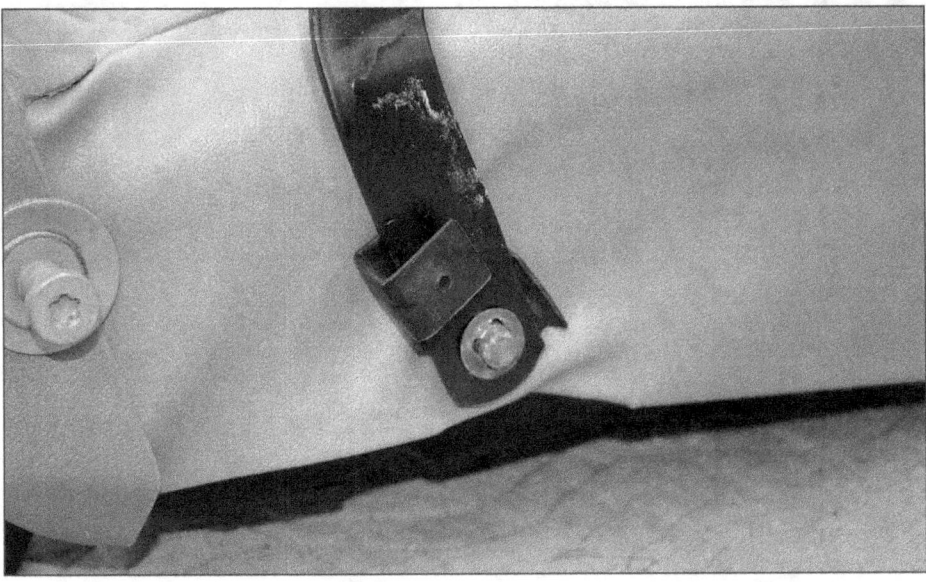

29 The seat-back brackets curve out and the holes align with the mounting hole in the bottom of the seat frame. Once aligned, use a 9/16-inch nut driver to press the bracket onto the mounting pins in the seat base. It's easier to turn the seat on its side and drive the bracket over the pin in the base. Do the same on the other side. Use a pair of pliers to install the C-clips under the head of the pin to lock the bracket to the pins and complete the installation.

Install Plastic Seat-Back Cover

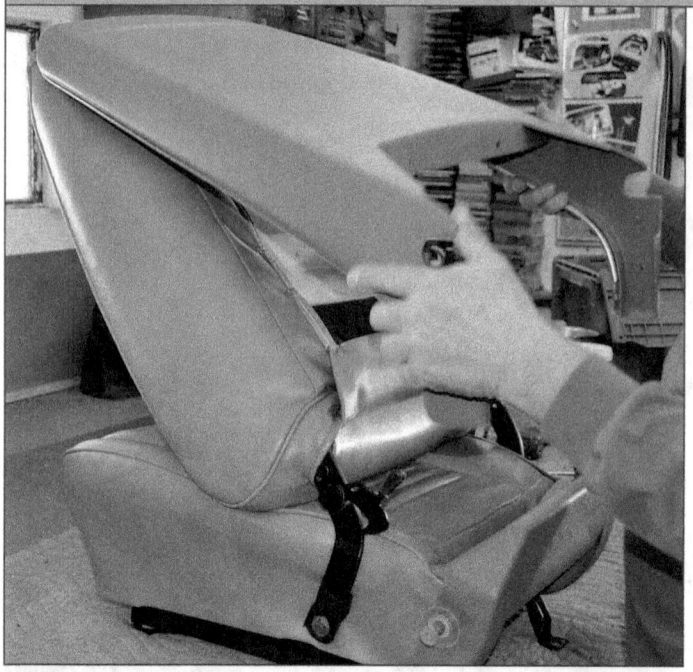

30 After you paint the plastic seat-back cover to look brand new (here, Original Equipment Reproduction's Camel Tan interior dye #PP820, available from Classic Industries), hook it over the bracket at the top. If your original seat-back covers are unusable they are available from restoration suppliers.

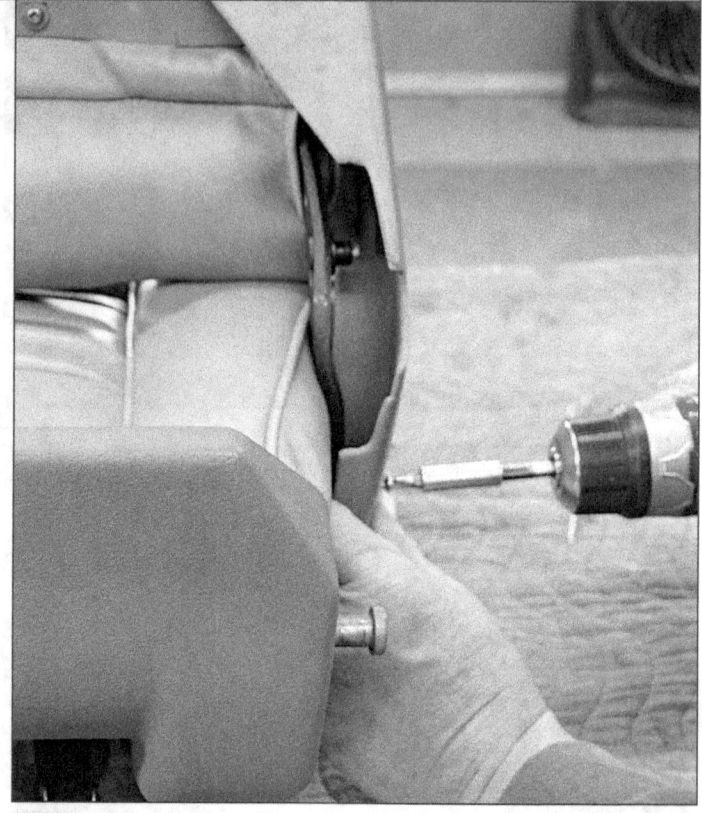

31 Connect the seat-back cover to the seat using two screws at the bottom.

This finished seat looks great and offers all of the side bolster support required for normal and mild road course driving. These seats are also very attractive and look nice in any F-Body, so early models can be upgraded with later seats that bolt right in.

INTERIOR

Dash and Gauges

It is difficult to beat the top-of-the-line interior designs and creature features offered in the later Camaros and Firebirds so many enthusiasts choose to use the original interiors. Fortunately, all of the parts are available, including dash assemblies, door panels, package trays, headliners, carpets, and even consoles for cars that are missing the parts or are equipped with damaged parts that can't be restored. Enthusiasts who own earlier cars can also completely restore their cars because every interior part imaginable is available, and that even includes many factory gauges.

The top-of-the-line Camaros and Firebirds had a nice factory gauge package and seemed to work fine. If you are building a restored or resto mod Camaro or Firebird you may want to upgrade the original gauges. If you are building a modified car, there are several companies making improvement kits that feature

Some of the early Camaros and Firebirds may be in good condition, but it is likely that they have cracked dash pads and unusable interior parts (top). This dash and panel were in poor condition, so plenty of work had to be done to restore them to perfect condition (bottom).

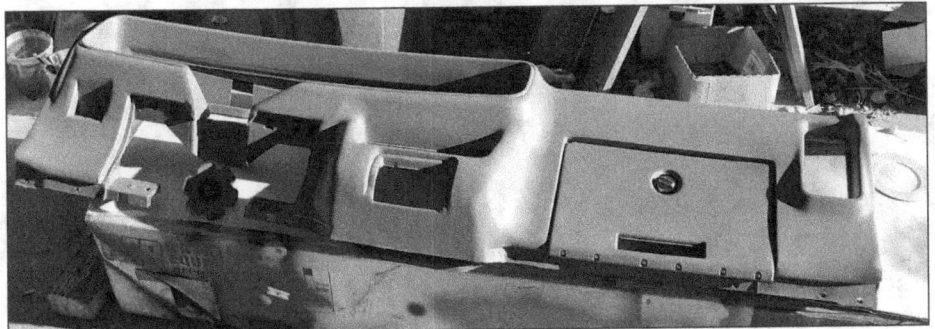

Companies such as Classic Industries offer reproduction dashes that look exactly like the originals. The dashes are all delivered black, so they have to be painted to match the original interior color. This dash has been painted Camel Tan.

CAMARO & FIREBIRD PERFORMANCE PROJECTS: 1970–1981

CHAPTER 16

The owner of this Camaro modified the gauge cluster to feature Auto Meter gauges because they provide accurate information about the engine's water temperature, oil pressure, electrical output, and fuel capacity.

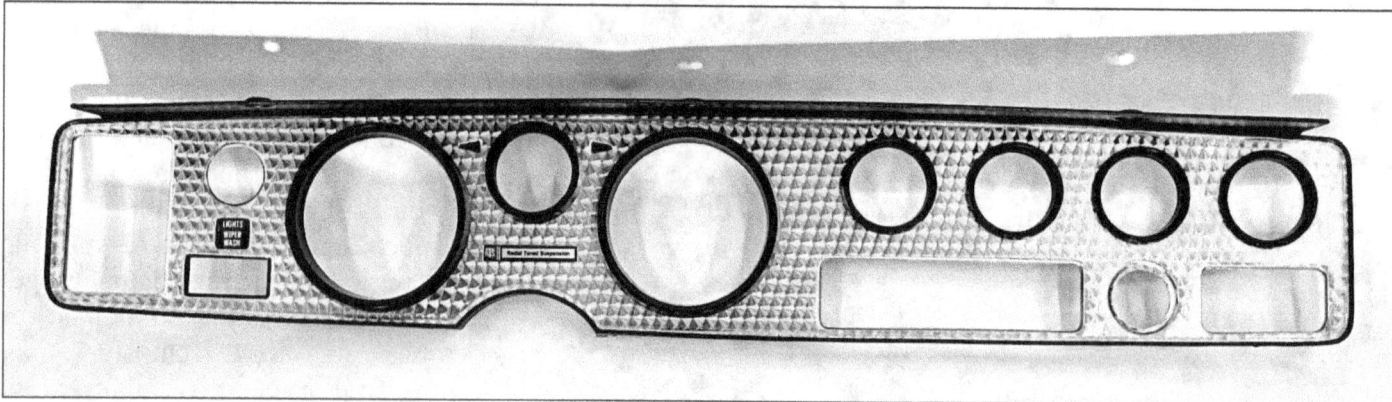

A Firebird Trans Am's engine-turned bezel can be restored. Trans Am Dash Bezels makes the gold-anodized, engine-turned panels that were found in the black and gold Special Edition models.

This Trans Am engine-turned panel was restored by Randy Combs. The gold color has been returned to the panel just like original, and the Radial Tuned Suspension emblem looks like brand new. The original gauges have also been restored.

INTERIOR

How wild do you want to go? This Camaro features a custom-fabricated metal dash with a billet aluminum gauge cluster.

Here is a 1970 Camaro that was upgraded with Auto Meter gauges. The panel was retained but the holes were opened up to house the custom gauges.

custom gauges that can be adapted to the original bezels. I have even seen some Pro Touring cars that were gutted and have entirely new dashboards filled with aftermarket gauges. It is all a matter of how wild you want to go when you are building a car for show or go.

Early Camaros had optional gauge packages, but by the 1970s the upgraded dash packages had all of the gauges a car required, including speedometer, tachometer, oil-pressure gauge, voltmeter, gas gauge, and small rally clock. In many cases the gauges in the cluster are the same size as the aftermarket gauges, and some builders install the aftermarket gauges using the original gauge bezel. Other builders make their own bezel to connect to the padded dash. There are some aftermarket companies that even make bolt-in gauge clusters that replace the originals. If you are building a wild Pro Touring Camaro or Firebird and want a dash that matches how wild the car is, you probably want a custom dash filled with competition-style gauges.

The covering on this stock steering wheel started coming off, and the rubber inside started crumbling, so the previous owner filled the depressions with silicone then wrapped the wheel with a steering wheel cover. It would be nice to restore this wheel but it is virtually impossible to do it for a reasonable price.

A reproduction steering wheel recently became available, and it looks just like the original. It was painted Camel Tan to match the Special Edition interior color.

If you are restoring a Firebird Trans Am and the engine-turned bezel is starting to look bad, you can have it restored by Trans Am Dash Bezels. After years of abuse, either being used or sitting in the weather, the panels can certainly deteriorate, so this is a handy company to know about.

Steering Wheel

Similar to the dash pad, a steering wheel takes a lot of abuse, and many wheels are found in poor condition, especially the plastic wheels that expand and contract in hot and cold weather. Plastic and leather coverings also deteriorate from use and weather conditions. If you are building a modified Camaro or Firebird, there are many excellent aftermarket steering wheels that are available from companies such as Le Carra, Grant, and Budnik.

Some aftermarket wheels are quite wild, and others are similar to original steering wheels. Recently, aftermarket restoration companies have started to reproduce the deluxe steering wheels found in the Pontiac and Firebird models starting with the first-generation Camaros through the second-generation cars. There were many popular aftermarket steering wheels and it's nice to see that they are available again.

Pontiac designed a racing-style steering wheel for the second-generation Trans Am Firebirds, and they remain popular today, but the originals are generally in poor condition. Today the steering wheels have been reproduced with both the standard centers and the gold-anodized centers for the Special Edition models. The wheels are available in black but they can be matched to the other interior colors using vinyl paint.

Sound System

In the process of upgrading a Camaro or Firebird most enthusiasts probably want to improve the sound system. Starting in the 1960s many muscle cars were equipped with optional AM/FM radios and 8-track tape players. As quality improved by the mid 1970s the cars were available with stereo radios with built-in cassette players. They were nice in their day and sounded fine but the radios built today are far superior and can be used together with CD players, and many have RCA inputs for iPod, MP3, or satellite radios.

There are many aftermarket radios that can be installed in one way or another, but the easiest way is to buy a radio from a restoration company that is designed to fit perfectly into a second-generation Camaro or Firebird. The radio units and systems I generally use in a wide variety of early cars (including Camaros and Firebirds) are made by Custom Auto Radios. They are designed to fit into the dash and look very original; but don't let the original appearance fool you because they are state-of-the-art radios that can be used with CD changers. The radios are also available with the RCA inputs for iPod, MP3, and satellite radios, so you can play all of your favorite tunes when you are cruising.

This Custom Auto Radios stereo radio unit looks original in the dash but it has many state-of-the-art features. The best part is the radio is very affordable, and the units are available for both the Camaros and Firebirds.

Roll Cage

If you are building a Pro Touring Camaro or Firebird that will see plenty of track time it is a good idea to outfit your car with a roll cage, just in case you run into trouble on the track. There are many companies that offer special roll-cage assemblies that can be bolted or welded into the car before the upholstery is installed. The roll cage can be adapted to accept a variety of custom seat belts and safety harness belts. The roll cage can be painted to match the interior or exterior of the car, or in some cases, the visible part of the cage can be wrapped for a softer appearance.

CHAPTER 17

ELECTRICAL SYSTEM AND WIRING

In the process of building a Camaro or Firebird, you have to think about improving the electrical system and what should be done to get it working properly. The electrical system can be somewhat simple when the car doesn't have a lot of options and very complicated when the car is loaded with power equipment. Many early second-generation Camaros and Firebirds were ordered with limited electrical options, such as a radio or a heater, and many that were ordered in warm areas such as on the West Coast and in southern states had air conditioning systems. Even with air conditioning the electrical systems were basic.

In the mid 1970s when luxury was more important than performance, Camaros and, especially, Firebirds and Trans Am models were generally available with many more options, such as power windows, power door locks, rear window defroster, power seat, power antenna, deluxe lighting systems, and cruise control. When all of the options are included, the electrical system becomes very complicated.

In an effort to make the wiring easier to understand and traceable for dealer mechanics and electricians, GM designers color-coded the wires so they can be followed to find a break in the wires or the other problems that can occur. The color-coding system works fine in an unmolested car, but so many Camaros and Firebirds have faded and cracked wiring in the engine compartment that makes it difficult to trace. In many cases an enthusiast finds "butchered" wiring under the dash that was caused by the installation of a custom radio or other electrical device, making it difficult to understand and fix the wiring system.

If you are building a mildly modified car or a restored Camaro or Firebird and want to use the original-style wiring system, there are a few wiring companies that reproduce and duplicate the factory wiring, so you can remove the original wiring harness and install a new reproduction wiring harness. I have found that the reproduction harnesses are almost identical and feature all of the correct wiring connections.

General Motors has designed its wiring so there is a separate and different plug for every connection, making it almost impossible to hook up the harness improperly. Using a reproduction factory harness is definitely the easiest and quickest way to get your wiring system working properly. This book provides help for the novice in the form of a full-color wiring diagram that can be followed during the wiring installation.

DIY or Outsource?

When it comes to working on the electrical system, most enthusiasts shy away from it because it looks very intimidating. In reality, the most intimidating part of the system is the harness that runs under the dash. And that's not so bad at all if you don't look at all of the wires as a whole but look at the individual leads separately.

Harnesses are ordered for the individual parts of a car, such as a front wiring harness for the headlights and an engine harness for the coil, starter motor, and alternator. Those individual harnesses plug into the firewall connection that is connected to the fuse box.

When the wires are laid out according to where the old harness was running it becomes obvious as to where the connections have to be made. Take pictures of how the original wiring was routed so you can put the new wiring back in the same location.

For example, when the light harness is routed properly the connections for the headlights can be seen along with those for the parking lights and the horns. It is really simple when a factory harness is used.

General Motors was intelligent when it came to using plugs that are different for each connection. Reproduction factory harnesses make it easy to wire a second-generation Camaro or Firebird, and fortunately, there are many different harnesses available.

If you have a car that is in rough condition and all of the wiring is gone you definitely have a more difficult situation. There are wiring shops that can rewire a car for you. That might be a good way to go if you are building a show car and want an extremely neat system, or what is referred to as a hidden system, where none of the wires can be seen.

Another way to go that saves you money is to purchase a wiring kit from an aftermarket wiring supplier such as Ron Francis Wiring, Painless Performance Products, EZ Wiring, and American Autowire. They all make kits with detailed instructions. Some kits allow you to install all of the wires to the panel and to the component; some kits have all the wires hooked to the fuse panel and you run them to where they are supposed to go.

If you plan to wire your own car with a kit you need a good supply of wiring tools. You need cutters, wire strippers, and crimping tools for small and large spark-plug wires, along with many other normal hand tools. The tools are available from many sources such as Sears, Snap-on, and Harbor Freight. The spark plug wire-crimping tool was supplied by MSD.

Even with the correct tools, it takes an average enthusiast several days to wire a Camaro or Firebird, and if you are working on a mid-1970s car with plenty of options it takes even longer. Again, the important thing to make the installation of a kit easier is to work on one circuit at a time and carefully follow the instruction sheet.

LS Engines

The hot option for Pro Touring cars is the installation of a new LS engine, which is used in Corvettes, GTOs, Camaros, Cadillacs, and even some trucks. The all-aluminum engines are very lightweight and compact, and depending on the LS model, they are able to deliver incredible net horsepower ratings.

In the past, horsepower figures were given as gross ratings, so a 435-hp Corvette engine had a net rating closer to 360. Today a base Corvette with an LS2 engine features a 400-hp net rating, making it stronger than the old engine.

The LS engines have been out for several years now, so they are becoming more available from auto wrecking establishments. They are also available from Chevrolet Performance, including all of the versions (such as LS1, LS2, LS6, LS7). If you are going to install one in your Camaro or Firebird you will have no problem getting it to fit.

The LS engines are easy to install but they are more difficult to get running because they are computer controlled and require a lot of wiring. A standard Chevrolet or Pontiac engine that came in a Camaro or Firebird required a wire going to the distributor, alternator wires, and a wire going to the starter motor. The wiring is very basic, and it worked fine. An LS engine requires a complete wiring harness with computers and electrical connections going to all of the fuel injectors and to the individual coils that are mounted over each cylinder.

LS engines are being used in a wide variety of cars, especially Camaros and Firebirds, so if you are building one check out the wiring suppliers to find the wiring kit that works efficiently and effectively with the Chevrolet Performance LS wiring. Enthusiasts who mildly modify or restore their Camaro or Firebird and use the original engine can improve the parts of their car's wiring system with new factory harnesses from a restoration supplier.

CHAPTER 17

Project 1: Power Window Installation

Today the early Camaros and Firebirds that weren't highly optioned are more desirable to enthusiasts when they are upgraded with more comfort and convenience options. Installing certain options adds a small amount of weight to a car but not enough to worry about because the chance of a boulevard confrontation isn't likely anymore.

The owner of this Z28 wanted to add power windows, and he wasn't worried about the slight increase in weight because the original LT-1 engine that was gross rated at 360 hp was replaced by an LS7 Corvette engine that is delivering 505 net hp. The addition of a few pounds makes no noticeable difference at all in the car's acceleration. The aftermarket offers direct bolt-in power window kits for Camaros and Firebirds, and so an early car can be converted in a matter of a few hours.

Electric-Life makes a bolt-in power window kit for early Camaros and Firebirds. The kit is easy to install and uses some of the standard window hardware.

Remove Door Handle

1 Begin the installation by removing the door handle as seen here. First remove the bezel, and then disconnect the small screw to remove the handle mechanism. Pull the door handle cup off the panel and guide it around the door handle mechanism. Properly store this part for reassembly or replace as needed.

2 To remove the door-handle mechanism from the rod actuator, remove the spring clip with a needle-nose pliers.

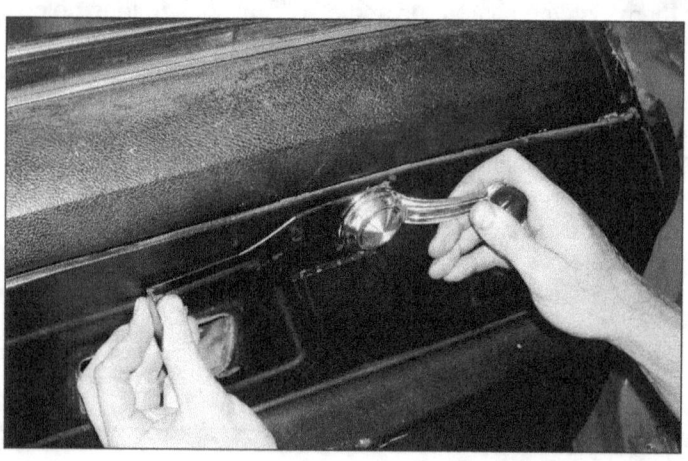

3 Before you remove the window crank handle, remove the armrest from the door panel. To do that, use a Phillips-head screwdriver to remove the three screws that fasten the armrest to the door.

ELECTRICAL SYSTEM AND WIRING

Remove Door Panel

4 *The door panel is held in with clips on the side and screws at the bottom. Remove the screws with a Phillips-head screwdriver. To remove the compression clips, use a needle-nose pliers. Pull the panel off the frame and grab onto the clip with the pliers and pull up. The bottom of the door panel simply pulls away from the door.*

Remove Window Molding

5 *Remove the plastic upper window molding by disconnecting the screws at the bottom. Use a Phillips-head screwdriver.*

Remove Window Mechanism

6 *Remove the window from the window crank mechanism and hold it in place with a piece of wood. Use a wrench with a 1/2-inch socket to remove the bolts fastening the mechanism to the inner door panel. Save the bolts and mark their locations because the new mechanism connects to the original holes.*

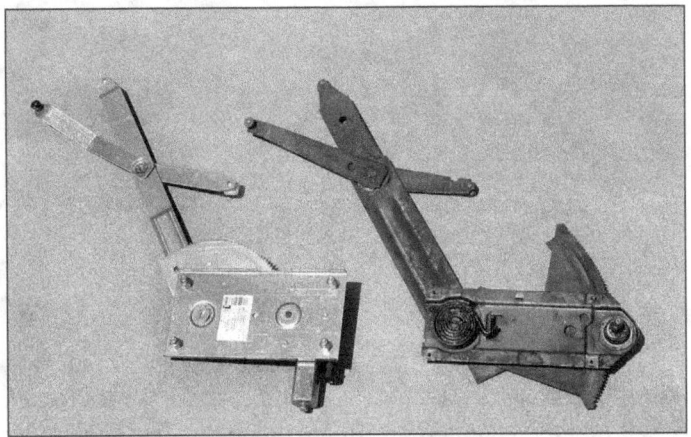

7 *Carefully remove the unit through the hole in the inner door panel (left). Here is a comparison between the original manual window crank mechanism and the new power unit (right). It is easy to see that the new power mechanism bolts in using the original mounting holes. There is only a miniscule weight difference between the mechanisms.*

CAMARO & FIREBIRD PERFORMANCE PROJECTS: 1970–1981

Install New Mechanism

8 To prop up the glass, insert a 2 x 4 block of wood through the door frame and under the glass. Install the new window regulator through the large hole in the inner door frame. Guide the mechanism to move it into position. Align the regulator behind the door frame with the mounting holes. Use a ratchet and 1/2-inch socket to install the mounting bolts. Be sure to route the wires up through the door frame and out through the hole for the motor switch.

Connect Window to Mechanism

9 Install the original window tracks to the regulator arms. Align the lower track to regulator arms and then install the bolts with a socket and ratchet. Bolt the upper arm to the door. Once the window tracks have been installed, carefully lift the window that's supported by the block of wood and remove the block of wood. Carefully lower the window glass into the door and slide it into the lower track on the regulator. Do not drop the glass because you could damage it. Make sure the regulator arms are properly lubricated.

Connect Window to Mechanism

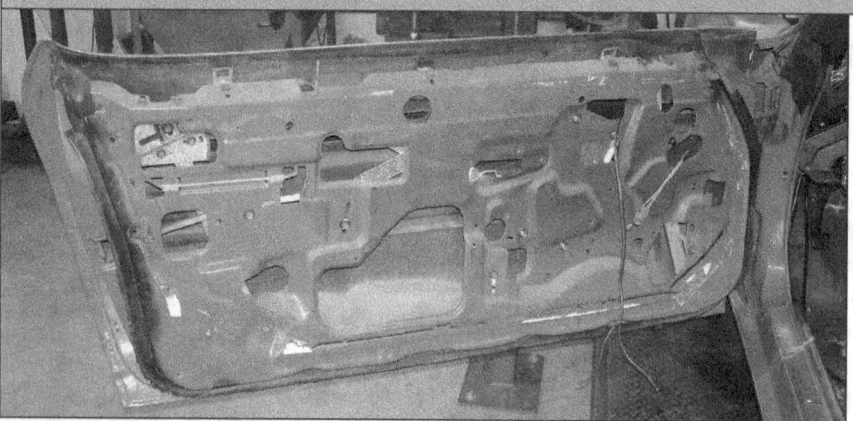

10 Inspect the felt window pads on the door. If these pads are worn out, replace them so the windows don't get scratched. The front, middle, and rear pads support the window as it slides in and out of the door. The pads are attached to brackets on the top of the door frame, and these are retained by hex bolts. Use a Sharpie marker to indicate the original position of the adjustable door guide brackets. When you reinstall the brackets, they can be aligned to the original position. Remove the hex bolts then grab and lift the brackets off the door frame. Attach the new pads to the brackets. Use a socket and ratchet to reinstall the bolts into the original position. You can adjust the location of the window tracks by adjusting the mounting bolt position within the doors. Adjust the window forward or aft so the window is level or up and down to set the desired window height.

ELECTRICAL SYSTEM AND WIRING

Install Switch in Door Panel

11 Enlarge the original window crank hole to house the power window switch. Install the switch in the door panel as seen here, or install it in the console similar to some of the later F-Bodies.

Install Wiring Plug in Door Panel

12 After you install and secure the window switch bezel, install the wiring plug.

Reinstall Door Panel and Door Handle

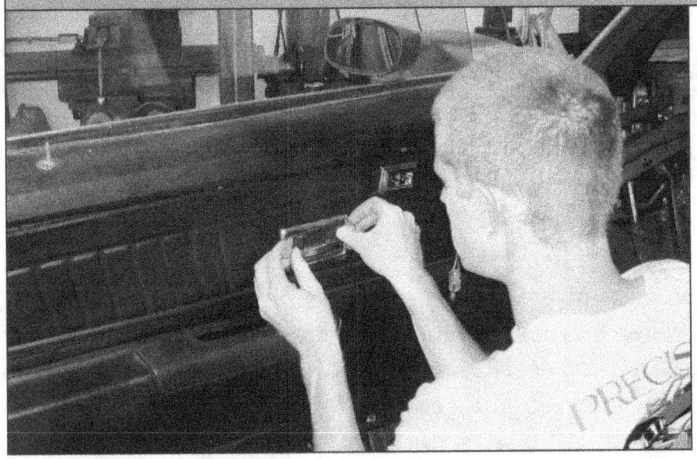

13 Install the door panel by first connecting the pop-in fasteners and then by attaching the bottom with Phillips-head sheet-metal screws. Install the door handle assembly and bezel.

Here is the finished door panel after the new windows have been installed. The panel looks as if it came with power windows because the switches are exactly like the ones used by General Motors in the 1970s.

AFTERWORD

Some great cars were built in the 1960s, starting with the full-size sedans that were competing in the Super Stock wars. When General Motors backed out of racing, Pontiac decided to build a street-performance car called the GTO, and before long all of the car manufacturers were building hot street drivers. With the introduction of the hot Camaros and Firebirds, it was a great time for young car enthusiasts. But things started to change in 1967 when the Vietnam War was heating up and young guys were being drafted to serve in the Army. Many of the would-be performance car buyers were being shipped overseas, so the sales of the performance cars started to go down.

The government introduced the Environmental Protection Agency (EPA) in 1970, and from an automotive standpoint, things started on a downhill slide. It took another 10 years for car manufacturers to come up with some solutions for the problems they faced but thanks to computer technology and fuel injection they did make a turnaround in the 1980s.

The 1970s were filled with cars trying to meet the emissions and gas mileage standards, but there were a few bright spots, such as the Camaro, the Firebird, and the Corvette. There were a few nice cars in the early 1970s but that started to really change by 1974. When you look at performance car production, the sales numbers in the early 1970s were low, and that was due to the fact that so many young guys were still in the service.

Chevrolet and Pontiac went in two different directions in the early 1970s. Chevrolet backed away from performance and even discontinued the Z28 Camaro. Chevrolet was adding luxury items to the Camaro to entice older buyers. Pontiac doubled down on the Firebird, especially the Trans Am, and when many fellows were getting out of the Army, Trans Am sales started increasing. Pontiac managed to keep installing big-block engines into the Trans Am Firebirds, along with luxury items, until 1979. Even though they weren't as fast as the early cars they still offered decent acceleration, good gas mileage, and excellent handling.

In 1980, Pontiac came out with a new small-block engine with a turbocharger, and it produced the same power as the discontinued 400 and 403 big-displacement engines. The turbocharged engine had plenty of potential but it was dropped after 1981. The management at Chevrolet saw the success Pontiac was having with the Trans Am, so in response it reintroduced the Z28 in 1977.

Today the 1967–1969 Camaros and Firebirds are difficult to find, and when you do, they are either in extremely poor condition or they have already been restored and are selling for a high price. If you are looking for a performance car to build I recommend looking for a 1970-and-newer Camaro or Firebird. I have built both and have found the newer cars to be much better than the early models in construction, handling, and even styling. The 1970-and-newer Camaros and Firebirds are lower, longer, and sleeker than the previous models, and I think they look better than the Camaros and Firebirds that followed in the 1980s and 1990s.

If you are looking for a 1970s Camaro or Firebird they are getting more difficult to find because they are more than 30 years old, but you can find them if you really look hard. Sometimes, you can drive around your own neighborhood and find them sitting in a driveway or parked on the street, and often the car hasn't been moved in years. I have seen five in my town that could possibly be for sale.

Another way to find the potential car of your dreams is to look on the Internet. I once found a 1978 Special Edition Trans Am on Craigslist, so I recommend checking that website in your area for a restorable Camaro or Firebird. Another possibility is eBay Motors because I have seen some nice Camaros and Firebirds selling there. You can bid, or sometimes the owner has a "buy now" price. There are

AFTERWORD

other sites, such as autotrader.com and goodguys.com, where you might be able to purchase a nice second-generation car.

You can also get the word out that you are looking for a certain kind of car, and there is always the chance that one of your friends knows of a car or locates one for you. You can always purchase a finished car, but if you want to completely rebuild a car to your own specifications—restored, resto mod, or Pro Touring—you really want a car that needs everything, and that means you can probably buy it for a reasonable price. If you plan on changing the engine and transmission you might be able to find a rolling chassis for an even lower price.

Before you start your project, check out the environmental laws in your state. Knowing those requirements, you can determine what kind of modifications can be made legally and design your car around those laws. In many states, pre-1981 cars are exempt, but in others, such as California, only pre-1975 cars are exempt.

I've covered everything from mild performance improvements to some wild ones. I have covered engine upgrades, transmission choices, suspension upgrades, and many other topics you should think about. I hope you find it helpful in selecting the kind of modifications you want to perform.

Good luck with your project car.

Source Guide

Baer Racing
2222 West Peoria Ave.
Phoenix, AZ 85029
602-233-1411
www.baer.com

Bowtie Overdrives
17359 Darwin Ave., Unit C
Hesperia, CA 92345
760-947-5240
www.bowtieoverdrives.com

B&M Racing & Performance
   Products
100 Stony Point Rd., Suite 125
Santa Rosa, CA 95401
800-544-4761
www.bmracing.com

Chris Alston's Chassisworks
8661 Younger Creek Dr.
Sacramento, CA 95828
888-388-0297
www.cachassisworks.com

Detroit Speed, Inc.
185 McKenzie Rd.
Mooresville, NC 23115
704-662-3272
www.detroitspeed.com

Dynomax Performance Exhaust
1 International Dr.
Monroe, MI 48161
734-384-7806
www.dynomax.com

Eaton Detroit Springs
1555 Michigan Ave.
Detroit, MI 48216
313-963-3839
www.eatonsprings.com

Edelbrock Corporation
2700 California St.
Torrance, CA 90503
800-416-8628
www.edelbrock.com

Energy Suspension, Inc.
1131 Via Callejon
San Clemente, CA 92673
888-913-6374
www.energysuspension.com

FB Performance Transmissions, Inc.
85 Cleveland Ave.
Bay Shore, NY 11706
800-769-1118
www.fbperformance.com

Flex-a-lite
Dept. SPR-SRB
P.O. Box 480
Milton, WA 98354
253-922-2700
www.flex-a-lite.com

Heidts Hot Rod & Muscle Car Parts
111 Kerry Ln.
Wauconda, IL 60084
800-841-8188
www.heidts.com

Holley
www.holley.com

Hotchkis Sport Suspension
8633 Sorensen Ave.
Santa Fe Springs, CA 90670
888-735-6425
www.hotchkis.net

Jim Meyer Racing Products
2795 S.E. 23rd
Lincoln City, OR 97367
800-824-1752
www.jimmeyerracing.com

SOURCE GUIDE

MagnaFlow Exhaust Products
22961 Arroyo Vista
Rancho Santa Margarita, CA 92688
800-824-8664
www.magnaflow.com

Mallory Ignition
10601 Memphis Ave., #12
Cleveland, OH 44144
216-688-8300
www.mallory-ignition.com

Mark 7 Machine & Radiator
102 S. Tuscola Rd.
Bay City, MI 48708-9644
989-992-7335
www.mark7machine.com

Mattson's, Inc.
7582 Industrial Way, Unit D
Stanton, CA 90680
866-435-6477
www.mattsonscustomradiator.com

Milodon Inc.
2250 Agate Ct.
Simi Valley, CA 93065
805-577-5950
www.milodon.com

MSD Ignition
1490 Henry Brannan Dr.
El Paso, TX 79936
915-857-5200
www.msdignition.com

PerTronix
440 E. Arrow Hwy.
San Dimas, CA 91773
909-599-5955
www.pertronix.com

Precision Street Rods & Machines
19158 Roscoe Blvd.
Northridge, CA 91324
818-886-5018

Proform Performance Parts
198 Industrial Park Rd.
Piny Flats, TN 37686
800-585-0683
www.proformparts.com

Recaro Automotive
www.recaro.com

RideTech
350 S. St. Charles St.
Jasper, IN 47546
812-481-4787
www.ridetech.com

Schwartz Performance, Inc.
1115 Rail Dr.
Woodstock, IL 60098
815-206-2230
www.schwartzperformance.com

Smeding Diesel
210-446-0888
www.smedingdiesel.com

Stainless Steel Brakes Corporation
11470 Main Rd.
Clarence, NY 14031
800-448-7722
www.ssbrakes.com

SW Performance Transmissions
2444 Fender Ave., #J
Ullerton, CA 92831
714-234-4271
sw-performance-transmissions.net

TCI Automotive
151 Industrial Dr.
Ashland, MS 38603
888-776-9824

The Roadster Shop
28775 N. Rte 83
Mundelein, IL 60060
847-949-7637
www.roadstershop.com

Tremec
14700 Helm Ct.
Plymouth, MI 48170
800-401-9866
www.tremec.com

U.S. Radiator Corp.
4423 District Blvd.
Vernon, CA 90058
323-826-0965
www.usradiator.com

Valley Head Service
19340 Londelius
Northridge, CA 91324
818-993-7000
www.valleyhead.com

Vintage Air, Inc.
18865 Goll St.
San Antonio, TX 78266
800-862-6658
www.vintageair.com

Wilwood Engineering, Inc.
4700 Calle Bolero
Camarillo, CA 93012
805-388-1188

World Products
19654 Eighth St. E.
Sonoma, CA 95476
707-996-5201
www.worldproducts.com

NOTES

www.ingramcontent.com/pod-product-compliance
Lightning Source LLC
Chambersburg PA
CBHW081446070526
44586CB00019B/2255